# BUDDHISM AS A RELIGION

# BUDDHISM AS A RELIGION

## ITS HISTORICAL DEVELOPMENT AND ITS PRESENT CONDITIONS

**H. HACKMANN, Lic Theol**

GYAN

*Published by*

Gyan Publishing House
5, Ansari Road
Daryaganj, New Delhi-110002
Phone: 011-47034999, 9811692060
E-mail: books@gyanbooks.com

*Distribution Network*
gyanbooks.com
India, USA, Canada, UK, Australia, France



ISBN: 978-81-212-9376-1 (PB)
First Published, 1910

2nd Impression 2023

*Printed at:* Gyan Press, Delhi.



**BUDDHISM AS A RELIGION**
AUTHOR: H. HACKMANN

# BUDDHISM AS A RELIGION

# BUDDHISM AS A RELIGION: ITS HISTORICAL DEVELOPMENT AND ITS PRESENT CONDITIONS.

By H. HACKMANN, Lic. Theol.

FROM THE GERMAN, REVISED AND ENLARGED BY THE AUTHOR

PROBSTHAIN & CO.
41, Great Russell St., London, W.C.
1910.

TO

BERNHARD DUHM,

*Doctor and Professor of Theology at the University of Basle,*

IN GRATEFUL REMEMBRANCE

DEDICATED BY AN OLD PUPIL.

# PREFACE

There seems to be no need of books on Buddhism, yet, though the literature on this subject is indeed immense, a serious gap remains to be filled. In vain one looks about for a book which represents Buddhism as a present-day religion, comprising all the countries under its sway. The writers on Buddhism either deal chiefly with the Buddha himself and with the old Indian Buddhism (as Oldenberg and Rhys Davids), or they put before us the Buddhism of one single country—Ceylon, or Burma, or Tibet, or China (as Spence Hardy, Bigandet, Waddell, Edkins, and others). Even Monier-Williams' well-known book, though more complete than many others, is far from being an exhaustive record. Northern Buddhism he only slightly touches upon. But there should be a work showing Buddhism *as a whole*, beginning with Gautama Buddha himself, tracing the line of historical development which his religion took over all the lands of its influence, and painting a vivid picture of its present-day conditions and organizations everywhere.

This is the scope of the volume now before us. The book is written for a general public, avoiding purposely display of scholarship as much as possible. At the same time it should be understood that it is entirely based, not only on the most recent scientific publications of our best scholars, but on long personal investigations made on the spot.

The author has studied Buddhism for more than twenty years. He has lived in Buddhist countries for nearly ten years, and has travelled a good deal in these lands with the special object of ascertaining the actual state of the Buddhist religion. He has been in personal contact with Chinese, Japanese, Korean, Tibetan, Burmese, and Singhalese Buddhism. Living in the monasteries, watching the monks and the lay-devotees, inquiring about rituals and institutions, he learnt thoroughly what Buddhism as a practical religion of the present day really is.

Having returned from Eastern Asia to Europe, the writer was asked by a publisher to contribute a book on Buddhism to a series of popular treatises. He gladly consented, as he thought it very necessary, at a time when Buddhism is discussed more and more in European countries, to make the general public acquainted with this religion *as a whole*, laying stress especially on the modern features of its life. The book is meant to give a fair and impartial statement. Of course that does not mean to restrain from criticism. Facts must be seen as they are. And some of the facts which one has to face in studying Buddhism as a living religion are not pleasant. Nevertheless, animosity and one-sidedness have been avoided. Also there is no arguing from the dogmatical point of view, which seems entirely useless. But the historical and the social character of Buddhism are the points to which attention is drawn.

The publication being in German,[1] friends suggested a translation into English, because the English-speaking people are those most interested in the topic. I had the privilege of finding a very congenial translator in a lady who herself is personally acquainted with the Far East, having travelled in China twice for a considerable time.

The book has been revised and much enlarged for this translation, there being no restriction of space, which hampered the German edition. But vast as the subject is, concentration seemed necessary. Particularly, the system of the Buddha himself has been stated in the most concise way, so as only to give a clear understanding of the ruling ideas. Who wants to go more deeply into details has books enough to help him on. To facilitate further studies, hints on the best literature are given at the end of the volume.

H. HACKMANN,

15, WINDSOR ROAD,
DENMARK HILL,
LONDON, S.E.

*October*, 1909.

[1] Published in 1905. Tübingen, J. C. B. Mohr (Paul Siebeck).

# CONTENTS

## BOOK I

### THE BUDDHA AND HIS DOCTRINE



## BOOK II

### SKETCH OF THE HISTORY OF BUDDHISM



## BOOK III

### THE MODERN BUDDHISM

## NOTE ON PRONUNCIATION

In *Indian* words pronounce:

*ś* as French *j* (in *jeu*, *jouer*).

*ṣ* as English *sh*.

*c* as English *ch*.

*ṃ*, *ṇ*, and *ṭ* as English *m*, *n* and *t*.

Double consonants are pronounced as two distinct sounds.

The *h* after a consonant is audible.

The vowels *e* and *o* are always long.

In *Tibetan* words the Tibetan orthography is not given, but the words are spelt as they are pronounced.

In *Chinese* words the transcription of Sir Thomas Wade (and Professor Giles in his Dictionary) is followed.

The vowels *a*, *e*, *i*, *o*, *u* are to be pronounced as in Italian or German.

# BOOK I

## THE BUDDHA AND HIS DOCTRINE

### CHAPTER I.—THE LIFE OF THE BUDDHA

THE founder of Buddhism is called *the Buddha.* It is the title of his rank, and not his own personal name. The one whom his followers, in reverence for him, speak of as *the Buddha* (the Enlightened One) came of the stock of an ancient noble Indian family which bore the name of Śâkya. From this family name was derived the poetical designation of *Śâkyamuni* (the Saint of the Śâkyas), by which he is widely known to-day. His personal name was *Siddhârtha;* but as he renounced it at the very beginning of his religious career, he is not called by it amongst his followers. The Buddhist only recognizes the Prince Siddhârtha as the young man living at his father's Court before the great religious transformation had taken place in him. There is, indeed, another name belonging to his family from the earliest times by which the Buddha was also known throughout his later holy life—viz., that of *Gautama.* This was a surname of his family derived from one of the famous bard families of Vedic times.

The father of Gautama was an Indian nobleman,

not exactly what we should understand to-day as a King. His name was Śuddhodana. The capital of his principality was called Kapilavastu. Although up to the present time there is no absolute certainty as to which of the ruined towns which dispute the honour of being the actual home of the Buddha is the real one, there is no doubt as to the neighbourhood in which it stood, nor as to the district over which the Śâkya family held sway; these points were fully established by discoveries made in 1896-97. The district was on the borders of the British and Nepalese territory, at both sides of the eighty-fourth degree of longitude, and undoubtedly Kapilavastu itself stood in Nepal. Gautama was not born in the capital. His mother, belonging to a side branch of the Śâkya family, came from the mountains lying to the north, and when she felt the time approaching for the birth of her firstborn, she desired to await her confinement in the paternal home; so she left Kapilavastu for her native place, Devadaha. On the way, however, in the grove of Lumbini, she was surprised to find that her hour had come. On the spot where the child was born, some hundreds of years later, King Aśoka raised a memorial tablet with an inscription commemorating the event, and it was this tablet which was discovered in December, 1896; so that both the event and the spot where it took place are beyond all doubt. The name of Gautama's mother was Mâyâ (also often called Mâyâdevî). She paid for the birth of her son with her own life. Her sister (Mahâprajâpatî), who was also one of the wives of Gautama's father, undertook the rearing of the child.

These events took place in the middle of the sixth century before Christ. It is only from what we know of the general condition of Indian culture at that period that we can form some conception of the way in which Gautama grew up. He was surrounded by the luxury due to his gentle birth. Crowds of servants; careful physical training; a splendid home, varied according to the three seasons of the Indian year (summer, winter, and the rains); the enjoyment of the beauties of nature which India offers; gardens containing a wealth of tropical vegetation; from time to time a festival or a hunting-party—such are the things which certainly belonged to his life. He was trained in the use of arms, and his military capacity was developed. His mental faculties were also developed by careful instruction, and certainly the Veda, the famous collection of old Indian sacred songs and texts, played a rôle in his education, though we can no longer ascertain to what extent.

When the youth was grown up he married. The name of his wife is not certain; we find it mentioned as Yaśodhara, but also as Bhaddakacca and as Gopa. She bore him a son, Râhula. Not long after this event Gautama left his home, his father, his wife and child, in order to withdraw into the solitude of the wilderness. He did it in opposition to the wishes of the family; certainly it could have been no easy matter for him thus to have broken the ties with his former life. He was driven to it by an overpowering inner longing to give himself up to the consideration of the fundamentals of human existence. For this purpose he desired to be quite free from external bonds.

Such a mode of action was not altogether uncommon in those days. The religious instinct of India had already produced hermits, ascetics, and people of monastic habits. Gautama took the usual way to solve the riddle of existence which pressed upon him: he associated with famous anchorites and sought their advice. It was the accepted opinion of the period that a deeper insight into the meaning of life could be obtained by the help of severe asceticism, which would free the soul from physical bondage. Gautama allowed himself to be driven into this course, but all such attempts failed to satisfy him. For seven years he wrestled strenuously, but in vain, till at last he gave up the struggle us a failure.

Soon afterwards a marked change came over him. Emerging from profound meditation, which had for many hours rendered him oblivious of all outward things as he sat under a peepul-tree, Gautama henceforth had a new outlook on the meaning of life and the highest task of humanity. He had received his revelation. At that time he was about thirty-six years of age. From now his whole life is devoted to the dissemination of his new doctrine. He has become the Awakened, the One who Knows, the Buddha.

For about forty-five years he worked amongst his people as the Buddha, wandering from place to place and preaching. With ever-increasing care he elaborated his system of thought by means of discussion with foes and friends alike. He won adherents. Soon he was surrounded by an inner circle of disciples faithfully devoted to him, and whom he taught and trained. He gained respect besides from a large number of outsiders, even if they did not accept his deeper instruction, and could not live up to his highest requirements. Although opposition was not altogether lacking, the impression gathered is mainly that of success and of the rapid spread of his doctrine. The Buddha also converted his own family, his father, his former wife, his son, and other relatives. The extent of country traversed by Gautama in his itinerary work far exceeded that of the paternal domain. He travelled in the eastern parts of North India, where the old kingdoms of Magadha and Kośala were situated, in a region the centre of which is the city of Benares. These tours, on which he was accompanied by his disciples, were interrupted every year for several months by the rainy season. Then they sought a shelter at a place where the gifts and care of adherents made a longer stay possible.

Thus four and a half decades had passed. The Buddha had become an old man while still engaged in his labours. He saw the result of a remarkable life-work surrounding him—a great community, obedient to the rule of salvation, framed by him. Death overtook him in or about the year 477 B.C. He happened to be in a village close to the noted city Vaiśâlî, when a severe illness attacked him; but after recovering a little, he still pursued his way. Arriving in a small place called Pâva, he was invited to a meal by a smith, Chunda by name. This meal (consisting of boar's flesh[1]) brought back his illness. He knew

[1] Some scholars disagree about the meaning of the term used for that meal (*sûkaramaddavam*), asserting that it was a kind of mushroom named after boars; but that is doubtful.

that the end had come, and held a farewell discourse, especially with his favourite disciple, Ânanda. Under some blossoming trees by the river-bank, near the city of Kuśinagara, his last resting-place was prepared. There he died. His corpse was cremated by his adherents with the greatest honour, and the remains of his body were divided among Princes and noble families. Some of these remains the family of the Śâkyas received, who buried them under a great monument. The place where these relics have been buried was found and opened in 1898, the old remains being left entirely untouched.

This is what may be asserted with confidence of the life of the Buddha Gautama.

In the traditions handed down by his followers there is a large addition of legendary embellishments tacked on to this kernel of truth. Already in the discourses of the master, carefully treasured by the first generation after his death, together with many interesting details of his life which are historic, a fantastic glorification crept in. We must here set aside the Buddha legends, as we are only concerned with historical information; but for those who desire to know more of the legendary Buddha, the following hints as to literature are annexed.

We possess four ancient records of the life of the Buddha:

1. The Nidânakathâ—that is, the introduction to the book of the Jâtakas, a work relating to the former lives of the Buddha. The Nidânakathâ, written in Pâli, has been translated into English under the editorship of E. B. Cowell. (The Jâtaka, or Stories of the Buddha's Former Births. Cambridge. Six vols. 1895-

1907. The Nidânakathâ is contained in vol. i.). See also Buddhist Birth Stories; or, Jâtaka Tales. Translated by T. W. Rhys Davids. London: Trübner. Vol. i. 1880.

2. P. E. Foucaux: Le Lalita Vistara trad. du Sanscrit. Ann. d. Mus. Guimet, tome 6. Paris, 1884.

3. The Mahâvastu, written in Gâthâ dialect. Edited and translated by E. Senart.

4. The Buddhacarita by Aśvaghoṣa. Sacred Books of the East, vol. xlix. Translated by E. B. Cowell, F. Max Müller, and J. Takakusu. The same work translated from the Chinese by S. Beal. (Sacred Books of the East, vol. xix. Oxford, 1883.)

Besides these original biographies of the Buddha, there should be mentioned some works based on old Oriental tradition:

R. Spence Hardy: A Manual of Buddhism. London, 1880. (Contains a Life of the Buddha on pp. 141-371.)

W. W. Rockhill: The Life of the Buddha . . . from Tibetan Works. 1884.

P. Bigandet: The Life or Legend of Gaudama, the Buddha of the Burmese. Third edition. London, 1880.

## Chapter II.—THE DOCTRINE OF THE BUDDHA

Of greater importance than the life of the Buddha is the question as to his teaching.

There is one point which from the first should not be overlooked. The teaching of the Buddha has a certain arbitrary limitation: it will give us no information as to many metaphysical and philosophical problems surrounding us—for instance, as to the origin of the world, the creating power, the deeper sense of existence, the character of good and evil, and such-like things. It always reverts to one cardinal point of practical importance, sweeping aside all other questions which man's thirst for knowledge may raise. The one cardinal point referred to is *the deliverance from suffering.*

For the very first statement which is at the root of all the Buddha's thought is this—*life is suffering.*

What, then, does Gautama mean by this phrase? The ideas and sentiments which grew up in the mind of the Buddha so as to form this fundamental conviction are partly due to his individual temperament, and partly to the spirit of the age in which he lived, to the inheritance he owed to his nation.

Personally, he certainly experienced life as burdensome. It must be borne in mind that the Indian genius is ripened by the Indian climate. There is a benumbing of existence under the tropical sun as well as under perpetual snow and ice. From the intellectual life of India there soon ebbed the joyous activity of primitive times, a passive receptivity taking its place, and a dull drifting on the stream of events. The exuberance of Nature also had something paralyzing in it. There can be no permanent satisfaction for man in the rest of satiety, our nature being rather formed for a life of endeavour and striving. Melancholy takes possession of him, a morbid scepticism, an overwhelming sensibility for everything destitute and afflicted. Such a mental attitude the Buddha must have had stamped upon him from the outset by his Indian parentage and surroundings, and it may have been unusually developed in him. What he saw as the curse of human existence more than anything else is plainly set forth in an old legend, which gives the motive for his abandonment of family and home. The legend describes how on three different occasions he took a drive from his palace: the first time he met with an old man, the second time with a sick man, the third time with a corpse. By each of these an indelible impression was made upon his mind. A fourth excursion showed him the apparition of a mendicant who had turned his back on the world—an indication of his appointed path. Old age, illness, and death are the terrible powers of destruction which hover over life; they are all included in the one word *transitoriness.*

This word leads up to the very heart of Gautama's experience, so far as it is connected with the world's suffering. There is no real happiness because everything in life is transitory. Behind every blossoming forth is a fading; behind every attainment, a loss; behind every life, death. This truth, though experienced to a certain extent by everybody and in every epoch in its ruthless irrevocability, takes such gigantic shape in this Indian mind that it overshadows all earthly gifts and values. Happiness is a mirage, a deception. Whoever really opens his eyes must recognize that all life is suffering.

This aspect of things is sharply intensified, moreover, by a doctrine which the Buddha received from the age in which he lived. This is the doctrine of *metempsychosis.* Nobody can ascertain at the present day at what time this conception, a hazy, fantastic idea at the outset, but in course of time strengthened by the pantheistic and pessimistic trend of ancient Indian thought, first took rise in the mind of man. The idea has undoubtedly something very natural and attractive for primitive philosophy. In any case, long before the Buddha's time it had become quite familiar to the speculative mind. It is a gloomy thought, well qualified to deepen the melancholy contemplation of existence to a degree that is terrible and unendurable. To be forced to pass through life again and again in a bodily form, predestined to the same imperfections, the same transitoriness, the same death—this is indeed a wearisome and formidable treadmill! Already thinkers before the Buddha had felt the torturing sting of this conception very deeply.

The doctrine of metempsychosis is therefore to be reckoned as an element of the atmosphere in which the Buddha grew up. He has, indeed, modified it somewhat, but he was unable to free himself from the main conception. He never thought of doubting the fact of reincarnation. Such universally accepted beliefs surround the single individual who is born into their midst with an impression of reality like that of heaven and earth. But it cannot be doubted that the belief in reincarnation most powerfully accentuated Gautama's view of life as suffering.

If one has realized as an unalterable truth that life means suffering, the next question arising must be as to the original cause of suffering; for it is only by coming to an understanding of this that anyone can hope to succeed in removing suffering. What, then, is the original fountain of all suffering? The answer to this question forms *the second fundamental truth* of the Buddha's teaching, and runs thus: *The cause of suffering is thirst (craving).*

It is worth attention that at this point already the system of the Buddha takes its turn to the personal and subjective side. The question is not how it may be explained that we find ourselves in such a world, which in reality is nothing else than a hell, a place of suffering for all its inhabitants; nor as to who or what may have originated such a phenomenon. We are not to look about for an external objective cause, to which this universal fate is due. The explanation is given entirely from the inner, the subjective, side of the phenomenon; it is merely psychological. Suffering originates in a certain psychological disposition of the individual, but this, disposition as it is, might be ruled and mastered by the individual who possesses it. Suffering originates from the thirst.

Before stating, further, how the thirst is the creative power of all suffering in the world, we must look at a certain doctrine of the Buddha intimately connected with that question, and at the same time a doctrine differing from the common mode of thought even in ancient India. Most philosophical systems of the pre-Buddhist period recognized a permanent soul as the active centre of the body, which represented the indestructible unit, this unit being led by Death from one habitation to another in the course of all its reincarnations. In order to come to rest, this soul of the individual must attain union with the All-Soul, the World-Soul, with Brahma, after which union the miserable wandering through ever new existences would cease. The Buddha emphatically rejected this conception. He denies both the individual soul and the All-Soul. Of the latter there need be no question, for, as we have remarked above, the Buddha does not deal with the explanation of the world's problem as a whole, but restricts himself to the teaching of salvation, which is the direct concern of mankind. So much the more vital, then, becomes the question as to the individual soul. The Buddha denies its existence, and impresses upon his followers that it is one of the most fatal errors to hold that a soul is the bearer of life in any living being. It is not a soul which migrates in reincarnation from one body to another, constituting a permanent entity. The new incarnation is only effected by—the thirst.

There is no soul. Man is merely a collection of bodily and mental occurrences. The co-operation of a group of forces creates an apparent unit, which has been taken as being something existing in itself, and has been called a soul. In reality that which exists is an ever-changing appearance in certain forms of combination. There is no permanent "I," to whom the events of my life are attached. That supposititious "I" is only the totality of a group of actions, and, inasmuch as these actions are perpetually new and different, it is in like manner perpetually new and different. Only inasmuch as one action always immediately succeeds another, there comes to be an appearance of unbroken continuity. But *thirst* is what holds together in a state of existence all living beings, leading them from one life to another as soon as the bonds of being are loosened by death. The thirst means that grasping clinging effort, that desire for life, by which all who live are attached in some way or other to their surroundings. How it comes to pass that this abstract idea of craving is sufficiently powerful to bring forth an actual new life the Buddha has tried to explain by a formula much revered by all Buddhists, but of very obscure meaning. It is called the Causal Nexus (Pratîtya Samutpâda) and runs thus:

Ignorance produces the syntheses;
The syntheses produce cognition;
Cognition produces name and form;
Name and form produce the sixfold sphere (sense surfaces and understanding);
The sixfold sphere produces contact;
Contact produces feeling;
Feeling produces craving;
Craving produces grasping;
Grasping produces renewed existence;
Renewed existence produces birth;
Birth produces old age and death, grief, lamentation, distress, melancholy and despair.

Thus a chain of twelve links is formed, the twelve Nidânas.[1] Though the ideas underlying the connection of these twelve links are much disputed, it is

[1] Scholars differ in translating the difficult Sanscrit terms. The above translation follows Mrs. C. A. F. Rhys Davids in her book, "A Buddhist Manual of Psychological Ethics" (London, 1909), p. 348. Compare also for deeper study De la Vallée Poussin, "Deux Notes sur le Pratîtyasamutpâda," 1906.

clear that some sort of natural law is maintained, resulting in a new existence, and that in the series of causes craving and grasping are those which immediately produce this new existence.

However, not only does the thirst by force of a natural law demand the fact of metempsychosis, but it also regulates the form of reincarnation. Here the Buddha emphasizes the value of the moral quality of our actions. On our moral attitude depends the form of our next existence. Good action produces subsequently more favourable and happier conditions of life; bad action results in the contrary. It is the never-failing accuracy of natural law again which is at work here. So all the different shapes of earthly existence are produced as the consequences of earlier good or bad lives. But not the earth only is the stage of this endless drama: it is the whole universe. There are other, both happier and unhappier, existences which might be popularly described as heavens and hells, or which are of an intermediate supernatural character. Already in the Dhanañjani, a discourse of the Majjhimanikâyo, part of the oldest canonical writings, we find an enumeration of the following grades of possible reincarnation: (1) In hell, (2) as animals, (3) as ghosts (spectres), (4) as man, (5) in seven kinds of heavenly abodes. In other parts of the canonical books the following six divisions are given: (1) Hell, (2) the sphere of the ghosts, (3) the animals, (4) the abode of the Asuras (spiritual beings of a rank lower than the gods), (5) the world of men, (6) the realm of the gods, itself divided into successive regions. (It is to be remarked that the Buddha did not include in his circle of reincarnation the vegetable life or the mineral kingdom.) But whatever may be the mode of existence to which a being is reborn, it is inevitably to a state of suffering, as all these states are transitory and uncertain. Therefore it does not really help a man even if he should become a god.

The question is rather how to escape entirely from the fate of reincarnation.

This is the next great theme in the Buddha's doctrine, and the answer to this question constitutes *the third fundamental truth.*

As we saw before, the eternal reshaping of beings is due to a subjective, inward root, the craving; therefore a subjective power also can destroy this root and prevent the reincarnation. *Where the thirst, the craving after life, is ultimately overcome, there no new existence can arise.* All effort must be concentrated on this object—to become completely free from every entanglement of life to such an extent that a man will feel no inclination, wish, or interest attracting him towards any physical or mental object. All the threads must be cut which attach the being to things existing, and even to existence itself. Through this utmost sundering of the individual from the stream of life there arises a new condition, which is the highest goal of Buddhism—*Nirvâṇa.*[1]

As to the meaning of this expression there has been a great deal of doubt, but a thorough-going inquiry has made it quite clear: Nirvâṇa is nothing else than a state of complete painlessness. But since in

[1] Compare "Buddhist Essays," by Paul Dahlke. Translated from the German by Bikkhu Silacara. London, 1908. Chap. v.

Buddhism pain is synonymous with existence, as existence with pain, Nirvâṇa may equally be described as non-existence. Here, indeed, our Western reasoning must not ignore the following reservation. The Buddha does not speak of existence in the absolute sense as our philosophy sometimes uses the word. He fixes his attention on the existence which we know experimentally—namely, the earthly existence; for the so-called supernatural states of being, to which reincarnation may lead, themselves embrace nothing more than modifications of earthly existence, strictly speaking. From this it follows that Nirvâṇa cannot be taken to mean extinction in the strictly philosophical sense of the word. Indeed, this is so little the case that a man who is still in outward appearance living may have already reached Nirvâṇa—namely, when he has completely overcome thirst in himself, which is the root of his union with existence. His visible earthly shape, then, is merely a kind of optical delusion in the estimation of the Buddhist. Thus it may be equally argued that after death Nirvâṇa leads to a kind of existence which is integrally different from anything that we know as existence. Such an assumption would form no contradiction to the conception of Nirvâṇa. But as to such a possibility the Buddha has not made any express statement either for or against, since it is an irrelevant question, merely distracting our attention from what is of vital importance—viz., the way of salvation. To be set free from suffering, and thereby to cease from any existence which is within the range of our experience and conception—that is all we need as human beings.

To state the possibility of an existence which did not include suffering would, by the way, have collided so sharply with the ever-present equation—life is suffering — that on this account alone one easily understands why Gautama avoided such a line of thought.

Man must therefore give up all thirst or desire. In what way can he attain this difficult goal? The answer to this question is the fourth fundamental truth which the Buddha discovered, and obviously it is the most important. At this point the system begins to take a practical direction.

It must be noted at the outset that the practical rules of Buddhism are not framed on an ascetic basis. Asceticism, the strenuous suppression of our bodily and sensual faculties, has no intrinsic value for the Buddha. Although one cannot but consider his religion ascetic in the deeper sense of the word, because of its ultimate tendency to turn away from the world, nevertheless the Buddhist method of attaining this end is not an ascetic one. The parting from the stream of existence must come from within; asceticism, on the other hand, would only be like chopping off the branches and twigs from the tree of life without uprooting it. As regards the physical and sensual conditions of living, it is sufficient if they are rendered helpful to the undertaking of the inward struggle. To this end one must seek an isolated and simple life, as it may be found in the monastic life. The purpose of monkhood for the Buddhist is, therefore, merely to provide congenial outward conditions for the struggle to escape from life; it constructs a kind of defensive coat of mail, behind which the real task must be accomplished.

The task which lay before the Buddha's disciples has been graphically set forth in the celebrated picture of "the eightfold path." It is described as right belief, right resolve, right speech, right behaviour, right occupation, right effort, right contemplation, right concentration.[1] A very old passage of the Buddhist canon (Dîgha-Nikâya, Sutta 22) explains these eight terms in an ampler way as follows:

"What, O priests, is right belief? The knowledge of misery, O priests, the knowledge of the origin of misery, the knowledge of the cessation of misery, and the knowledge of the path leading to the cessation of misery—this, O priests, is called right belief.

"And what, O priests, is right resolve? The resolve to renounce sensual pleasures, the resolve to have malice towards none, and the resolve to harm no living creature—this, O priests, is called right resolve.

"And what, O priests, is right speech? To abstain from falsehood, to abstain from backbiting, to abstain from harsh language, and to abstain from frivolous talk—this, O priests, is called right speech.

"And what, O priests, is right behaviour? To abstain from destroying of life, to abstain from taking that which is not given one, and to abstain from immorality—this, O priests, is called right behaviour.

[1] The translation of the Pâli terms is here given from Warren. It is very difficult to render the pregnant definition of the original with equal pregnancy. The translators therefore differ in some of them.

"And what, O priests, is right occupation? Whenever, O priests, a noble disciple, quitting a wrong occupation, gets his livelihood by a right occupation—this, O priests, is called right occupation.

"And what, O priests, is right effort? Whenever, O priests, a priest purposes, makes an effort, heroically endeavours, applies his mind, and exerts himself, that evil and demeritorious qualities not yet arisen may not arise; and . . . that evil and demeritorious qualities already arisen may be abandoned; and . . . that meritorious qualities not yet arisen may arise; and . . . exerts himself for the preservation, retention, growth, increase, development, and perfection, of meritorious qualities already arisen—this, O priests, is called right effort.

"And what, O priests, is right contemplation? Whenever, O priests, a priest lives, as respects the body, observant of the body, strenuous, conscious, contemplative, and has rid himself of lust and grief; as respects sensations, observant of sensations, strenuous . . .; as respects the mind, observant of the mind, strenuous . . .; as respects the elements of being, observant of the elements of being, strenuous . . .—this, O priests, is called right contemplation.

"And what, O priests, is right concentration? Whenever, O priests, a priest, having isolated himself from sensual pleasures, having isolated himself from demeritorious traits, and still exercising reasoning, still exercising reflection, enters upon the first trance which is produced by isolation and characterized by joy and happiness; when, through the subsidence of reasoning and reflection, and still retaining joy and happiness, he enters upon the second trance, which is an interior tranquilization and intentness of the thoughts, and is produced by concentration; when, through the paling of joy, indifferent, contemplative, conscious, and in the experience of bodily happiness—that state which eminent men describe when they say, 'Indifferent, contemplative, and living happily'—he enters upon the third trance; when, through the abandonment of happiness, through the abandonment of misery, through the disappearance of all antecedent gladness and grief, he enters upon the fourth trance, which has neither misery nor happiness, but is contemplation as refined by indifference—this, O priests, is called right concentration.

"This, O priests, is called the noble truth of the path leading to the cessation of misery."[1]

The foregoing passage contains an outline of the practical way which the Buddhist has to go. But it is only an outline. There are many writings treating this subject more fully and more in detail.

The practical directions of the Buddha begin with precepts, which are meant for people in general, for the whole of the lay world. For although the course of the true disciple narrows later on, so that only the monk who has forsworn the world can tread it, yet the Buddhist doctrine does not altogether keep aloof from the secular life. It is considered of high importance to prepare the layman for the higher path, even if the result of his striving only leads him to a happier reincarnation. Perhaps this reincarnation

[1] Quoted from Warren, "Buddhism in Translations," p. 373 *et seq.*

puts him in circumstances more favourable to his turning away from the world and reaching the ultimate goal as a monk. The precepts given to lay people are often expressed in the form of five commandments. They are as follows:

1. Not to take life.
2. Not to steal.
3. To refrain from unlawful sexual intercourse.
4. Not to tell lies.
5. Not to drink intoxicating liquors.

These five fundamental precepts form only the backbone of a very penetrative system of morality set up for lay people. It comprises all that was considered lawful, honourable, and obligatory in the social relations of life at the time of the Buddha. He who wants to get at the details of these duties may turn to writings such as the Mangala Sutta, the Dhammapada, the Sigâlowâda Sutta.[1] They set forth the duties of parent and child, of teacher and pupil, of husband and wife, of friend and friend, of master and servant, of laymen towards the religious institutions. Some of it would not be applicable to our day and manners, at other points there is something lacking in what we should expect; but most of it is beneficent, and appeals to our judgment as well, springing from a fine moral perception. The quintessence of this moral code for laymen is that their conduct should be governed by a careful observance of the moral norm prevailing in their days.

[1] Parts of these books are quoted in Rhys Davids' "Buddhism," chap. v., pp. 124-149, where the translation of the whole subject is to be found.

From this broadest basis of ethics (which is compulsory for all), the layman who wishes to do something special can, however, rise to a higher level by adding to the above five fundamental rules three further ones, which are these:

6. Only to take food at certain specified times.
7. Not to take part in dancing, music, performances.
8. Not to adorn the body with flowers nor use perfumes and unguents.

At the same time, he who accepts these rules must take a stricter form of the third precept given to laymen in general—namely, to restrain from *all* sexual intercourse. By the acceptance of these eight rules a minor stage of monkish life is entered. Lay people occasionally join the monastic Order for a limited time, subjecting themselves to these eight rules, and obtaining thereby a certain degree of merit, which will be accredited to them in their reincarnation.

But it is only within the monastic circle proper that the striving after the goal of Nirvâṇa can be fully carried out. The theoretical possibility of attaining the goal as a layman is not really disputed, for there are a few individual instances of such a thing happening in early times. But practically the possibility is held to be out of question on account of its extreme difficulty of attainment. The monk's life which the Buddha requires is founded on the fulfilment of ten precepts—namely, the foregoing eight and two others:

9. Not to sleep on any high or wide bed.
10. Not to possess either gold or silver.

When one looks at these commandments of Buddhist monasticism as a whole, they are seen to be partly prohibitions of an ethical nature, and partly such as aim at a certain isolation and simplicity of life, at the renouncing of family ties, of property and possessions, at the foregoing of outward beauty as a means of enjoyment, or of yielding to sensual desire. They characterize as such the tendency of Buddhist monastic life. But these fundamental laws are supplemented still by a number of other instructions requisite for the ordering of a common life, with its several obligations and relations. Thus, there are enactments as to dwellings, dress, occupation, food, the behaviour of one monk to another, his behaviour towards the laity, etc. These regulations cannot, of course, be dealt with here in detail;[1] but one particularly important point must be mentioned, and that is that the monk is supposed to be supported by mendicancy. For this purpose he goes forth every morning to beg. He eats what is given him: meat is not forbidden. A widespread error among Europeans is that the Buddha forbade the eating of meat; but he emphatically rejected this limitation, though it is manifest that he prohibited the *killing* of animals for food. It was only in its later development that Buddhism made it a principle (in some countries) of declining meat as food.

It must be observed that *the whole monastic organiza-*

[1] The whole of the precepts to be observed by monks may be studied in T. W. Rhys Davids' and H. Oldenberg's translations of the Vinayapiṭaka: Sacred Books of the East, vols. xiii., xvii., xx.

*tion is only a means to aid the Buddhist in his special task;* it is a sort of shelter. Without this shelter, without the previous purging of the passions which it made possible, and without the arresting of external hindering influences, the labour of the real task would be intensified so as to render it impossible of achievement. It is another common error for those at a distance to imagine that Buddhism ascribes a special merit to the monastic way of life in itself because of ascetic principles. On the contrary, even the rules of monkhood in themselves possess no saving value.

Saving value is only to be obtained by spiritual labour, which should begin under the protection of the monastic life.

The main factor of this spiritual labour is *meditation.* This is the name of a very great and important part of the Buddhist's actual work of salvation. The disciple steps right into the task of meditation when he has sufficiently prepared himself inwardly by the training of his spirit through the accomplishment of the external precepts of the monastic life. He must first have won a thorough inward watchfulness, self-control, power over his faculties, a discerning eye for faults and errors. For the one who thus possesses the right conduct the exercises of meditation now begin.

The character of Buddhist meditation cannot better be described than by again borrowing the words of one of the best authorities in this department, H. C. Warren, who in his work "Buddhism in Translations" (p. 280 *et seq.*) says:

"The Buddha analyzes man and things inanimate,

and finds nothing that is permanent, but only the concrete and perishable. All Karma, he says, is performed under the influence of greed after some desired object, with hatred of that which is not wanted, and of infatuation or delusion of mind that causes one to believe that satisfaction will result when the object is attained. Now, all these objects after which one strives are necessarily more or less concrete and definite, and the concrete and definite are not satisfying to the reflective mind. Every thinking man endeavours to pass from the things which are seen and temporal to something which is unseen and which he can picture to himself as eternal. Now, it is to be observed that, when we endeavour to pass in thought from the transitory and the phenomenal to something more permanent and real, we try to compass our object by passing from the concrete to the abstract. We try to reduce the multiplicity of phenomena to a few heads, and the more general we can make these heads, the nearer we seem to come to indefinite or everlasting verity. But what we gain in extension we lose in intension, and the nearer does our conception approach to being a conception of nothing at all. The Buddha evidently saw this; but as negation was what he was striving for, he considered he had found the way to salvation, and hence we have his elaborate system of meditation. But I ought to say that 'meditation' is here a very clumsy word, and does not properly cover all the ground. The meditations of the Buddhists were not simple reflections on abstract subjects, but trances of self-hypnotism as well, in which they tried to bring, not merely the conceptions of the mind, but also the emotions and feelings of the heart, to rarefied generalizations."

Thus far Professor Warren. There are forty different subjects of meditation enumerated. These meditations, if earnestly carried out, lead to a trance or to several kinds of trances. The Buddhist knows four such trances. To them are added four states, the so-called formless states. The trances and states are described by the Buddha himself as follows: Of one who has entered the first trance the voice has ceased; of one who has entered the second trance reasoning and reflection have ceased; of one who has entered the third trance joy has ceased; of one who has entered the fourth trance the inspirations and expirations have ceased; of one who has entered the realm of infinity of space the perception of form has ceased; of one who has entered the realm of the infinity of consciousness the perception of the realm of the infinity of space has ceased; of one who has entered the realm of nothingness the perception of the infinity of consciousness has ceased; of one who has entered the realm of neither perception nor yet non-perception, the perception of the realm of nothingness has ceased; of one who has entered the cessation of perception and sensation, perception and sensation have ceased. Of the priest who has lost all depravity, passion has ceased, hatred has ceased, infatuation has ceased.

The four trances and the four formless states are the eight attainments. But it is to be observed that there is a ninth attainment, which is based on wisdom or intellectual discipline. This consists in mastering the chief points of the Buddha's teaching, and applying them to the elements of being, especially the doctrine of the three characteristics which inhere in all things—viz., transitoriness, misery, and the lack of an ego. To this discipline belongs a special trance, the trance of cessation. Therefore the whole subject of meditation might be divided into two categories, of which the former might be called concentration, the latter wisdom.

It is impossible here to give more than these short hints on such a difficult, though most important, subject. All who wish to study it more thoroughly, will find a great help in chapter iv. ("Meditation and Nirvâna") of H. C. Warren's book cited above.

From the beginning onwards method and organization were the characteristics of the Buddha's teaching; this must be obvious to everyone who has thoughtfully studied the foregoing pages. It will therefore be no matter of surprise that soon after the master's death his disciples associated the system of his instructions and the organized body of his followers directly with his person: the Buddha, the Doctrine, and the Community (Buddha, Dharma, Saṇgha), composed the three precious fundaments. The Buddha's method of obtaining salvation, translated into a number of specific rules, was the priceless gift of an organization which the master had framed during his lifetime, and left behind to be the exponent of that method and the recipient of its contents.

At first the Buddha had only founded monastic

communities for *men*. At that time woman was hardly considered a responsible personality. Her existence appeared somewhat in the light of the remark made recently by Count Tolstoi: "Women are the greatest stumbling-blocks in the existence of a man." Nevertheless, the teaching of the Buddha in its earnest philosophical tenor, if one penetrates to the heart of it, results in a higher estimate of woman. In the same way as the Buddha's ideas admitted of no social class distinctions (caste), but sought man, as such, wherever he was to be found, so for woman also must the way of salvation be open, inasmuch as woman also is a member of the human race. But the Buddha was fully conscious of the pressing practical dangers of this view. He agreed reluctantly to the founding of nunneries, and made them from the beginning strictly subordinate to the monks.[1]

[1] The text on Admission of Women to the Order (Culla-Vagga, x.) is given by Warren, "Buddhism in Translations," pp. 441-447. The Buddha was asked to admit women by the repeated application of his aunt, Mahâprajâpatî (vide *supra*, p. 2). After having been denied her wish three times, Mahâprajâpatî had her hair cut off, put on yellow garments, and came sorrowful, sad, and weeping, to Ananda, who decided to plead her cause. To him the Buddha at last yielded. Eight rules were laid down, by which nuns were made strongly dependent on the male followers. But after giving his assent the Buddha expressed his sorrow on this new course. He expected that the admission of women would ruin his work. It is as mildew falling upon a flourishing field of rice, or as rust falling upon a flourishing field of sugar-cane. If women had not entered the community, the good doctrine would abide a thousand years; now it will abide only five hundred years.

Entrance into a community of monks or nuns was, theoretically, free to anyone. No caste distinction was made, as has been already mentioned. But of course there were practically some limitations. A number of dangerous diseases were prohibitory of admission. Besides this, people who were in any way bound (such as soldiers or debtors) were refused admission. The consent of parents was also usually required. The minimum age for entering the monkhood was twenty. But a provisional earlier retirement from the secular life was made possible. It was a purely private act when a scholar sought a monk as teacher to prepare him for admission to the monastic life. The profession of actual monkhood was entered with a certain solemnity. For that purpose a community of monks must be called together, and the request for admission be laid before them publicly; an exhortation as to the monastic mode of life must be delivered, and the aspirant's agreement to it obtained.

The candidate who had been admitted was at liberty to leave at any time subsequently, should he change his mind. The separation would necessarily be effected by gross violation of the most important

---

One should compare with this statement the attitude against women characterized by the following words of the Buddha: He is asked by Ananda, "How shall we behave toward a woman?" He answers, "You must avoid seeing one." "But if nevertheless we see her, what shall we do?" "You shall not talk to her, Ananda." "But if we nevertheless talk with her, what then?" "Then you must be very watchful over yourself, Ananda." (Oldenberg, Buddha, p. 187.)

outward commands. In the early times the four which follow were marked out as such:

1. A monk must have no sexual intercourse of any kind.
2. He must be guilty of no theft.
3. He must not wittingly destroy life.
4. He must not boast of supernatural powers (magic).

If an infringement of these rules were proved, the one concerned was expelled; undiscovered misdemeanours of this sort inevitably excluded the monk from the rank of true disciples (that is, all his work was fruitless), even though he maintained correctly the outward semblance. Minor infringements of the manifold regulations of the monastic life were expiated by all sorts of penances. The old revered collection of precepts, and of the penances by which transgressions may be purged, is the famous Prâtimoksha (or Pâtimokkha, in Pâli), not itself to be found in the sacred writings (as it was to be handed down orally as a kind of secret), but contained in the Sutta Vibhanga. Special days were appointed for the purpose of self-examination in the community by means of the Prâtimoksha, and of confessing possible shortcomings. This took place at the new and the full moon. (Later on they added to these two other days, so that four sacred days divided the month into four parts similar to the Christian Sundays and weeks.) The days of confession were called Uposatha, and they are observed up to the present time. These assemblies for confession are nearly the only distinct instance of united devout activity of the whole community.[1] But this, even, has nothing in common with the public worship of other religions. Here is only the feeling of all being pledged to the same rules of conduct, and the recognition of the authority of the assembly by the individual.

The whole Buddhist organization rested merely on verbal tradition. *Gautama left nothing in writing.* All his teaching was spread by word of mouth, and his followers impressed it on their memories. This is not so incredible as might appear to the modern Western mind. In the culture of the ancient Indian the memory played a far more important rôle than in our book-blessed days. It accomplished far more, and was much more keenly valued than at present. The form in which the Buddha cast his teaching was specially adapted for committing to memory. For his more important doctrines he constructed certain formulas which he continually repeated. Many of the amplifications naturally followed from what were already familiar categories to most of his hearers. A numerical sequence was used again and again. Other material was readily stamped on the mind by its connection with practical requirements which had to be carried out day by day. Yet again, other things were easily remembered by being embodied in the pictorial form which the master used, or by striking

[1] One might add the act of initiation of a new monk, and a festival called Pavâranâ at the end of the rainy season, when the monks, before parting for their journeys, asked forgiveness from one another for eventual transgressions.

comparisons, or by the relation of experiences drawn from his own life or that of some well-known personality. At the same time it was one of the most important forms of activity of the organized community of disciples that they should become living bearers of the teaching. So for some time Buddhism could forego the help of writing.

In the long-run, it is true, this became an impossible condition of affairs. After some centuries recourse was had to writing, which eventually resulted in a canon of sacred scriptures. Naturally, its formation under these circumstances was a somewhat dark process. The date of origin of the single books of the canon, and how much may be considered the very word of the Buddha, are questions which will long continue to be the subject of difficult historical investigation.

A preliminary word may here be added as to the contents of the Buddhist canonical writings. The canon is not identical in all countries where Buddhism prevails; the fundamental features, the most important books, the main divisions, are indeed to be found everywhere. Scholars generally agree that the canon of the so-called Southern Buddhism (prevailing in Ceylon, Burma, Siam), on the whole, presents the most original aspect of the sacred books. This canon is written in the Pâli language. It is called the Tipiṭaka (Sanskrit: Tripiṭaka)—that is, "The Three Baskets"; for it consists of three main parts of writings.

1. The first part is called the Vinayapiṭaka. It deals with the precepts and organization of the monastic life, and comprises three books:

(*a*) Suttavibhaṅga, a full exposition of the rules of the Pâtimokkha mentioned above.

(*b*) The Khandhakas, or smaller treatises, divided into two books: the Mahâvagga (great division) and the Cullavagga (small division). These books discuss some rules not contained in the Pâtimokkha, on admission into the Order, on the Uposatha ceremony, on duties in the rainy season, on clothing, dwelling, and similar points.

(*c*) Parivâra (appendix), a short manual of later addition, containing materials on the life of the community, arranged more for purposes of education.

2. The second part is called the Suttapiṭaka. The Buddha's doctrine of salvation is set forth in this, mostly in the form of dialogues, or discourses of the master to his disciples, frequently embodied in a historical setting. This part comprises the following collections:

(*a*) Dîghanikâya (collection of longer discourses), consisting of 34 long dialogues (suttas).

(*b*) Majjhimanikâya (collection of discourses of medium length, containing 152 suttas).

(*c*) Aṅguttaranikâya (collection of discourses arranged after numbers), containing more than 2,300 suttas in eleven divisions, so that the first division deals with things of which there exists only one kind, the second of such which exist twofold, the third of such which exist in threes, and so on.

(*d*) Samyuttanikâya (collection of discourses arranged in groups), containing 2,889 suttas in fifty-six groups, all suttas referring to one subject or one person brought together in one group.

Besides these four collections there is a fifth, which forms an appendix (some even count it as belonging to the next piṭaka), a collection of different materials, sayings of the Buddha, songs, tales, legends, and the like. This appendix is called:

(*e*) Khuddakanikâya (collection of smaller works); it consists of fifteen books, some of which belong to the best-known and most impressive works of the Buddhist literature. The books are these:

i. Khuddakapâtha (short recitations).
ii. Dhammapada (a kind of hymn-book).
iii. Udâna (ecstatic utterances).
iv. Itivuttakam (120 short stories, with sayings of the Buddha).
v. Suttanipâta (hymns).
vi. Vimânavatthu } (legends on future life in
vii. Petavatthu } heaven and hell).
viii. Theragâthâ } (songs of 107 monks and 73 nuns,
ix. Therîgâthâ } with biographical notes).
x. Jâtaka (legends on 550 former existences of the Buddha).
xi. Niddesa (commentary on the Suttanipâta).
xii. Paṭisambhidâmagga (on magic powers).
xiii. Apadâna (stories on saints).
xiv. Buddhavaṃsa (on 24 former Buddhas).
xv. Cariyâpiṭaka (on 34 former incarnations of the Buddha).

3. The third part of the Tipiṭaka is called Abhidhammapiṭaka. This part is of a psychological nature, discussing the psychological prolegomena of the Buddhist ethical system. It comprises seven books:

i. Dhammasaṃgani (compendium of states or phenomena).
ii. Vibhaṅga (continuation of the foregoing).
iii. Kathâvatthu (refutation of 252 heretical views).
iv. Puggalapaññatti (discrimination of men from the ethical point).
v. Dhâtukathâ
vi. Yamaka
vii. Patthâna

(v.–vii.: smaller treatises on psychological subjects).

Such is the contents of the Pâli canon of Buddhist scriptures. It seems that the whole of these scriptures has been reduced to writing towards the beginning of the first century before Christ, or somewhat later.[1] But there were certainly earlier collections of a similar kind, even at the time of King Aśoka (of whom we shall speak in the next chapter)—*i.e.*, about 250 B.C.

Very different from this Pâli canon is the canon of the Northern Buddhists—for instance, that of the Tibetans and the Chinese. Both the Tibetan and the Chinese Buddhist canons embrace a great many later works and commentaries, whilst those in common with the Pâli canon often differ very much in details.

[1] So it is stated by the Dîpavamsa, the old chronicle of Ceylon, written in the fourth century A.D. *Cf.* Rhys Davids, "Buddhist Suttas" ("Sacred Books of the East," xi.), p. xxii.

# BOOK II

# SKETCH OF THE HISTORY OF BUDDHISM

## CHAPTER I.—INDIA

DURING the lifetime of the Buddha the spread of his teaching extended not much beyond the kingdoms of Magadha and Kosala (see p. 5). During the succeeding centuries its influence slowly and gradually widened, but we are not able to follow the stages of its course, the next of which was the conquest of the whole peninsula. For a long time this great country was a sufficient task for it. By its spread in India Buddhism had by no means seriously set itself in opposition to the existing religions there. It rather appeared as a side-branch of the Brahmanistic system of thought. Despite some important differences (such as the teaching about the soul, the place held by caste), Buddha's mode of life and most of his doctrines were not received as anything new or unheard of. Superficially, therefore, it may not have been difficult for him to win possession of this territory, despite the controversies and passages of arms which would inevitably take place at the coming of Buddhism, owing to the rivalry of the Brahmans.

A greater difficulty lay in the successful passing through inward crises, so far, indeed, as this was possible. Some vague accounts of such crises have been handed down to us. From the very fact of the Buddha's long-continued labour, his withdrawal from the earthly stage, and the cessation of his personal direction and authority, were a severe test. It is true that when he lay a-dying he handed over the leadership to his most trusted disciple, who in his turn did the same at the time of his death, so that for many centuries there was a succession of so-called *patriarchs* at the head of Buddhism, who were leading personalities. But from the first these patriarchs were mainly of decorative value. A hierarchal development was too much opposed to the spirit of ancient Indian Buddhism. There was therefore no strong hand to keep an authoritative hold on the large numbers of monks. The doctrine on which the true basis of the society rested was, as we have already seen, a verbal tradition. Thus, it was but natural that its further growth produced various kinds of development.

Orthodox Buddhism emphatically maintains that immediately after the entrance of the Buddha into Nirvâṇa an accurate basis was defined on which this further development was to rest—namely, a council was held directly after the Buddha's death to establish the correct doctrine. Naturally this was oral, being delivered aloud by the two most highly esteemed disciples, and the others recited it in unison. This council is said to have taken place in a cave of the Vaihâra Mountain, in the neighbourhood of Râjagriha.

Five hundred monks are said to have taken part in it, and it was presided over by Kâśyapa, on whom the dying master had conferred the office of patriarch. This is the statement of orthodox Buddhist tradition.

We find a detailed account of this council in the book of the Sacred Canon called Cullavagga, chap. xi., and in the commentary on the Brahmajâlasutta, by Buddhaghoṣa. On the other hand, the main evidence against the fact of this council having taken place is the absolute silence on this point of the Mahâparinibbâna-sutta, one of the most important documents relating the death of the Buddha and some subsequent events. For further study see Rhys Davids' "Buddhist Suttas," pp. xi-xiii, and L. de la Vallée Poussin's "Les Conciles Bouddhiques": I. "Les Deux Premiers Conciles." In any case, the council, if it did take place, did not succeed by its decisions in putting a stop to the internal disagreement and dissension. In two respects we can prove that dissension characterized the new teaching during the first centuries. On the one hand, a lax party established itself along with a strict one in the practice of the monastic life. On the other hand, a number of differences of opinion crept in as to this or that philosophical point in the system.

Although the mode of life which Buddha had prescribed for his disciples was not, strictly speaking, an ascetic one, yet his instruction contained definite acts of renunciation, which in time were found to be very irksome and unattainable. This led to the formation of a group of adherents governed by laxer principles. They demanded a change in the rules, both as to their nature and the way in which they were to be carried out. Ten such "softening" requisitions were made, amongst which, for instance, were the following: That certain luxuries (fermented liquors) should be allowed; that meals might be taken after midday; that confession and the rite of admission should be allowed to take place in private houses; that comfortable beds might be used; and that the monks might own money. There was naturally a strong opposition to this relaxing of the old monastic austerity. At a second council which took place at Vaishâlî about a hundred years after the first one, a stern decree was passed utterly rejecting all those concessions, and reasserting the old basis of monastic discipline. But the opponents must have been already in the majority. They assembled in an opposition council, which far outnumbered the other, and decided the matter according to their own wishes. The existence of dissent became thus plainly evident.

The various opinions which arose at this time with regard to all sorts of doctrinal points, and the strife which they occasioned, were obviously of small importance. There were, indeed, eighteen different sects into which the faith had already split up, in the second century of its existence. These eighteen sects were subdivided into four main divisions called Mahâsânghika, Sthavira, Sarvâstivâda, and Sammitîya. Unquestionably, these were differences of minor importance, confined to the preference to be given to this or that interpretation of debatable points, or to this or that practical method, without (on such grounds) denying the fundamental right of anyone to the possession of the Buddhist truth of salvation.

In the second century of its existence, Buddhism saw great changes in the political conditions of its native land, which were not devoid of reflex action upon itself.

The journeys of Alexander the Great stirred India on its western frontier. It was, perhaps, due to these disturbing influences that a great united North Indian kingdom was formed in place of the many individual principalities, which both in the Buddha's lifetime and later had stood in rival and somewhat irritating proximity to one another. The founder of this united kingdom was Chandragupta, a gifted upstart of low caste, who became the hero of Indian folklore for many centuries owing to his heroic career. His kingdom extended from the borders of the present Afghanistan as far as Bengal, and from the Himalayas to the plateau of the Deccan. Chandragupta attained the summit of his glory in the year 315 B.C.

He had intimate dealings—first antagonistic, then friendly—with Seleucus Nicator, the mighty successor of Alexander the Great, who became India's neighbour on the western border. Seleucus Nicator attempted to renew Alexander's conquest of India, but was prevented from achieving this by Chandragupta. On the conclusion of peace, Seleucus consented to the marriage of one of his daughters with his former enemy. On this occasion the Greek Megasthenes was sent to the Court of Chandragupta at Pátaliputra, and his reports are one of the most important sources of our knowledge of the condition of India at that time. From the fragments of them, however, quoted by other writers we learn as to matters of importance very little about Buddhism. Megasthenes names the Buddhists as "Sarmanai," and says that they are opposed to the "Brahmanai." But his description of their mode of life is vague, and he seems to mix the Buddhists up with other Indian sects.[1]

Chandragupta himself was not a Buddhist; he was on far more friendly terms with the Brahmans, and it was the same with his son Bindusâra. His grandson, who was second in succession to the throne, became, however, the most famous patron of Buddhism. This was the King Aśoka (generally known by the Pâli form of his name, Asoka), who reigned about 270-233 B.C. It was after ascending the throne that he first came into contact with Buddhism, and only gradually that he awoke to an ardent zeal for the new religion. He always remained a mere lay adherent, but in the last twenty-seven years of his reign he became such an ideal and thorough promoter of Buddhism that no one since has come up to his level. He was originally called Priyadarśin, and may, perhaps, have adopted the name Aśoka (free from care) when he attained that condition by the acceptance of Buddhism.

Aśoka left behind him a large number of inscriptions on pillars and rock walls, which have recently been deciphered, and which form the most reliable material for the study of his character and for the

[1] *Cf.* "Megasthenis Indica," ed. Schwanbeck, pp. 136-140. Bonnæ, 1846.

Buddhism of that period. Thus we possess a fairly well-defined account of the development of Buddhism during Aśoka's reign.

During this period one traces a vigorous expansion of the strong young religion. King Aśoka in many of his edicts affirms the successful extension of Buddhist teaching beyond the borders of his kingdom. This refers to the relations he had entered into with several Western rulers, such as Antiochus II. of Syria (260-247 B.C.), Ptolemy Philadelphus of Egypt (285-247), Antigonus Gonatas of Macedonia (278-242), and others. These relations, which were of an essentially political nature, served at all events as a handle to the ardent Buddhist King, by means of which to introduce his religion, but the attempt led to no result worth mention. The attempt, however, is characteristic. It shows how the Buddhist of that time pushed forward into the unknown tracts of the world. The same spirit makes itself felt in the celebrated council which took place during his reign, the third according to Buddhist reckoning. It was held at Pâtaliputra in the year 252 B.C. Its main object was to safeguard afresh both doctrine and life from error and misuse. Here it was also resolved to send forth as missionaries a number of the most illustrious exponents of the faith beyond the limits of Aśoka's dominions. The following countries, indeed, were selected: Kashmir and Ghandara, the west of the Punjab, a district in the Deccan (the sources of the Godavari), Bactria, the territory of the Central Himalayas, the west coast of Farther India, Ceylon, besides some less certainly recognizable places in the same regions. A strenuous exodus from the homeland makes itself felt at this time, extending equally to the north, east, west, and south frontiers of India. It will not appear extraordinary that Buddhism, two hundred years after the death of its founder, should now for the first time set foot beyond the territory of India, considering the immense extent of that country and the length of time necessarily required to outgrow it.

As to the religious condition of Buddhism in India itself at this time we are well informed through the person of Aśoka, for in the inscriptions there is a clear account of what it meant to him. But one must never forget that Aśoka was a layman; that what concerned the innermost circle of followers cannot be demonstrated by reference to him. It is so much the more interesting, however, to see how Buddhism works through a gifted and influential layman, full of character. All the King's inscriptions prove that he draws from his religion a strengthening of moral effort, a consciousness of duty, a devotion to public welfare. Though Buddhism is certainly unable to express its doctrine of withdrawal from the world in the life of its lay adherents, yet in Aśoka it shows the moral and social training which form a preparation for this by means of the earnest accomplishment of all existing moral requirements. It is only by the respect he shows to monks, the fully-fledged disciples, and by the fact that many of his moral acts include the care and maintenance of the monastic community (the result, probably, of his esteeming these acts to be of the highest moral value), that Aśoka made it plain that the highest way must lead beyond the sphere of ordinary duties both for men and rulers.

Aśoka's moral apprehension is indeed somewhat idealistic. Thus, he says: "All men are my children. As I desire that my children may be partakers of all that is good and happy both in this world and the next, so I desire it also for mankind"; or, "There is no greater task than to strive for the universal welfare." What he urges on himself and on his dependents are mostly duties of real morality, the performance of which would not be questioned from the standpoint of any other religion: obedience and honour to parents, old people, and teachers; a rightful loyalty to friends; benevolence; effort for the public good (the planting of trees, digging of wells, the establishment of shelters, the distribution of medicinal herbs); the kindly treatment of servants and the poor; forbearance to all living things, even to animal life; truthfulness; patience; justice; curbing of sensuality; gratefulness, etc. No one can fail to be struck by his peculiarly keen moral attitude and impressive moral energy. He brings his own moral life into close touch with his religion, which he prizes over and over again. But he is no fanatic; he sees clearly the dangers of superstitious or bigoted action, and opposes it in a reasonable way.

But one must be careful not to generalize from the case of Aśoka as to the bulk of ordinary Buddhists of his day. The moral strength of purpose of Buddhism naturally exerted an influence on all laymen up to a certain point. There are traces even in Aśoka's inscriptions showing, on the other hand, that in popular Buddhism there already existed much extravagance and practices which caused moral declension.

Aśoka mentions in one of his inscriptions that he has for the second time caused a *stûpa*[1] of Kanakamuni to be enlarged. A stûpa means a memorial building, which often became also a place where relics were preserved. The above-mentioned personage, Kanakamuni, is looked upon as a bygone Buddha, who had appeared upon earth two generations before Buddha Gautama. This is an unhistorical dogmatic belief. But two facts are plainly demonstrated by this passage of Aśoka's inscription: first, that already in his day people had taken to building stûpas, and with them, no doubt, were connected all sorts of pious rites, pilgrimages, offerings, together with a belief in the efficacy of such things; secondly, that the mythological speculation of the Buddhism of that epoch had already developed a belief in a continuous series of Buddhas, each of whom had appeared at a particular time, one after the other in regular succession, till its consummation had been reached in the earthly existence of Buddha Gautama. From this we may draw some more general conclusions.

Soon after the rise of Buddhism in India it became weighted by that human dross which always, sooner or later, attaches itself to purely speculative religious conceptions, in so far as they are made serviceable to

1 *Stûpa*, a Sanskrit word, meaning originally "a tuft of hair," then "a dome-shaped monument." In Singhalese it is called *dâgaba* or *dagoba*, from the Pâli *dhâtu gabbha*, Sanskrit, *dhâtu garbha*, a casket for relics.

the common people. This is especially the case in the country of India. The natives of India, extremely religious as well as extremely superstitious, were surrounded with countless pious usages, which could by no means be set aside or ignored. Now, Buddhism made no effort to counteract them. This religion has from the very beginning always recognized a wider and a narrower circle of adherents. Even the monks divided themselves into groups, characterized by varying degrees of earnestness and efforts. If one looks farther afield, namely, at the lay adherents, Buddhism only aims at a certain ethical level and an outward support of the monkhood; beyond this, religious ideas and habits are considered unimportant. If they are foolish, if they are useless, it is no part of the scheme of enlightened adherents of Buddhism to combat them. If only those laymen, by means of moral zeal and thorough support of the Order, do their part, such a condition of existence will be granted to them in their next reincarnation (in accordance with the law of retribution) as to lead them into the path of pure doctrine. Then all superstitious practices will naturally disappear. It is on such grounds as these that the Buddhism of every period has shown itself singularly tolerant of foreign religious worship and conceptions, and it is this quality which gives it that particular Proteus-like gift of assimilation which has characterized it in every country where we have been able to study it in the light of history. This peculiarity has, indeed, been fatal to it, in the same degree as it has been the axle on which its historical movement turned.

That this was the case in the early times in India we have already observed from the account of the stûpa in Aśoka's inscription. The stûpa must then have been already some time in existence, for it was not erected by the King, but only twice enlarged. As this fact is well authenticated, the tradition gains a strong probability that there were many other stûpas in existence, and that Aśoka's name was connected with several of them. It is also evident that, at the time when stûpas were erected to the Buddha Kanakamuni (and besides him, doubtless, to other personages of the religious imagination), other places must already have had memorial buildings—namely, such places as those specially associated with the historical Buddha Gautama's life, and where relics of him were preserved.

Probably the first places to be marked by stûpas were the four which are most revered down to the present day: Gautama's birthplace (the grove of Lumbinî), the place where his great revelation took place (the Bo-tree), the place where he first preached (Benares), and the spot where he entered the perfect Nirvâṇa (Kuśinagara). But already in the days of Aśoka they had gone far beyond the limits of worshipping these places only. The need of the bulk of the people for places of prayer had found its satisfaction in the setting apart of numberless sacred shrines; and, furthermore, this coincided with the requirements of the monks. The worship of relics was attached to many of these places, and this is always the immediate cause of all sorts of superstition. Such superstitious offshoots were already so rife in Aśoka's time that he criticizes and tries to check them in some of his edicts.

Conceptions of the Buddhas of bygone periods (to which the name of Kanakamuni points) show equally an alienation from the modes of thought of this religion in its origin. Gautama had consciously and resolutely turned away from speculative thought, except such as was inseparably connected with the question of salvation; but in the intellectual atmosphere of India vague phantasies unconsciously sprang up which developed into universal history in the grand style. They played with measureless expanse of space and time; they created limitless worlds, to each of which they assigned their tale of fictitious Buddhas. The historical Gautama, Suddhodana's son, is foreshadowed by them in the whole limitless past. This sort of idea was already prevalent in Aśoka's day.

It is with Aśoka that one might begin the history of Buddhism outside India. But we will ignore this for the present, in order to trace further the development of this religion in its native land.

The large empire of Aśoka fell to pieces soon after his death. For some centuries Northern India was the scene of a similar drama to that which took place before Chandragupta's time, a large number of rival neighbouring States varying in power. During this time the Græco-Bactrian States were growing, as a by-product of the former empire of Alexander, on the western borders of India. This was an important fact for India. The Greek armies pressed forward eastward from Bactria, and temporarily seized large tracts of territory in North-West India. Under such circumstances, Greek and Indian culture became intimately fused. The high-water mark of the power and influence of the Græco-Bactrian empires was reached by King Menander (the Indian name is Milinda) about the middle of the second century B.C. The hindrance to the growth of this Greek confederacy of States, and to the growth of the petty States of Northern India, was the ever-increasing influx of Mongolian conquerors from the north and north-west towards the close of the second century. In the north and north-west of the Himalayas there was at that time a restless shifting of the aboriginal tribes. By this movement the so-called Sakhas (Scythians, the Chinese Ssŭ) were driven southward into Northern India, whence they extended small dependencies, like outposts, till they reached the Vindhya Mountains. Behind the Sakhas advanced the races of Yüeh-chi, also Mongols. After some encounters (of which our present knowledge forbids us to give a detailed account), a mighty empire was established in the North-West of India, composed of these invaders, which put an end to the Greek supremacy in Bactria. This is the so-called Indo-Scythian or Kushān Empire.

The most noted ruler of the Indo-Scythian Empire was Kaniśka. His reign was during the first or second century of the Christian era.[1] The extent of his empire was very considerable: it comprised mainly the bed of the Indus and of the Upper Ganges (as far as Agra),

[1] There has been much controversy as to the date of Kaniśka. Vincent A. Smith gives his accession as A.D. 78, or even as A.D. 120.

and extended also on the north as far as Yarkand, and on the west as far as Kabul. Kaniśka, like Aśoka, was an adherent of Buddhism. *During his reign it was that a new type of this religion came into existence,* which was partially opposed to the older form, and which was the cause of a great split among the followers of the Buddha; this division has controlled the whole course of Buddhist history. We must now consider this change more closely.

It has been already pointed out that the margin between Buddhism and the philosophico-religious tendencies of that period in India were from the beginning indeterminate in character. Also we have remarked already (p. 46), that the Buddhist did not separate himself entirely from the prevalent superstitious beliefs and customs common to the masses; on the contrary, he showed a strong inclination to adapt himself to the popular belief, and to weave foreign ideas into his own creed. This lack of sharply defined outlines of his spiritual territory was particularly disastrous in its results, since Buddhism—from the days of Aśoka onwards—spread over an ever-increasing area of India; while on the other hand foreign blood and foreign conceptions continually poured into India, together with the political changes to which we have already referred. The borderlands of India towards the Himalayas, towards Turan, and towards Iran in which the disciples of the Buddha were establishing themselves more and more securely, possessed their own individual, well-shaped religious characteristics, a remarkable cult and superstition, which enforced respect. At the same time all sorts of Greek, Persian, and other Asiatic influences poured freely from the west into India. The Indo-Scythian Empire freely absorbed all this medley.

In such a state of affairs the original trend of thought of Buddhist teaching became saturated with alien material and essentially changed. Conceptions totally at variance with those of its founder filtered into it. These new ideas were not only tolerated by the ignorant multitude, but they also took possession of the narrower circle of the monkhood; they were formed into a doctrinal system by speculative minds, which was given out as being thoroughly Buddhist, while others, indeed, recognized this as a dangerous innovation, and strenuously held themselves aloof from it.

The *most important of these new ideas* which had been incorporated into Buddhism were as follows:

(*a*) The *conception of an Eternal Deity*. Buddha did not combat the belief in gods which he found existing among his associates. The divine to him was but one among many forms of existence, a happy kind of existence, one of the rewards of a virtuous life. The gods, however, are also subject to change, no matter how long a time they may continue. They are capable also—according to the law of retribution—of sinking to a lower state of existence, or even to the lowest. The gods are far inferior to the Buddha; they have not yet reached the goal—Nirvâṇa—they still remain in the whirlpool of reincarnation. One easily recognizes that this is not a perfect conception of godhead, which embraces the highest, the entirely superhuman, the eternal. With such a conception of the gods, the

Buddha could afford to give full play to the superstition of the multitude, without his own ideas being thereby affected. But at the time of which we are speaking, another conception of the Divine Being had arisen, which is entirely opposed to the original Buddhist system of thought. By this is meant an Eternal God, superior to all things, who is the ultimate and supreme cause of all life. The historic Buddha Gautama is reduced to being but a transitory manifestation of this Eternal Being. One can only take this to be a reversion to the ancient Brahman theory of the world-soul, or perhaps the influence of a foreign (Persian, or even Christian) belief. The most prominent attributes of this highest Deity are those of infinitude (of absolute being, especially as regards the limitations of time) and of light.

(*b*) The *Bodhisattvas*—so called—now begin to assume an important rôle. The name of Bodhisattva (he whose essence, *sattva*, is becoming enlightment, *bodhi*) signifies those who, through the various stages of development, had by ever-increasing merit attained to the career of a Buddha in their next reincarnation. For instance, Gautama, when he came down from heaven (according to the legend) to become flesh in his mother Mâyâ, was a Bodhisattva. When a Bodhisattva undertakes the task of a Buddha, then his goal is Nirvâṇa: with that, naturally, all earthly relation comes to an end. For him who has reached Nirvâṇa, no faithful supplication can obtain anything further. But it is for the necessity of having a personality to which mankind can address itself in times of stress and sorrow that the following theory sprang. Many of those lofty beings, who are in a position to tread the last way of life, are possessed by a strong craving to aid their fellow-beings around them, to lead them into the true way of knowledge, and this craving determines them to willingly forego the Buddhaship which they might attain, in order to live for countless years in the state of a Bodhisattva engaged in tasks of ministry to lower beings. The Bodhisattva meanwhile exists in one of the many heavens, possesses divine powers, is filled with kindly intentions towards the suffering world below him, and is ready to help those who appeal to him. This is the kind of Bodhisattvas which the Buddhism of our period created in ever-increasing numbers, by which means it retained and remodelled frequently the popular deities of those countries into which it desired to gain admission.

(c) *By this theory the moral attitude of monasticism, as well as its ideals, was altered.* The ideal of the ancient monkhood was the so-called *Arhat*—namely, the Holy One—viz., a man who, through most perfect obedience to the teaching of the Buddha, had obtained entrance to Nirvâṇa. Now the attainment of the Bodhisattvahood takes the foremost place. The compassionate, helpful character of the Bodhisattva contributes to the moral aspect of sympathy with all beings, of a world-encompassing love, which becomes much more prominent now than in the earlier Buddhism, of which the morality was directed rather to the attainment of personal holiness.

(d) With regard to the laity, the *invocation of the Bodhisattva* now naturally becomes the central point.

Besides the emphasis laid on meritorious acts, remarkable stress is placed (for the laity) on *faith.* Whoever makes a trustful appeal to the Bodhisattva, and believes in him with strong conviction, may rely upon obtaining his compassion.

(*e*) This change into the usual religious belief in gods, countenanced by the ancient teaching of the Buddha, was still further strengthened by the fact that a happy state of existence—*a paradise*—was substituted for Nirvâṇa. Such is the reward (adorned with every imaginable joy) of virtuous conduct, and he who attains this blessed life is saved from the uncertainties of reincarnation. *Hell* is placed in contrast to this Paradise. A coarser delineation of reward and punishment in happy or unhappy surroundings replaces the old philosophical conception of existence being a state of suffering, and of the final release from it through the removal of all empirical being.

(*f*) Even the old fundamental rule of monastic life, which enjoined ten obligations, was now transformed, owing to the influence of the fact that in certain particulars the monk's life had been altered. The following ten obligations were now enjoined: Not to kill, not to steal, to avoid all unchastity, not to lie, not to slander, not to insult, not to chatter, not to covet, not to give way to anger, to harbour no scepticism. These ten commandments comprise three sins of the body, four sins of the tongue, and three sins of the mind.

These are the most important changes which took place during Kaniśka's reign in the Buddhist dogmatic system. It is also worthy of notice that this new phase was characterized by a change of language for the vehicle of its ideas. In the place of Pâli we find Sanskrit. For just at that time there was an artificial renaissance of this ancient and sacred language, in conjunction with definite efforts to fix the verbal tradition of the sacred records of Buddhism by written documents.

The King Kaniśka held again a council, which took place at Jâlandhara in Kashmir. At this council the above-mentioned new lines of Buddhism seem to have been established. Three great commentaries to the sacred canon were sanctioned. These commentaries were written in Sanskrit, and we may accept with confidence the fact that they were the expression of the new development.[1] This is the reason why Southern Buddhism refused to acknowledge this council.

The cleavage caused by this new development within Buddhism is marked by the names of *Mahâyâna* and *Hînayâna*. The names signify the big vehicle and the little vehicle. The picture of a vehicle was frequently used in Buddhism to symbolize the doctrine, which bore the disciples across the world to the goal of Nirvâṇa. The widened and transformed Buddhism, as it then found its centre in Kashmir, called itself Mahâyâna, and it called the older form Hînayâna. In India both schools of thought existed side by side for a long space of time, naturally not

[1] These writings have not yet been published; but in later times (for instance, by the Chinese pilgrims) they are mentioned as eminent works of the Mahâyâna division.

without a certain amount of friction ; this occasionally rose to an acute stage of denunciation and strife, but it was generally so slight as to allow monks of both persuasions to live together in the same monastery. Later historical development separated these two schools, so that the older and more original Buddhism — the Hînayâna — became the ruling one in the southern countries, Ceylon and Farther India, while Mahâyâna Buddhism won for itself the northern countries of Tibet, Mongolia, China, Korea, and Japan.

The whole scope of Mahâyâna Buddhism may be seen realized during the reign of Kaniśka in the personality of Aśvaghoṣa, who must be considered the most eminent exponent of this school. There is an important work of his which has been preserved for us in a Chinese translation. It has been translated by Teitaro Suzuki (Chicago, 1900), and lately by Dr. Timothy Richard (Shanghai, 1907), entitled "Treatise on the Awakening of Faith."[1] This work gives a systematic account of Buddhist principles, according to the Mahâyâna tenets. Other renowned masters of this school, of later date, were Nâgârjuna (in the later half of the second century A.D.), Âryadeva, and Vasubhandhu.

Despite the great cleft which from this time forward ran through Buddhism, it is nevertheless in the first centuries of the Christian era that it grew and flourished in India. At that time it seems to have

[1] Aśvaghoṣa also wrote a remarkable life of the Buddha of such a legendary character as to show how far men had already wandered from the historical conception of the founder of the religion (see p. 7).

largely superseded Brahmanism in the popular estimation. From 300 B.C. to A.D. 100, the many inscriptions as to gifts, sacrifices, and so on, which Kings, great and wealthy persons, or pious donors, presented, do not make mention of them in connection with any Brahmans or Brahman temples or Brahman worship. Also in the second and third centuries A.D. there is but seldom any mention of Brahmans. It is evident that Buddhism was until the fourth century A.D. the main and the ruling religion in India for the bulk of the population. The most noteworthy description which we possess from the Chinese Fa Hsian, when he traversed India as a pilgrim (about A.D. 400), shows us Indian Buddhism in its strength and pomp.

There was a large number of monasteries throughout the country, he tells us. They were specially numerous in the neighbourhood of those places connected either by historical or legendary association with the person of the Buddha Gautama. Thus, in the neighbourhood of the Jetavana Park, which is well known in connection with the Buddha's life, there were ninety-eight monasteries. Many of them must have been very large establishments, as the number of monks amounted to a thousand or more. Everywhere stûpas were to be found in close proximity to the monasteries, sometimes gigantic buildings, in which the art lent its brilliant service to religion. Monasteries and stûpas were beset by a dense tissue of superstition, which was by no means peculiar to the laity, but also shared by the monks both of the Hînayâna and the Mahâyâna schools. Relics, such as a tooth of the Buddha, or his begging-bowl, or his pilgrim staff, or a skull-bone of his, or some such thing, was said to be preserved in one place or another, and received great homage. The common faith overlaid them with miraculous powers. Thus, one hundred men were unable to lift the Buddha's stick. Five elephants could not drag his begging-bowl from its place. The account also of the Buddha's life is full of supernatural features. They showed places in the rocks where impressions of his footprints were to be seen. From existences of the Buddha previous to his last life, there is also drawn a wealth of legendary material. Not only are his portraits revered in the monasteries, but those also of many other holy persons, such as the three supposititious Buddhas, who preceded his epoch, and the one who was to follow him, besides the most noted of his disciples and others. All sorts of ingredients belonging to the earlier Indian mythology are melted together with Buddhism. The *devas* are worshipped as subordinate holy beings. From the very ancient serpent worship they adopted the *nâgas* (serpent spirits) and made them serviceable to Buddhism. Such a serpent, for instance, they would select to be the patron saint of a monastery, and a special room in it would be set apart for his worship.

The monks, according to Fa Hsian's record, find their main occupation in reciting sacred passages, in meditation, and in ascetic performances. They are frequently held in high estimation for their reputed supernatural powers of all kinds. Thus, they can affect the weather, and are applied to for this purpose. At festivals they form processions with great pomp. Naturally, it is the duty of the laity to provide for the maintenance of the monks. Illustrious personages and Princes occasionally give large donations, and in the ceremonies which take place at such times it is evident with what reverence the monks are treated by the laity. The ordinary person not only supplies food to the inmates of the monastery, but also material for clothes and other small requisites. In return for the maintenance of the monastery, the laity expect a blessing on their houses and families, success to their undertakings, as well as the reward of a happy future. The outward signs of the respect of the laity for the temple images is the bringing of flowers and fruit, the burning of incense, and the lighting of lamps and lanterns. This kind of offering is usually to be bought by visitors in the vicinity of the temples.

If one considers all these features as they appear in the description of his travels by Fa Hsian, it is quite evident that Indian Buddhism—full of vitality as it then was—had entirely been transformed into a popular religion, through amalgamation with an incalculable mass of material which was essentially alien to it. The supernatural and magical element had become extremely prominent.

This way is followed up still farther. Together with the statement of a divine world-soul, there was also the conception of the human soul (which Gautama had so strenuously denied), creeping in again at this time as popular assumption for the magical practices of Mahâyâna Buddhism. From here arose a new phase of doctrinal development—the so-called Yoga doctrine. The word Yoga means an ecstatic union of the individual soul with the world-soul. By certain methods, in which self-hypnotism played a large part, the soul of the individual was to be brought into union with the All-Soul, and would thereby participate in certain magic powers, so that the individual would be able at will to make his body lighter or heavier, larger or smaller, able to fly through the air, able to take on any appearance, and so on, until at last a condition of complete oneness with the highest would be attained. This doctrine found its connecting link in the old practice of meditation, which had been so essential in the early Buddhism. But in the Yoga doctrine the main stress is attached to miraculous powers. One aid to their attainment was the use of certain mystical formulæ (dhâranî) and short prayers (mantra), which were recited in special attitudes and with special attention paid to the position of fingers and hands, to the accompaniment of music. Owing to the use of mantras, this whole development of Buddhism has been called *mantrism*.

Into what a shallow and boundless superstition Buddhism had degenerated we can see from its present condition in Tibet, as Lamaism. It is to this that India has specially bequeathed this doctrine and type, as we shall see later on. From the height of a philosophical religion it had come down to the level of a blind superficial belief and coarse deceptions. This fall reached its lowest depth in some conceptions emanating from the Yoga teaching, which are known under the name of *Tantrism* (from *tantra*, verbally, "the book," a revelation).

In Tantrism the faith of the Buddha adopted a strongly marked sexual character. They set up pairs of deities, so that everywhere the male deity was accompanied by its female counterpart. These "female energies" were frequently represented with male deities in such a way that, notwithstanding a deeper meaning behind the conception of sex which might be pretended, practically it is certain that a strongly immoral attitude has been introduced by this symbolism.

The degeneracy of Buddhism which ensued from this influence we cannot trace step by step. But the light shed upon this period in the middle of the seventh century by the descriptions of the Chinese pilgrim Yüan Chuang shows this degeneracy in its whole extent. At the same time it emphasizes plainly certain symptoms showing the lack of vitality of Buddhism in the territory of India. Buddhism was completely choked by the increase of superstition, chimeras, and sensuality.

In the portrayal by Yüan Chuang of Indian Buddhism in the seventh century, we are confronted with relic worship, manifold legends, insipid stories of miracles, belief in the power of magic formulæ, arts of exorcism, fragments of ancient Indian nature worship, and all this is often expressed in the crudest manner. Alongside such traits are many observations as to the decay of religion, references to the once-renowned Buddhist monasteries and stûpas now in ruins, and to the paucity of monks. Some of the legends related by him are worthy of mention. One of these legends spoke of a certain garment bequeathed by an honoured monk to the community of the faithful as a relic, with the assurance that the garment would last till Buddhism ceased to exist. But in those days, remarked Yüan Chuang, there were already unmistakable signs of decay in the garment, and the faithful recognized, therefore, the truth of the prophetic statement! There was another record about a stûpa that the Buddha had foretold, that when it should have been seven times burnt down, and seven times rebuilt, then Buddhist teaching had reached its end. And Yüan Chuang maintained that in his time the stûpa had already been burnt down for the fourth time. Therefore the highest point of Buddhism had already been passed. This sort of legend shows plainly that the adherents of the religion themselves had the consciousness that they were living in a period of decadence.

Attacks from without also must have injured Buddhism in this century. A powerful tide of Brahmanism, which had long been held in check by Buddhism, now rose everywhere to a high mark. The hostile attitude of the Brahmans against their rivals can be as little doubted as the fact that the latter at this time could no more check it. The tradition telling of a sharp persecution of Buddhists by the Brahmans in the eighth century may, therefore, have historical accuracy. But it cannot be taken that this persecution or any other external cause has done away with Buddhism in India proper. It was of far greater importance that it laboured under a helpless inward decay. Its slow destruction continued from the eighth to the eleventh century A.D. When Islam penetrated at last into India (in the eleventh and twelfth centuries), all that still remained to be seen of the fallen religion was swept away utterly by the fanaticism of the iconoclastic Moslem. Since that time the religion of the Buddha Gautama no longer exists in its own native land. Only the ruined places of the old Buddhism preserve to the countries on the banks of the Ganges and of the Indus, down to the present day, the interest of all those who are nearer concerned with this remarkable religion.

## Chapter II.—THE SPREAD OF BUDDHISM

The period of the further spread of Buddhism begins with the above-mentioned council under Aśoka. It was an advancing and most eventful tide of conquest —stretching over whole centuries—by which the yellow-robed monks obtained the ascendancy over Central and Eastern Asia. Ceylon, followed by the Indian Peninsula containing Burma, Siam, Cambodia, Annam, besides the races in the Himalayas, Central Asia as far as Tien-Shan itself, Tibet, China and Mongolia, Korea and Japan—these are the countries which fell into the lap of Buddhist missions during the thousand years which ensued after the council of Aśoka. In most of these countries the result of the Buddhist mission is due to the fact that Gautama's disciples came to primitive, almost uncivilized peoples, to whom they brought, together with this new religion, a strong tinge of culture, so that the acceptance of Buddhism implies also the beginning of historical development. Where this was not the case—as in

China, where they encountered an already high degree of culture—the conquest of Buddhism was neither so rapid nor so complete.

In the following pages we shall trace the missionary history of Buddhism in the most important countries, though, naturally, it is only possible to give the outlines.

### Ceylon.

This island, which in prehistoric times was peopled by the primitive stock of the Vedda (of whom there still exist a few remains, as a rare proof of primitive man), was taken possession of in the sixth century B.C. (namely, about the lifetime of Gautama) by hordes of invaders who came from the mainland of India, and whose leader made himself ruler of the island. Thus Indian civilization touched the soil of Ceylon. A kingdom was developed and towns grew up. But the result of this cannot have been very great, since no building or design has been found of the period preceding the advent of Buddhism. In Aśoka's time the ruler of Ceylon was Tissa, who began to reign about 251 B.C. It is reported that there existed a friendship between these two, since Tissa, without ever having seen the King of Magadha, had conceived an ardent admiration for him, owing to a description of his person and deeds. Directly after his accession to the throne, Tissa sent, therefore, an embassy to Aśoka, and an embassy was sent to him in return. The latter is said to have come with the object of communicating to Tissa Aśoka's Buddhist creed. In any case, it was from Aśoka's kingdom that Buddhism was introduced into Ceylon. One cannot doubt the assertion of the Singhalese chronicle, the Mahâvamsa, to which we owe all this information, that the bringer of the new doctrine was Aśoka's own son, Mahendra, who had himself entered the monastic Order. If meagre accounts of Buddhism had already reached the island in consequence of the existing intercourse with Northern India, they were completely thrown into the shade by the brilliant entrance of the new religion with Mahendra. A prominent teacher—a monk—had carefully prepared him in his own home for this important missionary task. Mahendra came to Ceylon with a large number of others about 250 B.C. The Singhalese chronicle relates how he met King Tissa out hunting not far from the capital of Anuradhapura, and at once announced to him the sublime teaching, whereupon he was led with honour to the city in order to give further instruction to the King and to the Court. The place where Mahendra afterwards lived for many years is, according to the tradition which has been handed down to the present day, a picturesque spot, where huge boulders surmount the top of a peak near Mihintale, to the east of the city of Anuradhapura, whose extensive ruins have recently been excavated. Some time after Mahendra came he was followed by his sister Samghamitrâ, who herself belonged to the Order as a nun. She came from her father's Court to found a nunnery. She brought as a present from Aśoka to Tissa a branch of that celebrated and much-revered tree, under which the Buddha sat when he received the revelation of his new doctrine, and which was therefore called the Bo-tree. The branch was planted in Ceylon, and grew to be a tree, which outlived the original Bo-tree, and which still blooms among the ruins of Anuradhapura, a symbol of the fact that Buddhism has been stronger and more lasting outside its native land than in North India itself.

Buddhism soon blossomed forth in Ceylon. The Prince and his Court became adherents, and the common people was drawn after them. A lively religious culture and art developed themselves in connection with the monastic communities, in the shape of cloisters, dagabas, sacred images, and religious outfit. King Tissa himself presented a large garden for them to live in, and provided land for buildings and halls for meditation. He also built one of those huge dagabas, which still exists, namely, the Thuparama Dagaba, under which one of Gautama's collarbones is said to have been preserved as a relic. Anuradhapura, the capital, was for centuries the brilliant centre of Buddhist life. The dagabas which in course of time were erected there are considered amongst the greatest monuments in the world, and down to the present time give astonishing proof of the achievements of art in the service of religion by their many temples, halls, baths, palaces, and irrigation works. At the beginning of the third century A.D., a tooth of the Buddha was brought as a relic from India to Ceylon, and a magnificent place was built for its reception. The holy tooth was removed later on to Pollunarua, which became the capital in the eighth century A.D.; and finally it was sent to Candy, where a spurious one (for the original tooth was destroyed) is venerated to the present day.

In all important respects Buddhism remained unchanged in Ceylon from the early days, and its history is mainly that of changing circumstances (of which there were many), for it was closely bound up with the history of the Singhalese rulers and their kingdom. Important invasions of conquest-hunters from the mainland, especially from the south-east coast, had a fateful effect, and wrought ever fresh disaster on the splendour and power of Ceylon. A fall in the political power of its patron meant invariably a corresponding fall in the position of Buddhism; whereas a more powerful and prosperous ruler added new lustre to religion. After a rapid declension, a great revival took place during the reign of the mighty ruler Parakrama-Bahu (in the twelfth century). But after the Portuguese had laid a heavy hand on the island in the sixteenth century—to be displaced and robbed of their plunder later on by the Dutch, from whose hands Ceylon passed yet again to the British in 1796—Buddhism lost more and more of its ancient splendour. It still remained an important factor in the intellectual life of the island within its natural limits.

## Farther India.

This section deals with Burma, Siam, and Cambodia. Annam and Cochin China are not included in it. These last belong rather to the China sphere of influence, and their Buddhism has taken the Chinese shape. As to the spread of Buddhism in the three above-mentioned countries, not much can be determined with certainty from the standpoint of our present knowledge. The many legendary and fabulous stories which these people possess about their own history are of very little use to us with regard to early times. The study of buildings and inscriptions provides us with our principal material, but there is not yet much done in this direction.

As regards Burma, we are confronted with two accounts of the advent of Buddhism. In the first place we are told that, after the council of Aśoka, two men were sent here as missionaries. The accuracy of this account is not to be doubted. The country designated by the name of Suvarna-bhûmi (gold land) certainly is Burma—that is to say, the strip of land on its north-west sea-border, Arakan and Pegu. On the other hand, Burmese tradition attributes the introduction of Buddhism to the celebrated Buddhaghoṣa. This man was born in Northern India in the fifth century A.D., in the ancient country of Magadha; was converted from Brahmanism to being an ardent adherent of Buddhism; and owes his great reputation to the excellent commentaries which he wrote, and to his translation into Pâli of the then existing Singhalese commentaries. He lived for a long time in Ceylon. One of the ruined temples of Anuradhapura is still shown as the place where, for many years, he was occupied with the work of translation. There is ground for doubting the statement that this man brought Buddhism to Burma. The chronicles of Ceylon, to which we owe the information about Buddhaghoṣa, and which must have been well informed on the subject, give no account of his journeys to Farther India. Indeed, one of the most important inscriptions in Burma, which was erected at the end of the fifteenth century A.D., at the instigation of a King of Pegu, who was among the most devoted adherents of Buddhism, and which throws a backward glance over the history of Buddhism in Burma, makes no mention whatever of Buddhaghoṣa. The Burmese tradition which refers to him does so on account of his translations and writings having become fundamentals in the country, probably also because his intellectual influence may have inaugurated a new epoch in Burmese Buddhism.

The Buddhist missionaries sent out by the council of Aśoka must have been the first to plant this religion in the soil of Farther India. They found there primitive, uncultured peoples. Indian culture went with them, and flowed increasingly across to the Burmese. In the next centuries the Buddhism of Burma developed in a manner analogous to that which we have already observed in Northern India. It was invaded by a strong admixture of rough popular conceptions, to which not only the lower Indian religious life, but also the coarse ideas of the ancient Burmese inhabitants, contributed. The Burmese traditions themselves state that their Buddhism had a troubled course for many centuries, mixed with serpent worship, magic beings, horrible and debauched customs. The Himalayan tribes also—especially the Assamese—have in this time exercised an influence on Burmese Buddhism. The sacred language (as in the whole Mahâyâna school) was then Sanskrit, and it has been observed, as a survival of that epoch, that even to-day there are many names in Burmese Buddhism which still retain the Sanskrit form, although later on the sacred language was changed to Pâli. Through a strong reaction this old phase of Burmese Buddhism was overmastered. This new foundation may have been laid during the time succeeding Buddhaghoṣa, and it may be related to his intellectual influence. The purer southern type of doctrine now obtained the predominance, which it has maintained down to the present day.

The older form of Burmese Buddhism must have corresponded somewhat to that which we meet still amongst the so-called Shan tribes. These are mountain races in the north and east of Burma, adherents of Buddhism, but of a type strictly different from Hînayâna.

Siam and Cambodia were associated with Northern Indian culture from an early date. They owe to it all the fundamentals of their life. Brahmanism and other religious forms came over with that culture, and especially the former was very strong at the beginning. Of Buddhism, on the other hand, we hear only after the middle of the seventh century A.D., as gaining ground in Cambodia. It then slowly advanced in ways which tradition has not preserved. There are numerous Buddhist inscriptions in Cambodia, dating from the ninth century. The stronger influx of Buddhism at that time appears to stand in intimate connection with its decline in Northern India. Whereas it was obliged to give way there to Brahmanism, here it succeeded from the end of the tenth century in showing itself the tenacious opponent of Brahmanism, and eventually, in the twelfth century, its master. After it had continued for a long period to grow in strength—thanks to the powerful protection of the Court—it finally reached the throne itself. But in Cambodia also there are evident traces that this older Buddhism has been Mahâyâna Buddhism disfigured by many external influences (perhaps from Nepal, and even Tibet, using Sanskrit as its language). It was only in the fifteenth century that a great change took place. This resulted from contact with Ceylon, and the Southern Buddhism, with its Pâli literature, its more original doctrine, and its higher moral level, displaced completely the older relations. The Siamese kingdom (which only came into existence in the fourteenth century) from that time begins to be one of the main strongholds of Hînayâna Buddhism.

### Tibet.

Tibetan history begins when Buddhism penetrated into that wild mountainous country. In the seventh century A.D. a chief called Srong Tsan Gampo succeeded in reducing the rough tribes of that inaccessible land to a stricter discipline, and it was this chieftain who accepted Buddhism and introduced it into the country. This was owing to his two wives, one of whom sprang from the Chinese royal house (this was a marriage arranged for political reasons, as the Tibetan chieftain was always making difficulties on the Chinese frontier); while the other was Nepalese. Both of the wives, therefore, came from countries where already Buddhism had long been established. From the outset Indian influence was predominant, as can be most clearly proved by the fact that Tibetan writing was founded on Sanskrit. In such utterly unprepared soil the spread of the new religion was far from rapid. Only the sixth follower of Srong Tsan Gampo (about a hundred years after him) could effect a more general spread of Buddhism in his country. He sent to India in order to obtain monks, books, and advice. Indian Buddhism was in the last stage of decay, and it was exactly in this condition that it made its entrance into Tibet. A renowned adherent of Tantrism is said to have been the man, who at the head of a band of companions entered Tibet and undertook to disseminate his doctrines under the patronage of the King. He was called Padma-Sambhava (the lotos-born), but is usually known among the Tibetans as Guru Rimpo Che (the glorious teacher). Tradition states that he built the first monastery in the year A.D. 749. In the preceding period Buddhism had not thoroughly taken root; from now on it caught firm hold.

The Indian teachers found a primitive form of religion previously existing in these regions, which was known under the name of *Bon*. The Bon belief recognized nature spirits, which were worshipped by all sorts of powerful and terrible offerings; and it also paid reverence to the spirits of the dead. The religious functions were performed by priests, and there were the elements of a magic cult, the knowledge of which was a secret confined to the Bon priests. Sacrifices — especially human sacrifices —

were obligatory. This religion, which at first opposed the imported Tantric Buddhism, was subsequently completely mixed up with it. The Bon religion did not die out, but remained as an undercurrent, tinged with Buddhism.

The Buddhist writings imported from India were translated into Tibetan in the following century, and from this emerged the Tibetan canon. Monasteries and monks received their privileges from the Kings. They continually won a stronger hold over the people. In the tenth century their progress received a slight check from one of the rulers; but the persecutor was murdered by a lama,[1] and his traces were soon obliterated. Intercourse with India and the smaller Buddhist States of the Himalayas long remained a standing feature of Lamaism. We soon hear of the formation of different sects, which partially, at all events, were founded by the influence of noted teachers, who had wandered thither from India. Thus, in the eleventh century one of these, a very illustrious teacher called Atîśa, who was personally acquainted with the Buddhism of India, came to Tibet and spread a new doctrine, which extended still further in manifold ramifications. An important period in the spread of Lamaism is that of the supremacy of the Mongol dynasty in China (from the middle of the thirteenth to the middle of the fourteenth century). The wide conquests of the

[1] The Tibetan monks are called "lamas." The word (in Tibetan it is spelt *blama*) means "superior," "better" (Sanskrit *uttara*). Originally it was only applied to the Abbot of a monastery. This is why Tibetan Buddhism is called Lamaism.

Mongols had reached as far as Tibet. The Emperor Kublai Khan—the well-known patron of the traveller Marco Polo—showed himself particularly interested in the religious condition of his subjects. Lamaism appeared to him a very useful religion—from the political standpoint—for his countries; he therefore encouraged it, and under his rule it took possession of the wide-spreading territory of Mongolia, which down to the present day is completely dominated by it. The Tibetan canon was translated at that time into Mongolian.

Already in the time of Kublai Khan there was plainly visible a tendency to hierarchical concentration, which in later times became the most marked feature of Lamaism. For we hear that the Emperor recognized the principal lama of one of the sects then existing, the so-called Saskya school, as Primate of Buddhism throughout Tibet. Afterwards, indeed—in the middle of the fourteenth century the Mongols having been replaced by the Ming dynasty—the latter found it a wiser policy to diminish the power of the Saskya sect by raising the leaders of the other sects to a similar position.

The most important change experienced by Lamaism was the reformation undertaken by the lama Tsong Kapa in the fifteenth century. This reformation was at first restricted to that sect which had been mostly influenced by Atîśa's ideas. Tsong Kapa's new sect was called Gelugpa, and became by far the most powerful of the various Lamaistic developments. It is quite possible, and even probable, that Tsong Kapa's new ideas were touched by the Christian spirit of the

West. For already Catholic missionaries had unmistakably made an impression in East and Central Asia, and a knowledge of the forms and doctrine of Romish Christendom were doubtless no longer unfamiliar to the well-informed inhabitants of Tibet, owing to the strenuousness of such men as John of Montecorvino and Odoric. The efforts of Tsong Kapa's new teaching were specially directed to a more detailed ritual and a stricter organization. Especially with regard to the question of organization, the party of his adherents developed the most surprising results. The influential position of leader—possessed by Tsong Kapa himself—was to be bequeathed to his successor through his own reincarnation. The fifth of these successors attained the supreme goal in the middle of the seventeenth century, by widening out his religious leadership to a temporal supremacy: the regency of Tibet was handed over to him by China, with the title of Dalai Lama.[1] Meanwhile he ruled under Chinese suzerainty. From this time the conception of reincarnation became somewhat different. It was established from this time onwards that one of the most popular Bodhisattvas of Lamaism, the Bodhisattva Avalokiteśvara (also called Padmapani), who was a sort of tutelary deity of the country, was incarnate in the Dalai Lama of the day. Avalokiteśvara is the Indian name for the well-known Chinese and Japanese Buddhist deity, Kwan Yin

[1] *Dalai*, *dale*, is a Mongolian word which means "ocean." Thus, the title is of Mongolo-Tibetan origin. It was a Mongolian Prince from the Koko-Nor territory who practically conquered Tibet for the Dalai Lama in one of his warlike expeditions.

(Kwannon), the most conspicuous figure in the mythology of Northern Buddhism.

Through the installation of the Dalai Lama, the Gelugpa sect obtained an unconditional supremacy over the whole of Tibet; it persecuted the other sects for a time, till it eventually established a *modus vivendi* with them. The other sects also followed its example, and set up perpetually reincarnated Bodhisattvas at their head. Though none of these mystically conceived Grand Lamas could enter into rivalry with the one residing at Lhassa in temporal power, one at least of them—the Grand Lama of Tashi Lhumpo, near Shigatze, whose usual title is Panchen Erdeni (a Mongolo-Tibetan combination like that of the Dalai Lama)—was his equal in holiness. The Court of Pekin has always maintained a nominal supremacy over the dominion of the Dalai Lama, and its representative has a small military force at Lhassa; he has a paramount influence in determining the choice of the child in whom—after the death of a Dalai Lama—the pretended reincarnation of Avalokiteśvara is to take place.

The rule of Lamaism has extended in the course of centuries far beyond the limits of Tibet. It has already been pointed out that this form of Buddhism was accepted by the Mongols. It became, also, strong in Manchuria. Both in and round Pekin—from the time of the Mongol dynasty—there sprang up many lama monasteries, and even to-day there is a Tibetan admixture in the otherwise differently constituted Chinese Buddhism. In the same way the Himalayan States, such as Nepal, Bhotan, Sikkhim,

Kashmīr — from whose decadent Mahâyâna Buddhism the faith once found entrance into Tibet—in the course of time succumbed completely to the influence of the daughter Church. Lamaism actually reached so far as into European territory, for its adherents are still to be found amongst the Kalmucks of the Volga and the Don. But since the beginning of the nineteenth century these Russian Buddhists are no longer under the control of the Dalai Lama.

### China.

There is a Chinese record which tells of the entrance of Buddhism into that country so early as the year 217 B.C. The first messengers of the new faith were put in prison by the Emperor. Supernatural intervention set them at liberty. It is probable that these legends contain the record of some weak, individual efforts to carry the teaching of the Buddha into the Chinese Empire at that time. Such attempts cannot have had any serious results. The commonly accepted date of the real entrance of Buddhism into China is during the reign of Emperor Ming-Ti (A.D. 58-76; the title of reign was Yung-P'ing). This ruler is said to have had a dream in which a high, shining gold image of a god appeared to him, which entered his palace. The interpreter of the dream—a brother of the Emperor—attributed this apparition to the Buddha Śâkyamuni, who was revered in Central Asia and India, and who demanded worship in China also. There is no question that warlike expeditions into Central Asia as well as peaceful intercourse had by that time familiarized many of the Chinese with the knowledge of the Buddhist religion, and also Buddhist pictures may have reached the Court of the Emperor as spoils of war. Whether in the interpretation of the dream a stronger religious current may have found expression it is now impossible to determine, or whether there existed already at the Court a silent band of adherents of Gautama's religion. At all events, the Emperor Ming-Ti sent an embassy through Central Asia to Khotan (the land of the Yüeh-chi) to procure the things requisite for the practice of the new religion. The emissaries—eighteen in number—left the imperial Court in the year A.D. 65, and returned in 67, accompanied by two monks, Kâśiapa Mâtanga and Gobharana (the latter arriving a little after the former), as well as in possession of Buddha images and scriptures. A temple was built for the new religion, in which the two representatives lived, and gave themselves to the work of translating the most important Buddhist instructions into Chinese. The imperial place of residence at that time was Loyang, the present Honan Fu. It was here that Buddhism first took root in Northern China.

Buddhism did not spread so rapidly in China as elsewhere. The most striking fact, to which too little notice has so far been given, is that it was not till the beginning of the fourth century A.D. that the Chinese were allowed to become monks in the Buddhist religion.[1] The authorized representatives, therefore, of the new religion were foreigners during

[1] Even at a later date the number of his subjects allowed to enter the monastic Order was frequently much limited by the Emperor.

the first two and a half centuries. A roll of names of foreigners has been handed down to us who came from India, from the Himalayan States, and from Central Asia, to take charge of Buddhism in China. For a long time their most important labours consisted in translations of the books of the Buddhist canon, in which the first messengers had already been engaged. These translations, however, made but slow progress. Kâśiapa Mâtanga only translated a single important work; his companion Gobharana completed five others, which have since been lost. But from that time forward we hear of no further translations being made for a hundred years. Till about A.D. 300 the translators were all foreigners (with the exception of one Chinese layman); but from the fourth century onward there were also Chinese monks among their number. This appears to be the epoch when Buddhism first took a strong hold of China. They no longer waited for messengers to be sent, but sought to win knowledge and stimulus for themselves from the original home of the religion. Pilgrimages of deeply interested Chinese monks began to flow to India, whence they returned laden with books, relics, and pictures. The most renowned of these pilgrims were Fa Hsian, Yüan Chuang, and I Tsing; with them deserves also to be mentioned Sung Yün, a layman, who was sent as a messenger by a Prince of the Wei State to study Indian Buddhism. These journeys took place in the fifth, sixth, and seventh centuries.[1]

[1] Fa Hsien's journey took place A.D. 399-413; Yüan Chuang's, A.D. 629-645; I Tsing's, A.D. 671-695. Sung Yün was sent in the year A.D. 518.

At the same time that Fa Hsian, the first of these pilgrims, was thus engaged, the most noted of the Indian translators, Kumarajiva, was labouring in China; with the help of many Chinese monks he disseminated the knowledge of a large number of the canonical works and commentaries. The great revival of Buddhism in China during the fifth century was marked by embassies from India and Ceylon to the Emperor, congratulating him on the success of the new movement. It is also noteworthy that at this time an Emperor himself entered the cloister as a monk. Perhaps the renown attained by the Chinese Buddhism of that period is best demonstrated by the striking event that in the year A.D. 526 the Patriarch of Indian Buddhism, Bodhidharma, the twenty-eighth in the list of the Buddha's successors, left his native land and migrated to China, which thenceforward became the seat of the patriarchate. Eventually Bodhidharma took up his residence at Loyang (a Buddhist centre from the beginning), but he first visited Nanking, the Court of the Emperor at that time, Wu-Ti, of the Liang dynasty, who ruled over Southern China, and he made a great impression on that Prince, who had already accepted Buddhism. The successors of Bodhidharma in the patriarchate lived in monasteries not far from the Yangtze, in the neighbourhood of the present Kiukiang. These monasteries still preserve the old tradition (though under very decadent conditions) of their former illustrious inhabitants. During the time of Bodhidharma and his successors, Buddhism spread in Central and Southern China.

The form of Buddhism which won its way on Chinese soil was the Mahâyâna school. This is plainly shown by the choice of works introduced there by the translators. While the translations of the two first monks sent to the Emperor Ming-Ti were confined to the rules of monastic life, the Buddhist legends and similar uncontroversial matter, the catalogue of later translations shows a number of characteristically Mahâyâna writings. Also the records of the Chinese pilgrims to India are written entirely from the Mahâyâna point of view. In China the Mahâyâna school, in the course of time, divided itself into a number of sects; finally there were ten main divisions. The impulse for the formation of these different schools was mainly due to the authority of an unusually influential teacher. A group of adherents gathered round him with a new understanding of old truths, generally evincing a special predilection for individual parts of the canon and the commentaries attached to them, which had been written by their master.

The attitude of the Chinese Emperors towards Buddhism varied considerably; consequently its external position varied in the same degree. One of its most conspicuous promoters was the above-mentioned Emperor Wu-Ti, of the Liang dynasty, who ruled from A.D. 502-550. Three times he took monastic vows (for a certain period) and earnestly studied the sacred writings. It is also stated of other rulers and Princes that they entered monasteries for a time or permanently. On the other hand, it was very easy for Confucianists—and they were not sparing in good arguments—to rouse the popular Chinese instinct against the unnatural loosening of family and patriotic ties, engendered by the monastic way of life. They made use of the lofty persuasiveness of the wise and unrivalled excellence of their own ancient classics as a powerful weapon against the somewhat abstruse doctrinal teaching of Buddhism. By means of such arguments even many rulers were influenced. Also numerous abuses in the monasteries, and amongst the monks themselves, gave reason for the protests against them and for energetic action. This is not the place, however, to enter into the details as to the favour or disfavour of the rulers; it is sufficient to note that Chinese Buddhism passed through various stages of martyrdom. In the beginning of the eighth century an official persecution broke out against it, in which 12,000 monks and nuns were said to have been compelled to return to the secular state, and all Buddhist worship was prohibited for a long time. Another persecution took place in the middle of the ninth century. Chinese records relate that 4,600 monasteries were then destroyed. All the property of the monastic communities was confiscated. More than 260,000 monks and nuns were compelled to return to secular life. Then again in the first half of the tenth century there was a period of severe depression of religion. Thirty thousand temples were then closed, while a very small number, which had obtained special privileges under previous rulers, were allowed to continue only under strict State surveillance.

From this period of trial Chinese Buddhism emerged

after a while with fresh vigour. It had struck already too deep a root in the religious and superstitious demands of the great mass of the people, so that the opposition of the great and the rationalistic confutations of the literati were unable to extirpate it.

Buddhism confronted an element in China which responded to it much more readily than Confucianism did, and, indeed, blended with it to a very high degree. This was Taoism. This religion—indigenous to China—which is usually attributed to Laotze, the elder contemporary of Confucius, sprang in reality from an earlier source, and had in the course of centuries become the vehicle in which an ancient nature and spirit worship was embodied; it was a chequered superstition void of system, a kind of philosophy of nature, formulated in a rude, fantastic way. The character of Taoism so far resembled Buddhism that it also possessed supernatural features, that it attributed great merit to the hermit or monastic life, and maintained the possibility of averting distress and danger by means of magic, and that it described the future life after death in vivid colouring. Buddhism and Taoism have approached very closely to one another by means of this common basis, but Taoism is perhaps rather the recipient than the donor.[1] Competition, it is true, frequently set them at variance

[1] The monastic monkhood in which one line of Taoism has been perpetuated down to the present day appears, from many of the details of its organization, to have been derived from Buddhism, though Taoism may have possessed ascetic hermits from the earliest times. On the other hand, a number of deities peculiar to Taoism are found under another guise in Buddhism.

with one another, so that they were not always in friendly relationship. But in the main their ways lay parallel to one another, although they did not combine in the popular consciousness. It is related of the ruler of the kingdom of Ts'i, that he attempted by forcible means to unite the two religions into one. And a persecution of the sixth century fell upon both Buddhism and Taoism alike, in the kingdom of Chou, where they both appeared equally objectionable to the ruler. Again, there is a very popular book, Hsi-yu-chi, a narrative of the journeys and experiences of Yüan-Chuang (the above-mentioned Buddhist traveller), written by a Taoist, and liberally interspersed with material drawn from the Taoist mythology, though the subject-matter is derived from Buddhism.

Buddhism must also to a certain extent have come in contact with Christianity in China. For the Nestorian form of Christianity had penetrated China possibly as early as the sixth century, and in the seventh and eighth centuries it made a great step forward, as is proved by the celebrated inscription on the tablet at Si-ngan-fu. It was also referred to by Marco Polo as still plainly in existence in the thirteenth century. Nestorian Christianity was completely lost in China later on, and left no traces behind it. But in the seventh to the eighth entury, when it certainly played a rôle in that country, it may have mixed with Buddhism to a certain degree, as likely as there has been a colouring of Buddhism by Taoism. The Dominican mission also (John of Monte Corvino and his followers), which for a time had a powerful influence on the Court of the Mongolian Emperor in the fourteenth century, may have had its effect upon Buddhism, which was always impressionable. Things were very different when the modern phase of Christian missions commenced with the coming of the Jesuits at the end of the sixteenth century. At that time opposing conditions were too strongly developed in Europe and in China to admit of Christian art and thought commending themselves for acceptance to the popular religion.

### Korea.

Korea received Buddhism from China. Its entrance took place during a period of Korean history when the peninsula was divided into three distinct kingdoms. The northern part, about as far as to the Tatong River, was included in the kingdom of Kokurai. In the south were the kingdoms of Pakchi (the west coast) and Silla (the east coast). In the northern kingdom, which always maintained the closest intercourse with China, Buddhism first made its entrance in A.D. 372, according to Korean annals. A Buddhist monk called Sundo came to Korea with images of the Buddha and a sacred book, from the small feudal State of Tsin in Northern China (in the south of the present province of Shensi). As he directed his course at once to the Court of the King of Kokurai, it may be supposed that he was sent by the Chinese Prince of Tsin. A few years later two monasteries were built in the capital of Kokurai. This example appears to have been followed; for shortly afterwards the ruler of the kingdom of Pakchi sent messengers to China to ask for exponents of the new religion; indeed, he sent directly to the Emperor, who belonged to the so-called Eastern Tsin dynasty. In A.D. 385 there came, therefore, the Buddhist monk Marânanda, with ten companions and the customary requisites for worship, in order to pave the way for Buddhism in Southern Korea. The south-east country of Silla only accepted Buddhism about fifty years later, direct from China. In all three kingdoms the acceptance of Buddhism was associated with political intentions. They wanted the support of the powerful neighbouring kingdom. From this very reason Korea adopted, together with the new religion, much of the higher Chinese culture—for instance, the use of the Chinese written character.

Buddhism had its golden age in this country at the time when a new Korean Empire was formed after the destruction of the three older kingdoms. The soul of the movement which led to this result was a Buddhist monk, who indeed failed to reap the reward of his labour, as he was murdered by a rival. The latter, who succeeded in placing himself on the throne of the newly united kingdom of Korai (with Songdo as its capital), founded a dynasty which lasted about five hundred years (912-1392). He thoroughly supported Buddhism; monasteries and monks increased rapidly in numbers, and won a strong hold over the whole nation. There was a law at that time in existence urging that one out of three sons in a family should become a monk. During this epoch of its prosperity, Korean Buddhism on certain occasions even had some influence on China, its motherland. Important documents belonging to a noted Chinese school, which had been lost by the fate of war, were restored by an embassy sent from China to Korea, and this gave a new impetus to that school. It is equally worthy of notice that the two systems of alphabetical writing invented for the Korean language both show some connection with Buddhism.[1] The first, the so-called Nido alphabet, an adaptation of Chinese characters employed for their phonetic value, was the work of a Buddhist monk and great scholar called Syel Ch'ong, living towards the close of the eighth century A.D. Some six centuries later the present Korean script, the Un men alphabet, was invented under the auspices of the King Se Jong (A.D. 1447). This alphabet was derived from the Tibetan (which itself is an offspring of the Sanskrit), the knowledge of which was due to Buddhism. It is well known that the Korean Un men is very likely the most simple and most perfect alphabet in the world.

At the end of the fourteenth century the Korean royal house came to an end owing to a political revolution springing up from the great change in China, whereby the Mongol dynasty was overthrown and replaced by the Ming dynasty: a new family

[1] There are many incongruous statements regarding the Korean script in the common literature on Korea. The best information on the subjects is to be found in an article by James Scott ("Stray Notes on Korean History and Literature") in the Journal of the China Branch of the Royal Asiatic Society, vol. xxviii., p. 214 *et seq.* *Cf.* also H. Giles, "Chinese-English Dictionary," vol. i., p. xix *et seq.*

(with Hanyang or Seoul as capital) mounted the throne of Korea, whose successors rule there down to the present day, if they can be said to rule under the present strict Japanese suzerainty. The revolution was also a social one; other intellectual movements came into existence. Buddhism, which so far had been a support to the throne, was abandoned by the State, while an attempt was made to substitute the teaching of Confucius as an intellectual backbone to the people. Buddhism therefore declined more and more, but it continued to hold fast the main outlines of its shape—even if in a very subordinate position—and is up to this day one of the few characteristics of the Korean intellectual life.

### Japan.

Japan owes the entrance of Buddhism to the missionary ardour of Korea. The south-western of the three above-mentioned ancient Korean kingdoms, Pakchi (called by the Japanese Hiakusai or Kudara) was the starting-point of the mission. According to the account given in the old Japanese historical work Nihongi, in A.D. 552 a Korean King sent an embassy to the ruler of Japan to commend the new religion to him, and to convey to him objects for worship and sacred books. It is true that an unreliable Japanese authority speaks of an earlier advent of Buddhism in A.D. 522 (another authority says A.D. 534). It could at the most have been but an abortive attempt. Even after A.D. 552 Buddhism only advanced slowly and with many struggles. A party gathered about it, which the adherents of the native religion of Shintoism most strenuously opposed. A further importation of priests and sacred objects kept it in close connection with the land of its origin. The struggle about it resulted in its favour since A.D. 588. The greatest help to the rising Buddhism was Prince Shotoku Daishi (he died 621), whose memory is still firmly cherished in history and legend. The Buddhist monks and nuns who streamed into the country from Korea continued coming for a long time, and the influence of Korean art is still plainly visible at such places as Hôriuji, or in the museum at Nara, in the most ancient Buddhist statues. As Korean Buddhism had adopted the Chinese form of the Mahâyâna school, so in like manner it transmitted this to Japan. That it was Mahâyâna Buddhism which entered Japan is confirmed by some details in the old story of its introduction, such as the nomenclature of certain divinities (Amitabha, Kwanyin, Tashihchi).

In the first half of the seventh century A.D. communication with China took place directly, instead of via Korea. Zealous monks made the difficult journey to the Middle Kingdom, which at that time was increasingly passing over to Japan; they sought out celebrated teachers of the doctrine, and took back with them new opinions and new writings. The predominant schools of Chinese Buddhism were transplanted into Japanese soil. But Japan itself also produced a number of new, and in some cases remarkable, schools.

The Buddhist canon of Japan always remained

Chinese, for the knowledge of that language was at the root of all deeper learning in the kingdom of the Rising Sun.

The centre of Buddhism was in the imperial Court, for a time situated at Nara, and then for many generations in Kyôto. But there were other places, such as the renowned Nikko and the sacred mountain Kôyasan, which became noted centres of worship.

In Japan Buddhism had to find its way alongside with Shintoism, which was the indigenous religion of the country. Shintoism was a religion rich in legends, and full of fantastic worship of the powers of nature, amongst which the sun held a conspicuous position. The tradition which derived the imperial dynasty from the sun-goddess had been the means of establishing the worship of the ruler, which, coupled with the ancient ancestor worship, was further developed into a kind of hero worship. It is to be observed that Shintoism possessed no dogmatic tenets or ethical system, and had not even established any formal religious observances; but its development had stopped at the early stage, where religion is only a free play of the imagination. The imported Buddhism, as already shown, naturally appeared to Shintoism as an opposing force in the first instance. But the position of this vague and primitive nature worship was from the beginning a difficult one, when compared with the doctrine of the Indian thinker, a comprehensive system teeming with ideas, and reinforced by literature, art, and ceremonial. Buddhism, indeed, achieved its master-stroke when it absorbed and completely incorporated its rival with itself, by means of a clever adaptation. The Shinto divinities were raised to the position of earlier incarnations of Buddhist Bodhisattvas, and the baldness of Shinto worship and temple decoration was gilded by Buddhist splendour. Thus originated the so-called Ryobu-Shintoism—namely, the mixed Shintoism (also called Ryobu-Buddhism)—which was in reality only a variety of Buddhism. The man who was the principal promoter of this transformation was Kobo Daishi (as he is usually known with his posthumous honorary title), a remarkable leader of the eighth century, and down to the present day one of the most popular of Buddhist-Japanese saints.

The highest culture in Japan was for centuries almost entirely rooted in Buddhism. Here as well as in Korea Buddhism gave the popular language its written form, the Hiragana as well as the Katakana system. All grades of society were equally influenced by Buddhist ideas. From the seventeenth century, however, Chinese Confucianism came into the foreground, especially among the upper classes, and drove Buddhism back without disturbing its hold on the bulk of the populace. A more dangerous rival made its appearance in the shape of the Jesuit Mission, which began with Xavier in the middle of the sixteenth century. During the brilliant successes of the first years, Buddhism gave ground before Christian influence. But soon persecution set in, which is partly to be attributed to the hatred of the Buddhists, and what still remained of the life of the Christian communities during the years of oppression was concealed, and could be of no real danger to Buddhism. A very severe blow indeed was dealt to the latter by the great revolution in Japanese history which took place in the years 1867 and 1868, when the new era of modernization began. The State support was then mostly withdrawn from Buddhism, and the old connection of it with Shintoism was broken up; in an almost fanatical way Shintoism was "restored," and was placed in sharp antagonism to Buddhism as being the true native religion. It appears so far that Buddhism, thrown back on its own resources, retains sufficient hold over the Japanese nation to enter the lists against Christianity with energy and ability in the fight for supremacy, while the reinstated "independent" Shintoism, in utter powerlessness, falls rapidly and miserably to pieces under the stress of modern life.

Here we reach the end of our survey of the spread of Buddhism in the principal countries where it took root. The account of its present position and condition in these various Buddhist countries will be the subject of the next part.

# BOOK III

## THE MODERN BUDDHISM

### Chapter I.—GENERAL REMARKS ON SOUTHERN AND NORTHERN BUDDHISM

Since the time of Eugène Burnouf[1] it has become usual to divide the whole domain of the Buddhist religion into the two classes of Southern and Northern Buddhism. This is done not only from a geographical point of view, but it is based on a fundamental internal difference, as the southern countries are governed by that aspect of the religion which is known as Hînayâna Buddhism, while the northern countries represent the Mahâyâna Buddhism. Ceylon and the countries of Farther India—Burma, Siam, and Cambodia—belong to Southern Buddhism; while Tibet, together with the Himalayan States, Mongolia, China, Korea, and Japan, belong to Northern Buddhism.

Although there is good reason for the division into Southern and Northern Buddhism, one must guard carefully against mistaken ideas creeping into it.

[1] Eugène Burnouf (1801-1852), the excellent French Orientalist, has prepared the ground for a thoroughly scientific study of Buddhism, especially by his book entitled "Introduction à l'Histoire du Bouddhisme indien" (1845).

The expressions Hînayâna and Mahâyâna do not imply two absolute types of Buddhist doctrine—they rather indicate a twofold tendency of development: on the one hand, adherence to the original modes of thought and the old habits of life and action; on the other hand, the blending of new ideas with the old ones, and the adaptation to the ways of foreign nations. But this difference has worked itself out in various ways, according to the countries where it has operated. Those two great groups are not to be considered as absolute units; they did not each organize a complete system for themselves, they do not stand opposed as rivals to one another. Southern Buddhism, indeed, could perhaps be considered as uniform. In it the sacred canon is everywhere the same; it is written in the same language—Pâli—though the letters used may be Singhalese, or Burmese, or Siamese. The character and organization of the monastic communities, the arrangements of the monasteries, the attitude of the laity towards the monks—all such things are very similar to one another in the southern countries. But at the other side, if one glances at the so-called Northern Buddhism, the differences in these countries are much more marked. Here there are at least two distinct branches, running side by side: one is the Lamaism, to which belong the peoples of Tibet, the Himalayas, and Mongolia; the other is the Chinese Buddhism, which has often been given the special name of Foism (from Fo, the Chinese name of Buddha), and which is the fundamental type also of Japanese and Korean Buddhism.

From this state of affairs, it is evident that the division into Northern and Southern Buddhism can only be accepted with reservations. Indeed, recently one of the best authorities—Professor Rhys Davids, in his book "Buddhist India"—has declared that he entirely repudiates this classification. On the other hand, the Buddhists themselves maintain it.[1] For our purpose we may acquiesce in the old classification, as there can be no danger of misunderstanding when the reader keeps in mind that neither of the two divisions of Northern and Southern Buddhism forms a determined unity—a Church of its own. The one certainty is, that everywhere the aspect of Buddhism in detail was determined by the country in which it found itself, while at the same time there exists a deeper diversity between South and North.

The countries held by Southern Buddhism are in general supposed to represent the religion in its true and original conception. This reputation is well founded, when they are set in comparison *as a whole* with Northern Buddhism. Many later changes of doctrine, of the habits of daily life, and of ritual, which have given such a new character to Northern Buddhism, are unknown in southern countries. At the same time a certain admixture of foreign elements is to be found in Southern Buddhism also. These are specially obvious to the observer when living in the simple monasteries of the remote country places.

---

[1] See the article by the Burmese writer Taw Sein Ko, "The Introduction of Buddhism into Burma," in the periodical called *Buddhism*, published at Rangoon by Ananda Metteya, vol. i., No. 4, p. 598. Compare also Teitaro Suzuki in his "Outlines of Mahâyâna Buddhism" (London, 1907), who (pp. 3, 4) prefers to divide Buddhism into three sections—Southern, Northern, and Eastern.

Features of animistic and nature worship which governed these people before the advent of Buddhism are still evident to-day, working not only in Buddhist lay devotees, but also in many of the monks. A European who, in countries as Ceylon or Burma, expects to find "pure Buddhism," as taught by the Buddha Gautama, will often be disappointed. The true adherents are few; but there are some who may be taken as genuine disciples of the old teacher, and who give us some impression of what the Buddha himself must have been.

The three countries of Southern Buddhism—Ceylon, Burma, and Siam—may generally be characterized by saying that in Ceylon are to be found the most learned representatives of this religion, that Burma is the most thoroughly impregnated by the Buddhist atmosphere in popular life, and that Siam (and Cambodia) is of special interest as showing Buddhism a still living State religion under a Buddhist King, a condition which no longer exists in any other countries.

## Chapter II.—THE BUDDHISM OF CEYLON

### A. Entrance into the Monastic Order.

Whoever wishes to enter the monastic Order as a novice is handed over to the care of a monk to be educated at the age of about eight years. Naturally, it is in most cases the parents who have induced the child at such a tender age to enter on the spiritual career. The motive is, for most of them, the maintenance of the child, as the novices generally come from poor families. The child enters a monastery by means of an entirely private agreement between the parents and a monk. After some years of elementary learning, at the age of eleven or twelve the boy is admitted to the noviciate by a simple ceremony (called *pabbajjâ*) taking place in the monastery, at which the parents and some friends assist. The boy's hair is cut. He asks the permission of his parents, and begs to be admitted as a novice; then the robes of monkish life are given to him by his tutor, he repeats some formulas, the ten precepts are handed over to him, and so he becomes a novice. The robes of the monks consist of three pieces. The first is an undergarment extending from the waist to the knees; over that is worn a garment covering the whole body, to which is added a wide garment for full equipment. The mantle is often worn so as to leave the right shoulder uncovered, but some sects cover both shoulders. The clothing must be made of a woollen, not a silk, material, according to regulation, not only on the ground of simplicity, but also because a silken material involves the killing of silkworms. Nevertheless, silken robes are frequently worn. The colour of the clothing is either orange or yellow-brown of various shades. The early rule was that the monks were to make it from rags and pieces of stuff which were worn out or thrown away. That rule is no longer observed. There is a formal recognition of it in the fact that the material from which the clothing is to be made is first cut into a number of pieces and then sewn together again. The novice, as well as the full monk, is only permitted to possess one set of clothing (consisting of the three garments).

The novice, as a rule, lives with the monk whom

he has chosen as his tutor. It may happen that he lives in a large monastery, in which case he will probably associate with a number of other novices; but it may equally well happen that he lives alone with one of the monks, who has the solitary charge of a village temple. His work is pursued daily according to the ancient rules, which in the main are very much the same as those regulating the daily course of the monk, only that he has in addition many services to perform for the monk. He must get up in the morning before sunrise; he must cleanse himself and the temple, must fetch water and filter it. Then he must spend some time in meditation. With this exercise he combines worship of the Buddha images and the fetching of flowers to put before them. After that he prepares to go through the village with the begging-bowl in his hand, or makes his way among the adjacent huts in order to obtain the daily sustenance for his tutor. The novice, it is true, does not undertake as yet the begging for himself, but should be there only in company with his master, whose bowl he has to carry, and to whom in other ways also he must make himself useful. Indeed, it not infrequently happens that the monk sends out his novice alone. On his return the novice devotes himself to the service of his teacher, washes his feet, brings him drinking water, prepares his meal, and also eats his own. Then he washes the utensils and immerses himself again for a time in meditation. He next begins to read in certain prescribed sacred books, or to copy something out of them. And in this he both may and should receive instruction from his teacher as to any points that may not be clear to him. If it is the season of the year when the monk reads Bana (a kind of recitation before lay people which is mentioned later on), then the novice has to prepare everything in readiness for it, and to assist his teacher. He must in all things serve his master with great reverence, as also the other monks (if he is stationed in one of the large monasteries), as if he were serving the Buddha himself. Meditation—specially as to whether he has fulfilled all his duties accurately—closes the day.

A certain number of writings has been selected for the novice to study and to learn by heart. These writings are partly in Elu, an ancient Singhalese dialect, partly in Pâli, the sacred language of Southern Buddhism. Singhalese letters (derived from the Devanâgarî alphabet) have been used for the Pâli writings. Most of the writings selected for the use of novices contain practical instruction, commands, and prohibitions, which are more explicit about the details of daily life than the ten fundamental precepts. Others make it their object to deepen the moral sense, and this is particularly the case in the celebrated work Dhammapada, one of the best-known parts of the Buddhist canon. Directions for the exercise of meditation are also contained in the books for novices. One of the books for beginners leads to the art of exorcism; it is called Piruvânâ-pota. In it is a collection of sayings from the sacred canon, the recital of which when accompanied by certain external ceremonials is warranted to be a safeguard against evil influences, and to bring down a blessing. It is worthy of notice that such kind of instruction is included already in the novice's learning.

However earnest and profound many of the precepts and observations in these writings may sound, however emphatically the highest motives are inculcated, yet one would be much mistaken if one supposed it to correspond to the standpoint of the average novice. Most of them take an entirely external view of things. Certainly they read and learn by heart; outward decorum is observed, the obligations to the monks are fulfilled; but they do all this on purpose to get a livelihood and to become members of a monastery. Those whose endeavour is more serious are exceptions to the rule.

By the time he has attained his twentieth year the novice can be admitted to full monkhood in the inner community. This necessitates a public ceremony, which is called Upasampadâ. It is performed in accordance with the ancient ritual.[1] The novice first dons his secular clothing again. His monastic habit, together with various other accessories, are placed in a special spot, whence they are given back to him afterwards. As the day is kept as a high festival, friends of the candidate accompany him in joyous procession to the monastery where the ceremony is to take place. All the monks assemble in a large hall. The first part of the ceremony is a repetition of the *pabbajjâ* (*cf.* p. 96). After that the candidate, assisted by his tutor (*upajjhâya*) and his instructor (*âcâriya*), applies for ordination. He is

[1] Compare the report of an eye-witness in Warren's "Buddhism in Translations," pp. 395-401; also *Journal of the Royal Asiatic Society*, 1893, p. 159 *et seq.*

asked a number of questions as to the alms-bowl and robes, whether they are his own; whether he is free from certain diseases (leprosy, boils, itch, asthma, epilepsy); whether he is a human being, a male, a free man, free from debt, exempt from military service; whether he has obtained the permission of his parents, and is of the full age of twenty years. Next he is asked his name and that of his tutor. He must now step forward and thrice ask the whole assemblage of monks for admission to their Order. The tutor states that there is nothing to prevent it, and requests that, if anyone has a protest to make, he will now speak. If no one makes any opposition, the novice is held to be accepted. The tutor briefly states to him the duties of his new life in a somewhat antiquated formula, for some of these are no longer observed (as, for instance, that the clothing must be made of rags sewn together, that in cases of illnesses only certain nauseous medicaments might be used, and that the dwelling is at the foot of a tree). The property of a monk shall consist only of eight specified articles—that is, in addition to his three garments, a girdle, an alms-bowl, a razor, a needle, a filter-cloth (through which to strain the water before drinking).[1] These requsites the monk must be able to produce at his admission. He generally receives them as presents from his nearest friends.

If a full-grown man—over twenty years of age—seeks admission to a monastic Order, he has first to undergo a probation as novice, which may be very

[1] This is the old rule of the Pâli texts (Abhidhânappadîpikâ, 439), but there is a slight variation in modern practice sometimes.

short. During this time he is instructed in the most necessary observances. There is no set rule as to the minimum of instruction required; but the president of the admission ceremonial can require proof that the aspirant possesses the most requisite knowledge. The ceremony of full admission is the same as given above.

In the whole island of Ceylon, the festival of full admission into the monastic Order is only held as a rule in Candy, the ancient capital, and there at only two of the monasteries, Malwatte and Asgiri, which have a prominent position. Both monasteries contain a special room for this purpose—an open, right-angled, pillared hall called *poyage*. The president of the ceremony is the Abbot of the monastery where it takes place, the Mahâ Nâyaka; the monks who have the functions of *upajjhâya* and *âcâriya* must have been full monks for at least ten years; the number of monks taking part in the ceremony must be not less than ten. The proceeding is a public one; generally there are many laymen, relatives and friends of the candidate for ordination, taking part in it. There is naturally always a large number of novices admitted at the same time. It is customary to have these ceremonies only four times a year, and they take place during four consecutive weeks in the month of Wesak (our May-June), beginning with the day of the full moon of that month, the day assigned as that on which the Buddha attained Nirvâṇa.

Entrance into monkhood is not binding for lifetime. Indeed, entire freedom is granted to every monk to return to secular life if he feels himself unable to fulfil the duties of the monastic life or loses his belief in it. He is also at liberty to quit it for a time under certain circumstances, so as to rejoin later on. But, in order to guard against the wanton misuse of such liberty, it is ordained that he who leaves must state in the presence of the assembled monks of the monastery his determination to do so, and give his reasons for it.

### B. The Sacred Buildings.

It is difficult to know what to call, with any degree of accuracy, the places where the monks live. Neither of the terms "monastery" or "temple" is quite correct. The word "monastery" cannot be used, because it is frequently the dwelling of a single individual. The temple, again, is always a separate building, apart from the dwelling of the monk or monks. The monk's house is called *pansala*, the temple hall is called *vihâra;* there are always these two buildings to be found where monks live.

*Pansala* originally means a "hut of leaves," and points back to the primitive character of the monastic dwellings. Even at the present time they are quite meagre little houses, built of lath and plaster, with a roof of straw or palm-leaves. At least, such is the case with the numerous ordinary *pansalas* seen dotted all over Ceylon in the shade of palms and ebony-trees, surrounded by bananas and blossoming tropical flowers. In their artless unpretentiousness these humble brown-and-white buildings are no blot on the beautiful harmony of nature. It is a different matter, indeed, as regards certain big monasteries in such places as Colombo or Candy; there they have several storied houses, built in European style and containing modern furniture.

The temple hall—*vihâra*—always stands apart, frequently on a hill-top or other conspicuous place. In large monasteries there are, indeed, several *vihâras*. The *vihâra* is the place where the Buddha images are put up. The building is usually a more solid structure than the dwellings of the monks, and has a tiled roof; frequently it is surrounded by a mud wall, on which are painted simple mythological subjects. Similarly, sacred subjects are used to decorate the inner walls of the sanctuary, but the painting has small artistic merit. As regards colour, dress, pose, the delineation of faces, and the grouping of figures, it is of the old Indian style. There is no trace of a peculiar development of the art of painting under Buddhist influence.

The statues of the Buddha are limited to a few fixed types. There are mainly three kinds of Buddha statues—the sitting, the standing, and the recumbent. In all three forms the Buddha wears the conventional monastic habit, the outer garment being the mantle which is thrown back from the right shoulder, leaving it bare. The lobes of the ear are so long that they rest on the shoulders. The surface of the head is covered with a number of short, regular stumps, which were originally meant to represent the ends of hair left when the Buddha, in the night of his flight from home, cut off his hair by his sword, but which in the course of time have been so conventionalized as to become quite unrecognizable. On the crown of the head there is usually a special erection which takes the form of a fivefold flame. This cranial protuberance, called the *uśnîśa,* was one of the thirty-two distinguishing marks which the legend assigns to every Buddha.[1] Another of these marks is a small twist of hair between the eyebrows, called *ûrnâ* (wool). The features are generally formal and stiff, copied from a traditional type. The seated Buddha is cross-legged, the feet laid on one another, the left under the right, the hands, likewise left under right, lying in the lap above the feet. This is the attitude of meditation, in which one pictures the Buddha under the Bo-tree, at the time when he received his revelation (see p. 47).

The standing Buddha is represented in an upright position, the feet placed close together, the right hand raised with the palm turned towards the spectator; the left hand hangs down alongside the body, grasping the robe. He is in the attitude of the preacher.

The recumbent Buddha is represented at the moment when the great teacher entered Nirvâṇa—namely, when he died. He lies fully outstretched on his right side, with the right hand under his head and the left arm stretched out along the body.

Here and there one meets some slight deviation from these three representations,[2] but as a rule this

[1] Originally it is a representation of the hair done up into a coil on the top of the head, but, as the Buddha had his hair cut off, it had to be explained in another way.

[2] Among these deviations may be noted that of the Buddha guarded by a cobra. The position is the sitting one; the seat is formed by the curled-up body of the cobra, that snake which

is how they are depicted, varying in size, o course, from colossal figures, ten times the height of a man, to tiny ones that may be conveniently carried in the pocket. Huge figures of the Buddha are sometimes carved on the face of rocks. The figures in the *vihâras* are usually made of burnt clay, covered with a veneer of special cement, the so-called *chunam*, which is very durable and takes a good polish. Statues are also made in wood, copper, bronze, ivory, and stone. They are usually gilded, and the more important ones ornamented with real or imitation precious stones. The eyes and other features are generally painted in order to emphasize them.

Accompanying the figures of Buddha are several of his chief disciples, sometimes merely painted on the adjacent walls. With the seated Buddha two favourite followers, Maudgalyâyana (Môgallâna) and Śâriputra (Sâriputta) are frequently represented, and with the dying Buddha Ânanda is sometimes found.

The *vihâras* contain, besides these Buddha representations, not infrequently also all sorts of Hindu (Brahmanistic) mythological figures. Especially common are those of Vishnu and Brahma. The admission of such deities is a concession to the popular combination of Buddhism and Hinduism,

---

is so common in Ceylon, and the head of the reptile, with its broad erect hood, waves protectingly over Gautama's head. Legend relates that a serpent demon protected the Buddha when he was seated in meditation, surrounded by menacing powers of rain and thunder. Similar legends are in vogue of the gods Brahma and Siva. Representations of five- or seven-headed cobras may not infrequently also be seen on rocks and in temples.

which the monks are not slow to justify. The Hindu gods (*devas*) play a many-sided rôle in Buddhism as the worshippers and servants of the Buddha. Not infrequently the Hindu deities are to be found in an adjacent building, called *devâle*, but which belongs to the Buddhist sanctuary.

Besides *pansala* and *vihâra*, at every fairly large monastery there is a special hall set apart for preaching. This hall is called *banage*, from *bana* the word—namely, the sacred canon. The hall is generally devoid of all ornament, with a kind of platform in the centre for the officiating monk. The audience require no seats or forms, as they sit on mats on the ground in Singhalese fashion. The preaching for which these halls are designed takes place during the three months of the so-called *was* (*varsa*), hence it is also known as *was*. The name originally meant the rainy season, at which time the Buddha had commanded the monks to give up their wanderings and to settle down quietly in one place.

In Ceylon they observe the same months which the Buddha had selected on account of the climate in Northern India—about the middle of July to the middle of October—although in Ceylon they are climatically rather pleasant months, so that preaching can be held under a light wooden shed, or equally well in the open air, if there happen to be no special hall for it in the sanctuary. The preaching takes place in the evening, and the sight of these gatherings is highly weird and picturesque. The people, dressed as far as possible in bright and festive garments, bring many lamps and lanterns with them, as it is reckoned a meritorious deed to add to the illumination. The spectacle is enlivened with flowers, flags, bright draperies, sometimes with music and with fireworks. The "preaching" mainly consists in the recitation of the sacred Pâli texts with their Singhalese comment. Favourite parts are the Jâtaka stories of the Buddha's former existences. As often as the name of the Buddha is mentioned, the whole people shouts "Sâdhu!" (Good!)[1] At the time of the full moon the meeting often lasts from eve till morn.

In the court which surrounds *pansala*, *vihâra*, and *banage*, various kinds of artistic workmanship (in the larger monasteries) are worthy of notice and study. There is a bell in its bell-tower; there is a pond containing lotos-flowers; there is a small dagaba; there grows a Bo-tree, such as the monks plant everywhere, a specimen of the genus under which the Buddha sat when he was illuminated—*Ficus religiosa*. Every monastery boasts such a tree, while the venerated progenitor of all these trees—the Bo-tree dating back to the time of Mahendra, which Aśoka sent to Ceylon (see p. 65)—still survives as a two-thousand-year-old rarity in the remarkable ruins of Anuradhapura (see p. 112). In the courtyards of many monasteries may be found a pavilion in which is an interesting specimen of what is a frequent object of worship in Ceylon—the footprint of the Buddha (*srîpâda*, on account of which the pavilion is called *srîpâdula*).

[1] Already the Chinese pilgrim I Tsing mentions this exclamation as usual at similar occasions (see I Tsing, "A Record of the Buddhist Religion," translated by J. Takakusu, p. 49).

This singular object is connected with a mountain of unique formation, called Adam's Peak, which has been an object of worship from very early times. The religious fancy has discovered something supernatural in a peculiarly-shaped hollow on the summit, which Buddhist legend asserts to be the impress of the Buddha's foot on his third wonderful flight from Northern India to Ceylon. At the request of a demon, he made a footprint on the island as a seal by which he claimed it as his own property. Similarly Hindus claimed that this impress had been made by the god Siva; the Mohammedans said Alî or Adam, the Christians (Portuguese) St. Thomas, or the "man of Ethiopia," from the Acts of the Apostles, chap. viii. The actual place on Adam's Peak, which is still visited annually by many pilgrims, is a flat hollow about 1½ metres long and ¾ metre broad. Representations of this "footprint," usually executed in wood and painted, are set up in many monasteries. The sole of the foot is usually divided into 108 small fields, each of which encloses a special figure, mostly those of animals. According to the popular interpretation, these figures are symbolic of the past earthly careers of the Buddha Gautama, those various incarnations which he experienced in the course of time, and which are narrated in the Jâtaka tales. The 108 fields are usually grouped round the wheel, which is the ancient symbol of Buddhist doctrine.

As the more celebrated temples receive votive offerings from many devotees, mainly images of the Buddha, there is often a special building erected to house these gifts.

## C. Special Noteworthy Sanctuaries.

The most noted sanctuary of Ceylon is the temple of the "Holy Tooth" (*Daladawa Maligawa*) at Candy. The building dates, perhaps, from the sixteenth century (the time when Candy was founded by King Vira Vikkama), and presents a charming picture, lying on the edge of the lake of Candy, in the midst of one of the pleasantest scenes on earth, with its uncommon-looking architectural lines, which far excel the usual style of the average monastery. The temple owes both its name and fame to the Buddha relic which has been guarded there for centuries, and which up to the present day (although the modern relic is not genuine) brings devotees in crowds. A tooth of Gautama, which was picked out of the remains of his funeral pile, and preserved for a long time in India, came to Ceylon in the fourth century A.D.; was taken again to India later on; was won back by a noted Singhalese ruler of the Middle Ages, Parakrama Bahu II.; and later on was handed over to the monastery at Candy for safe guardianship. But the Portuguese seized the holy tooth in order to prevent its veneration by the Singhalese, and, at the instigation of the then Archbishop of Goa, burnt it there in public. The Oriental gift of imagination made good indeed the loss through the audacious story that from the remains of the destroyed tooth of their founder a new one had been miraculously formed. Other more plausible apologists relate that the Portuguese had been deceived, and had burnt a false tooth, while the genuine one had been saved. But historical documents leave no room for doubt that the fanatical deed of the Archbishop was executed with all care and absolute certainty, and also that the present guarded specimen-tooth is, to judge by its shape, of anything but human origin. It measures nearly 2 inches in length, and less than 1 inch in diameter at the base, "resembling the tooth of a crocodile rather than that of a man" (Sir Emerson Tennent). It is kept concealed in a casket which is shrouded from the light of day in a dark hall. By dim, uncertain lamplight the doors of the casket are opened for the faithful to see it, and amidst the benumbing perfume of countless flowers (which are brought here daily as offerings) the devotee kneels before it and allows his uncritical gaze to fall upon what may rather be imagined than actually seen.

Two other very noted monasteries at Candy are *Malwatte* and *Asgiri*. For a long time these two places have claimed a sort of supremacy over all the sanctuaries of Ceylon, so that almost every monk in the island is reckoned as belonging to one or the other. The difference between them is not on theological grounds, but is rather a matter of jurisdiction. The monastery of Malwatte has its adherents mainly in the south, and Asgiri in the north. In many neighbourhoods the adherents of both jurisdictions are to be found together. The Abbots of both these chief sancturies bear the title of Mahanâyaka (High-priest). To them alone belongs the right to admit monks to the Order, as is mentioned above.

In *Colombo*, where there are many temples worthy of mention, the most noteworthy is that of *Maligakanda*, because there is an institute attached to it for the study of Pâli and Sanskrit, the *Vidyôdaya College* (Vidyôdaya Parivêna) a widely known seat of learning. Here the monks are given the opportunity of obtaining a thorough knowledge of the sacred canon, and Buddhists also from other countries—from Siam, China, and Japan—come here for periods of study. At the head of the school is the venerable Hikkaduwe Sri Sumangala, a man of widespread reputation, known by the honorary title of 'High Priest of Adam's Peak and of Galle.' In all questions of scholarship he is the ultimate authority in Ceylon. The number of students in the institute in 1903 was over fifty. A considerable library is at their disposal, containing works in Pâli and in Sanskrit; there are not lacking, also, all the best works of European authors.

When enumerating the renowned Buddhist places in Ceylon, the towns which now lie in ruins must not be forgotten, for sufficient traces are left to indicate what a conspicuous rôle they played in the early history of Singhalese Buddhism. The most important of these is *Anuradhapura*. For centuries (from the third century B.C. to the eighth A.D.) this was the flourishing centre of Buddhism, and magnificently adorned with buildings, pagodas, temples, palaces, and monuments. Valuable remains of old buildings have been brought to light during the last twenty years by careful restoration, and give an excellent idea of what early Buddhism created in the way of art and culture. Next in importance to Anuradhapura is *Mihintale*, with its reminiscences of Mahendra, the founder of Singhalese Buddhism; after that comes *Pollunarua*, the capital in later times; *Dambulla,* where are some of the most singular and ancient cave temples; and *Sigiri*, a remarkable mountain fortress.

### D. Life and Character of the Monks.

The usual daily routine of the monks is very similar to that which has already been described in the account of the novices' duties: certain domestic work, reading and learning the sacred text, meditation, simple devotion before the images, and begging for the necessary food. For nine months of the year the monks must beg their food at the doors of the houses; only during the three months of Was, which correspond to the Indian rainy season, they remain at the temple and their needs are supplied by the laity. At the present day the monks can daily be observed begging. It usually takes place between nine and eleven o'clock in the morning. From the larger monasteries they go about in groups of six and eight; the inhabitants of the small sanctuaries go singly. The monks stand with their begging bowls—round earthenware or iron pots, holding about 3 quarts—in front of a house, and wait, without saying a word, for someone to come out and give them something. As they are, to a certain extent, regular guests, many households reckon for them in the preparation of meals; and when they come and stand outside, the housewife or a servant immediately goes out and puts rice and vegetables into their receptacle, and bows down after doing so, with reverential salutation. The monk returns no word of thanks, he stands in a completely indifferent attitude, and after receiving the gift he goes away silently—at least, such is the custom of some of them; others utter a short formula of blessing when they depart. The act of alms-begging is looked upon as an act of benevolence to the laity, by thus giving them the opportunity of obtaining merit as benefactors of the disciples of the Buddha. As Singhalese food is fairly uniform—consisting of rice and curry (a spicey sauce), together with fish and vegetables—the mass accumulated in one receptacle is not so unpalatable as a European might suppose. However, it is not always that the monk really lives on the food which he begged for. In the large monasteries of Candy the monks have meals prepared at home, while the food collected by begging goes to the poor and to animals. The begging for food with them has become a mere form.

That some larger monasteries are independent of the supply of food obtained by begging is not merely due to the fact that they receive gifts from lay visitors, but also because such monasteries possess no inconsiderable amount of property. For the rule which forbids a monk to possess property after he has entered the Order only applies to him as an individual; on the other hand, the monastic community as such may possess much property, and is, in fact, sometimes a wealthy body. This is seen to be the case in the more noted monasteries, by the beautiful and costly fittings of the building, by the magnificent votive offerings, adorned with gold and precious stones. Not a few monasteries have land let out on rent, by which they receive good profits. Even in early times Princes frequently gave the monks land for their maintenance, when the feeding of the monks direct from the royal table became an impossibility owing to their number. And down to the present day most of the sanctuaries own landed property. The monastic lands are still exempt from the otherwise universal land-tax. It is reckoned that about one-third of the cultivated land of Ceylon is temple property.

Field labour is not one of the occupations assigned to monks, and scarcely more so is the manual labour of transcribing the sacred writings. They generally leave such work to paid laymen. On the other hand, the monks are often engaged in school-teaching, and also in certain medical service, which imperceptibly merges into exorcism and maledictory practices.

The instruction of children, as undertaken by the monks, is naturally characterized by all the desultoriness and irregularity common to the Asiatic nature. The children learn to read and write their own language, Singhalese; here and there one may also be introduced to the poetic old Singhalese language, Elu, as well as to the sacred language, Pâli. The books which they read with their priestly teachers mainly consist of narratives, legends, and poems, in honour of the Buddha or of one of the Hindu deities, as well as of rules of conduct and proverbs. The method of instruction is the most primitive one in the world: recitation and repetition, recitation in unison, writing on sand or on the leaves of trees; such are the forms of teaching in use until the scholar is sufficiently advanced to read palm-leaf manuscripts.

In cases of illness, a layman often sends for a

monk. Many of them have the reputation of being able to supply valuable remedies; they must also read *bana,* the sacred word which binds the layman to faith in its miraculous healing properties.

Real preaching (not only reading of the sacred text) is done in some temples on the so-called *poya* days, the four quarters of the moon, when lay people assemble in the *vihâras* to present their gift. On these days, also, the confession of the monks takes place. For this purpose a number of monks from neighbouring temples come together and form a chapter. They go through the ceremony of confession exactly after the form of the sacred book, the Pâtimokkha, which is recited by one of them. The confession made by twos to one another is merely formal.

It is not possible to have a high estimate of the intellectual and moral level of the Singhalese monkhood in general. Of course the man who takes as his criterion the members of the Vidyôdaya Institute at Colombo, or otherwise selected individual monks of a learned and strenuous character (as they may be found in the most highly reputed monasteries), on which alone to base his opinion, may reach a very incorrect conclusion, such as one often reads in European works; but they do not represent the ordinary facts. On the occasion of a more exact settlement of the temple landed property being made (during the nineties), the British Government appointed a special representative for a term of years to make himself thoroughly acquainted with the condition of the monasteries. In the course of four years this official visited about thirteen hundred different temples and monasteries, and won such an intimate knowledge of the people and conditions as seldom falls to the lot of any individual. His verdict is, on the whole, very unfavourable.[1] The observations of other authorities, as well as the present writer's personal inquiries, fully corroborate his statements. The average monk leads an idle life, and has no interest even in the deeper questions of Buddhism, since the reading and reciting of the sacred text soon becomes purely mechanical, and the exercise of meditation is not practised by most. Even the ten fundamental rules of the monkhood are often ignored. It is not uncommon to find monks possessing money, and even following a money-making calling. Theft and immorality are but too common. The well-known authority on Singhalese monkhood, Spence Hardy, wrote the following words forty-five years ago, in "Eastern Monachism" (p. 319): "In no part of the island that I have visited do the priests, as a body, appear to be respected by the people, though there are individual exceptions in which a priest is popular, either from his learning, his skill in medicine, the sweetness of his voice, or his attentions to the duties of his profession. I feel unwilling to make any positive statement as to their moral conduct, as it was generally described to me by interested persons. . . . But when I have heard them spoken against, it has been rather on account of their rapacity than their licentiousness; though I have sometimes, and

[1] Dr. Bowles Daly's Final Report on the Buddhist Temporalities Ordinance, Galle, 1894.

especially in certain districts, heard them accused of a great crime." The above-mentioned official adds to his testimony, quite recently, the words: "There are about nine thousand monks; among them a few—very few—great scholars; the majority are illiterate, and some, to avoid labour, seek a life of indolence sheltered by the yellow robes of priesthood; many are depraved. There are, however, some examples of personal piety, devotion, and self-denial, which would be an ornament to any Church." Similar is the statement of R. S. Copleston, from his very intimate acquaintance with the subject.

The body of a dead monk is cremated. Very soon after his death a pile is erected on a neighbouring spot, and the dead body is borne there in solemn procession. The body is unclothed and placed on the top of the funeral pyre, with the face turned downwards. Then a friend or near relative sets fire to the pile with a torch. The ashes of the corpse afterwards are collected and buried, and the place is frequently marked by a simple monument.

The total number of monks in Ceylon, after the census of 1891, was 9,598; after the census of 1901, 7,331; so a considerable decrease has taken place within ten years.

### E. Sects and Reforms.

There is little to be said about the division of Singhalese Buddhism into various sects. Generally one counts three different bodies—the Siamese, the Rangoon (or Râmanya), and the Amarapura monks. The Siamese society exists down from A.D. 1750, when some monks from Siam came over to Ceylon to regenerate the Buddhism. This sect confined the entrance to monkhood to one particular caste—the Vellala. Against this restriction there arose the Amarapura society at the beginning of the nineteenth century, admitting also three other castes, but not the lowest. The Râmanya society, again, founded in modern times, is remarkable as being more genuine in point of discipline. They reject the admixture of Buddhism with Hinduism as it is found in many temples, live in a purer and stricter way, possessing no lands, no costly robes, or other forbidden property. There are also other small points of distinction between the three sects—a difference in the way of reading *bana,* a different mode of wearing the yellow mantle (either over the left shoulder only, the right shoulder being uncovered, as the Siamese do, or covering both shoulders, as the other two divisions do), a different mode of behaviour when receiving alms (the Siamese uttering a word of blessing, the other two departing in silence). The Râmanya sect is very small, and keeps aloof from the other two.

Besides these three divisions, there is one reform movement of quite modern date in the Singhalese Buddhism, which takes the name of Buddhasâsana Samâgama. Its chief seat is Burma (Rangoon), but in Ceylon also it has a certain importance. Its adherents—mostly cultured people of Ceylon—strive after a purer, more inward Buddhism, one more in accordance, in many respects, with European taste. They have built a preaching-hall, in which on Sunday (!) evening there is usually a Singhalese sermon on Buddhist questions, at which the audience —mostly attired in European clothes—sit on benches as in a Christian church, the monk preaching from a kind of platform. They do not sing, but a creed is recited in unison at the close. In the background of the hall—somewhat in the position of a Christian altar—is a statue of the Buddha. At one of these assemblies when I was present in 1903 there was a large attendance. The preacher spoke on the absolute validity and obligation of the first Buddhist commandment—not to kill any living being. This party of Reformed Buddhism is not antagonistic to the Singhalese Buddhism of the present day, but has the friendliest relations with its most prominent adherents.

### F. Influence on the Laity.

There is not a sufficient reason for describing the population of Ceylon as entirely Buddhist, though this is frequently done in a superficial way. For, firstly, there are whole parts of the island where Hinduism prevails, so that few traces of Buddhism can be found. This is the case in the north. Secondly, even where Buddhism is strong among the population, this religion has not been sufficiently powerful to bring the laity into close union with their ideals, or to indoctrinate them with their conceptions. What the laity accepted from Buddhism they have adapted to their capacity, and alongside this vague Buddhism they follow other lines of religious life—more or less openly—which the tolerance of a superstitious mind enables them to hold in combination. It is the same combination or juxtaposition of different religious conceptions which we find amongst almost all Asiatic races to a certain degree.

That by which the layman is attached to Buddhism consists mostly in certain outward observances. He visits temples, brings little lamps for the worship of the Buddha,[1] and offerings of flowers (the *champac*—*Michelia champaca*—and jasmine are specially used for this purpose, and the temple halls are often filled with their overwhelming perfume), and he gives the requisite gifts to the monks—namely, food and clothing. The ordinary food is given to mendicant monks at the house door, but many people make extraordinary contributions of rice, sugar, honey, butter, fish, or meat, which they carry to the sanctuaries. The special season appointed for giving clothing to the monks is the month after Was, which is therefore called the "clothing month." Many laymen buy one or more pieces of stuff to present them to the monks. Each monk may only accept *one* outfit, consisting of the three garments mentioned above. But what is left over of the gift belongs to the temple and the whole community. A remarkable custom is that by which sometimes a number of monks' habits are entirely made in the course of a single day—between sunrise and sunset—from the raw material, cotton-wool. This is done by means of many hands.

[1] The commonest of these little lamps consists merely of a piece of cocoanut shell filled with oil, in which a wick is laid. They are set in niches of the temple wall or in the sanctuary itself, to illuminate it at night, especially for any festive occasion.

A large number of people, especially women, meet in a preaching-hall of one of the temples, and while some bring in cotton-wool, which they have gathered from the bushes, others prepare it; others, again, spin it; then it is woven, cut out, sewn, and dyed, the last process being performed by the monks themselves.

A special performance of the layman consists in his submitting for a short space of time to certain forms of abstinence, approximating to the life of the monkhood. This religious observance is known as *poya*, because it takes place on the four quarter days of the moon, which are so called. Whoever desires to observe *poya* must notify his determination to a monk early in the morning of the day specified, when he goes to the sanctuary and announces: "I will observe the commands." By the "commands" are meant those eight which have been mentioned above as a kind of preparatory stage of monkhood (see p. 22). On the day of *poya* the layman refrains from work and business; he listens to the sacred word recited by the monk, or reads it; he passes the time in silent meditation; he also performs special good deeds to parents, relations, or the needy, and takes offerings to temples and pagodas.

All these kinds of action are considered by the common people as a means for obtaining religious merit and for averting disaster. Religion is here, as anywhere else for the common people, a way of winning the favour of the unseen powers. For this purpose also the sacred canon, the Word, is used. *Bana* is a kind of charm which brings a blessing by the mere reading and hearing, even although utterly unintelligible to the hearer, and which averts illnesses and exorcises evil spirits. There is a remarkable custom called *pirit* (Pâli *pâritta*), which consists in laymen hiring a number of monks to read *bana* uninterruptedly day and night—usually for the space of seven days—either in the preaching-hall of a monastery or in some other building suitable for the purpose, the object being the obtaining of a beneficent influence. The monks relieve one another in such a way that no smallest pause occurs to break the charm. A Buddhist relic lies on the platform where the monk is reciting, and a sacred cord encircles the whole building, beginning at the place of recitation and leading back to it again, so that by its means the working of the incantation may be substantially held together. Besides the two monks who read the *bana* simultaneously, there are usually others assembled in the building, who murmur with them and keep hold of the cord which encircles the sacred area. The festival ends with a procession and a mythological performance, which is often the cause of lavish expenditure. Thus the word of the Buddha's doctrine is perverted into a magic formula.

No one can be surprised that under these circumstances nothing of the deeper spirit of Buddhist teaching has penetrated the laity. Buddhism has been entirely unable, for instance, to influence the Singhalese by making kindness to animals natural to them, although such influence would seem to lie closest to the foundations of their religion. One may read in Sir Emerson Tennent's book (that profound and accurate student of Ceylon, who for many years as a high official had every opportunity for observation and information)[1] how they obtain tortoiseshell in the most inhuman manner from the living turtle by burning ("Ceylon," vol. i., p. 190), and how in the markets and streets animals are cruelly treated without the slightest consideration or for any valid reason ("Ceylon," vol. ii., p. 177). The very careful and moderate record of Buddhist influence on the Singhalese people, which R. S. Copleston ("Buddhism Primitive and Present," second edition, pp. 284-286), after long personal observation, gives, may be read by those who are interested in this question.

The simple Singhalese are not really affected by Buddhism in their innermost life, but far more by their ancient nature and demon worship. Buddhism has done nothing to displace that, but has rather encouraged it. From a very early period the people of Ceylon believed in the working of all sorts of spirits (*sanne*), who are responsible for every misfortune, every illness, every threatening appearance. A class of exorcists, the Kattadias, are employed to mollify the evil spirits. People are specially driven to make use of these exorcists in case of drought, or scarcity, or severe illness. An altar is erected to these formidable powers, an offering is brought (often a fowl), and gifts of food and flowers are presented at special hours—sunset, midnight, and sunrise. Between these hours the Kattadias—

[1] See the two volumes of "Ceylon: an Account of the Island; Physical, Historical, Topographical," fourth edition, London, 1860. This is still the foundation for more recent works, even if out of date as to details.

arrayed in disguises and wearing frightful masks—perform dances till they work themselves up to a state of frenzy, in which they believe themselves to be possessed by the demon, who thereupon specifies the cause of the disaster and the means of deliverance. This demon worship is down to the present day the only one that has religious weight among the people. It has allied itself with the manifestations of Hinduism as well as with the ideas and figures peculiar to Buddhism. But these two religions have only served to introduce new classes of demons to it, to invent new incantations, new magic formulæ ; it is, in reality, the old dread belief in nature spirits which governs the ordinary man. Whether the Buddha, or Brahma, or Viśnu, or Siva, the friendly or the hostile imaginary beings of the Buddhist legends (*yakśa* and *râkśasa*), they are all equally included among the crowd of ancient demons, with whom one must deal discreetly from day to day.

A striking example of the syncretism prevailing amongst the Singhalese laity is to be seen at the great annual festival called Perahera or Esalakeliya. It is in commemoration of the birth of the god Vishnu, or of his victory over the Asuras, the enemies of the gods. But notwithstanding this Hinduistic origin, Buddhism takes part in the ceremonies very freely, and at the same time the "devil-dancers" have to play their rôle.

On the other hand, it should not be left unnoticed that Buddhism of late has tried to emphasize its original pure ways even on the lay people of Ceylon. This certainly has been done under European influence and after European methods. Temples and dagabas are kept in better repair, books and tracts are distributed, education is more cared for, abuses are reformed, and the people are taught how to become real promoters and protectors of the religion. Whether this striving will have a deeper effect on the masses, and whether it will work also where European civilization and the English language are not co-agencies, cannot be said so far.

## Chapter III.—THE BUDDHISM OF BURMA

In Burma, Buddhism has penetrated more deeply than in Ceylon into the life of the people, and has given it more of its colour. Perhaps it is here that the religion of Gautama won its most real and attractive presentment; and the visitor to this country cannot fail, in looking back on the religious life of the Burmese, to retain an impression of sunny brightness. Whoever is inclined to let himself fall under the spell of Buddhism finds here a certain inducement to do so—that is to say, if he penetrates into the country, and does not confine his view to the semi-Europeanized city of Rangoon. As a whole it appears harmless and antique, kindly and considerate, and it is only to a keen observer that its weaknesses and limitations soon become obvious.

### A. Novices and Monks.

As in Ceylon, the influence of Buddhism in Burma begins with the educational activity exhibited by the monks. Every village, every hamlet, without exception, possesses a temple, where at least one monk is in residence. Here is the Burmese child's school. It is customary for every child to receive a certain amount of instruction in the monk's abode. This training is indeed as limited, and of the same quality, as that of the young Singhalese. It consists in reading and writing Burmese and a little of the sacred language, Pâli (here written in Burmese characters), learning by heart sacred formulæ and prayers, the conduct of religious ceremonies, first acquaintance with the fantastic world of Buddhist legend and mythology, moral maxims, and something of popular poetry. By means of this teaching the individual is brought into early and friendly relationship with the religion of his country. The monks are generally honourable and esteemed, and their instruction is a pleasure to the children. It begins when they are eight or nine years old. The scholars may be lodged in the monastery itself, and are not required to become novices, but remain simply pupils, wearing secular clothing, and with no other duties than that of instruction.

A few years later comes the hour for decision of the young human being, when he may fully take monastic vows and monastic responsibilities. In Burma it is, indeed, the ordinary custom for every layman, even when he has no intention of permanently renouncing a worldly calling, to dedicate a certain time during his youth to monastic life. This passing through monasticism signifies his entrance into full manhood. The boy then receives a new name, to be dropped later on when he returns to the world. The age for the monastic period should be fifteen, according to the rules laid down, but for practical reasons the majority enter on it earlier—at about twelve. The entrance usually takes place at the beginning of Was—namely, about the middle of July. The entrance ceremony is a great festival, in which relatives and friends of both sexes take part. A pretty procession introduces the proceedings, when the aspirant to the noviciate takes leave of the spectators, as if renouncing the world. After this he returns to the paternal residence. A number of monks, besides other people taking part in it, are all assembled there. The novice's hair is shaved off, his secular clothing is exchanged for the monastic habit, the youth begs thrice for admission into the holy community, the monk's utensils are handed to him, and then he walks in procession to the monastery. In his father's house further hospitality is dispensed to the guests, and it usually ends with what is so much enjoyed in Burma—a pantomimic dance called *pwe*.

The duration of stay of such novices in a monastery varies according to their earnestness of purpose. There are cases in which it is such a purely perfunctory matter that the youth merely remains one day with the monks. Others remain at least a few weeks or a month. The correct thing, however, is to belong to the monastery for the Was season—namely, three months—and whoever is desirous of satisfying the highest requirements of strong religious convictions can only do so by spending three rainy seasons with the monks; this is explained as the first was being for the purpose of obtaining merit for his father, the second for his mother, and the third for himself.

The common name for the novice in Burma is *shin*. He follows the mode of life of the monks, and must not venture to transgress the ten fundamental commandments, or he will lay himself open to punishment, frequently to corporal punishment. But the burden laid upon him by monastic life is not in reality a heavy one, owing to the simplicity of Burmese life, especially when it is only for a short space of time.

Whoever wishes to enter the monastic community permanently has to be admitted by a second ceremony, when his noviciate is ended, which corresponds with that which takes place in Ceylon (see p. 100). Here also the lowest age prescribed is twenty.

The dress and other equipment of monks is the same as that of Singhalese Buddhism. The daily routine is also similar. They rise at daybreak, wash, say the morning prayer, accomplish the necessary domestic labour, eat a light meal, and betake themselves to meditation or the study of a sacred work. At eight or nine o'clock the prescribed begging takes place, from which only the sick and very aged are exempt. As in Ceylon, the food obtained by begging is not always eaten by the monks, unless under the compulsion of poverty; it is preferably given to the poor or to animals; not infrequently the monks empty their well-filled bowls in the street in the course of their begging, for the benefit of the dogs or other recipients. This is not considered as contemptuous of the giver, since the feeding of animals is also an act of merit.

After they have accomplished the duty of begging for an hour or two, they return to the monastery, and take the meal which has meanwhile been prepared for them. Afterwards the time is spent in reading or religious conversation, or the reception of visitors, or in any other way they please. Towards midday they have another light meal, since after midday they are not allowed to eat anything more. The afternoon is spent in all sorts of simple duties—the teaching of pupils, learning the sacred text, meditation, the superintendence of copyists, who prepare manuscripts for the monastery. A considerable part of the time is passed in gossip and chewing betel-nut. For the younger ones, especially the novices, there are several menial duties to be performed during this time. At sunset all who wear the yellow robe, even those who have been outside paying visits, must assemble within the monastery. A certain supervision is maintained over what the disciples have learnt, and the day closes with a united act of worship of the Buddha images.

### B. Grades of Rank.

Theoretically all the monks are alike in rank, except for the difference made by the time they have spent in the monkhood. They reckon it by the Was seasons, and say of a monk: "He has so many Was." Whoever has the largest number of Was is held in the most esteem; otherwise there should be no distinction. Nevertheless they have practically established distinct grades on a hierarchical system, even more completely than in Ceylon. The full monk holds the title of *Yahan*, or is called *Pyit-Shin*. If he has had more than ten Was he receives the honorific title of *Hpongyi* (great renown), a name which foreigners often mistakenly bestow upon the monks in general. From the Hpongyi monks alone can the Abbot of a monastery be chosen. He has the honorary title of *Sayadaw* (royal teacher). The monasteries of a certain district form a union under the presidency of an older and specially venerated Abbot, who is called *Gaing-douk*. A yet higher group is formed of the monks named *Gaing-ok;* above these is the rank of the *Gaing-gyok*. Finally the guidance of the whole Burmese Buddhist Church is in the hands of the so-called *Thathanabaing*. He formerly was chosen by the King of Burma.

Since the time when Burma lost her King, and the British supremacy was established, a certain confusion invaded this hierarchical system, especially since the death of the last Thathanabaing (in 1895) belonging to the royal times. For a long period he had no successor, as the British rule did not recognize as one of its functions the selection of a religious head for Buddhism, while the monks of the country could not agree in their choice. At last, however, a new Thathanabaing has been appointed by the monks, and has received the official confirmation of his appointment by the British Government. He resides at Mandalay, the former capital. Originally his supremacy was confined to Upper Burma, but Lord Curzon—the Viceroy of India at the time of his appointment—extended the area of his jurisdiction, so as henceforth to include Lower Burma.[1]

## C. Sacred Buildings.

The monasteries and temple buildings vary considerably both in extent and in value. With few exceptions they are built of wood,[2] and for this purpose they make use of the excellent and very durable teak wood, in which Burma is so rich. The buildings are raised on pillars three or four yards in height, and are one-storied, although the picturesque roofs are divided into several stages, of diminishing size as they ascend, which gives an impression of stories. The principal building of a monastery, *kyoung*, is a hall divided into two parts, surrounded by a veranda. One division serves the inmates as a general abode; frequently they even sleep there on the mats, which serve as beds, and which during the daytime lie rolled up alongside the walls.

The other division contains the Buddha images, altars bearing candles or little lamps, flowers, and other adornments, besides the chests in which the sacred writings are kept, manuscripts on palm-leaves of varying value. This is the more important room of the two; its floor is raised higher than the surrounding veranda

[1] Compare the article in the periodical *Buddhism*, vol. ii., No. 1, p. 107 *et seq.*: "Reorganization of the Sangha in Upper Burma."

[2] Both in Rangoon and in Mandalay may be seen buildings of stone erected in a somewhat European style, but farther inland there are also old monasteries which are occasionally built of brick.

and the room used for living in. Visitors are generally conducted there, unless they are well-known acquaintances of the monks.

The *kyoungs* contain no other images than those of the Buddha. Generally a large one stands in the centre, and countless others are ranged round the walls on the floor; sometimes small ones are on shelves or brackets against the wall. They are made of wood, brass, alabaster, as well as silver or gold. In their representation of the figure of the Buddha, they agree with the above-mentioned three poses of the Singhalese Buddhism—the seated (meditation), the standing (preaching), the recumbent (entering Nirvâṇa, see p. 105). The seated Buddha is usually represented in Burma with the hands in a different position from what the Singhalese images show. The right hand hangs down over the right leg close beside the knee, the palm facing the body, while the left hand lies palm uppermost in the lap.[1] Usually in front of this Buddha kneel his two disciples, Maudgalyâyana and Shâriputra, the one with his ear turned towards the master, as if in the act of listening, the other with folded hands in the attitude of worship. Besides the figures of the Buddha Gautama, one sees here and there in the shrines some of the noted earlier Buddhas, as, for

[1] There is a specified number of positions of the hands and arms of the seated Buddha, about which many theories are held. The position is called *mudrâ* (seal), and each *mudrâ* has its peculiar significance. The one mentioned above is the *mudrâ* of witness, because the Buddha is thereby said to have called the earth as witness when he sat under the Bo-tree fighting with the tempter.

instance, Gautama with his three predecessors of this world epoch: Kakusandha, Konâgamana, and Kassapa. Also the fourth figure in the complete series of the twenty-eight former Buddhas, Dîpamkara (the Light-bringer) is sometimes represented.

Besides the *kyoung*, in most of the monasteries a sort of steeple meets the eye, which rises in a series of stories. This is the *thein*, which is set apart for special purposes, in particular for meditation and for the rite of admission. Frequently there are legends attached to the spot on which the *thein* is erected, in order to show the connection of the monastery with some holy being of ancient times or with some celebrated King.

The whole of the monastic grounds are usually surrounded by a wooden or stone wall, within which the layman dares only to penetrate after removing his sandals or shoes, as it is holy ground. A certain circumference outside the enclosure is also frequently marked off by the Abbot as sacred ground. Above all things, no living creature must be killed there, and passers-by are warned of this fact by notices. It is here that people like to place tanks in which fish are kept, or tortoises and other water beasts, which are fed and tamed. It is reckoned an act of merit for visitors to the monastery to feed them, and, naturally, they soon become extremely tame. In some cases laymen send animals (which they have rescued from being killed) to a monastery to be taken care of by the monks. They are then suitably housed and fed in close proximity to the monastery.

The appearance of the more important monasteries

is extremely picturesque. The great skill of the Burmese in wooden architecture and wood-carving attains its highest success in them. The different roofs, balusters, walls, posts—everything is carved and painted with marvellous elaboration and dexterity; even where the style of architecture is not characterized by originality or any remarkable imaginative power, yet the whole effect is highly pleasing, and worthy of admiration in its fine, laborious, and thoughtful decorative art. The "golden monastery of the Queen" at Mandalay is one of the most charming examples of this kind of Burmese building.

### D. Dagabas.

A special chapter is requisite for the description of the Buddhists' buildings in Burma, called dagabas (Burmese *Zaydee*, from Pâli *chaitya; or paya*).[1] No other country has such a wealth of these religious monuments. When one goes down the river Irrawaddy, and glides through the beautiful scenery on its banks, from the forest-clad mountains in the north, with their rocky peaks, down to the rice-fields surrounding Rangoon, the spires of the dagabas, frequently gilded, emerge one by one in ever new variety from among the palms or thick underwood. They are the distinguishing feature of the country. The reason why the dagabas are so numerous, and why new ones are always being erected alongside countless old ones, which are falling to pieces without anyone taking the

[1] On the original character of this building, see above, p. 45.

trouble to restore them, is the popular belief in the supreme meritorious efficacy of building a dagaba; naturally, everyone desirous of obtaining merit builds his own dagaba.

Many of the dagabas are built in the neighbourhood of monasteries, but it is quite permissible to set them up away from them. In each dagaba a revered object is placed in a kind of mausoleum; originally these were relics. Now they are generally a costly statue of the Buddha or a valuable specimen of a sacred writing. Sometimes besides there are costly votive offerings, models of sacred places formed in silver or gold, precious stones, vases, and such-like. The consecration of a dagaba is carried out with great pomp. A remarkable feature on such occasions, and which is also present at the reception of important gifts, is the libation of water on the soil, while a sacred formula is recited. Thereby the earth and its spirits are taken as witnesses of the transaction.

The shape of the dagaba varies considerably in detail, but the fundamental architectural design is usually the same. The basis is a four-sided pyramid, with a row of additions in the shape of steps. From this rises the conical part, probably meant to represent a lotos bud, which tapers abruptly upwards, with parallel furrows running round it all the way up. The top bears an ornament, the so-called umbrella, Burmese *hti*, frequently adorned with a covering of gold and precious stones. At the entrance or beside the flight of steps leading to it there may frequently be seen, at the more important dagabas, grotesque animals on either side, carved in stone, combinations of dragons and lions, showing the influence of Chinese art. As guardians of the dagabas you may notice certain demons (*nats*, of which there is more to be said later on). The walls are not infrequently decorated with simple drawings, scenes from the legendary life of the Buddha Gautama, or (for the purpose of awakening the conscience) the various torments which the wicked dead suffer in innumerable hells.

At the present day the most celebrated of all Burmese dagabas is the Shway Dagon dagaba at Rangoon. Under it there are said to be buried not only eight veritable hairs of the Buddha Gautama, but also a begging-bowl, a garment, and a pilgrim staff, of each of the three earlier Buddhas of this world epoch. The Shway Dagon boasts an extraordinary wealth of specimens of Oriental art. It is an imposing collection of temples, chapels, monuments, and shrines, with the principal dagaba in the centre, a never-ending exhibition of Buddhist art and skill, embowered in a wealth of tropical vegetation, daily visited by thousands of pilgrims, monks, suppliants, sight-seers, business people, a fantastic picture of the attractive force of the Southern Buddhist religious life. Japanese, Chinese, and Korean pilgrims make their way here, and leave behind them in the sacred place both offerings and buildings in token of their veneration.

Besides the Shway Dagon, mention must be made of two others which are considered equally important by the Burmese at all events—the Shway Maw Daw at Pegu, and the Shway San Daw at Prome. At

Mandalay the so-called Arakan dagaba is highly esteemed; the Burmese call it Maha Myat Muni. The ancient capital Pagan, on the Irrawaddy, should also be mentioned in this connection; it is deserted and ruined since the close of the thirteenth century, but its walls enclose the remains of 9,999 dagabas.

The dagabas are the usual places of worship for the laity. Attached to them is a hall containing some Buddha images, where laymen can pay their homage. At noted dagabas there are several such halls; sometimes there are four, each of which looks to a point of the compass, and they are full of Buddhas large and small, the presents of pious laymen. For the protection of all these ever-recurring gifts which are brought by the faithful, special houses are erected at much-visited sanctuaries, if the dagaba cannot contain them all. These houses, which are under the care of an old man, are also much frequented by zealous laymen, who perform their devotions in front of the images. But they are far less venerated than the dagabas.

A necessary requirement at the dagaba is a bell. Large dagabas possess several of them. They are struck by worshippers when they have finished their praise of the Buddha, bringing their merit to the notice of the invisible ones. The biggest bell in all Burma is that of the Mingon dagaba in Mandalay.

The representation of the Buddha's footprint, which we have already mentioned as found in Ceylon, is also seen in many of the dagabas of Burma.

### E. Character of the Monkhood.

Monasticism in Burma, according to common consent, is taken seriously, at all events, as the monastic rules must be strictly observed. Small misdemeanours are expiated by penance appointed by the eldest monk (the Abbot), the penance consisting in physical labour for the monastery, or nocturnal vigils, or a more austere way of living, or ascetic deeds, or other such things. If, on the other hand, it is a heinous offence, especially if it is one of the four great sins—a great sexual crime, theft of a valuable object, murder, or the misuse of supernatural power—then, unless there are extenuating circumstances, the member is expelled publicly from the community by unfrocking and the taking away of his begging-bowl. The consequences of this are serious, for an expelled monk is not only subject to universal contempt, but even to the hatred of the populace. He is outlawed.

A monk is at liberty, however, to leave the monastery by his own will, and here and there one is to be found who chooses to do so when he is severely tempted, so as to be able to gratify his cravings.

Although the monks on the whole keep a pretty careful watch on their outward behaviour, yet a number of lax habits have crept in which are not severely condemned. It has been already pointed out that many monks do not eat the food which has been begged, but only beg for the sake of form. Furthermore, silk clothing is in common use, which is, strictly speaking, prohibited. The monks also frequently take part in plays, especially in the very popular *pwe*, the pantomimic dances. Above all, many of them are extremely covetous, and are eager for the personal possession of money and presents; indeed, they themselves carry on business transactions. Law-suits are by no means uncommon, both with one another and with the laity, even in the English law-courts. Such shortcomings of the monastic ideal are open to the public gaze. If one probe deeper and examine the inward maturity and grasp of the most vital requirements of Buddha Gautama, one must equally admit a deficit in the majority of cases. The monks are satisfied with the accomplishment of what is the prescribed mode of life, with reading and committing to memory sacred writings, with the outward appearance of meditation. Monks possessed of inward zeal and real knowledge are always exceptional; they spring more from the simple, retired monasteries of the interior, especially of Upper Burma, but they often attain a career (when they have sufficient ability) by being selected as the leaders for the large monasteries at Mandalay or elsewhere.

The fact that most of the Burmese monks are lacking in real earnestness in their career has long since given rise to the formation of a reform party, which is called Chulla-gandi. The adherents of this party try to enforce a stricter observance of the monastic rules, as, for instance, that no luxurious gowns should be worn, even going so far as to prohibit the use of umbrellas and sandals, and to require that they should live on the food obtained by begging, that no one should accept money or gifts to himself personally, and that he should take no part in dances or popular festivals. The Chulla-gandi is in the minority, and has the bulk of the monastic communities—the Maha-gandi—ranged against it. The controversy has sometimes been carried on with much heat, not only in speech and in writing, but even in street brawls, when the English authorities were obliged to interfere.

Another more modern reform party is the society of Buddhasâsana Samâgama, which we mentioned already in connection with Ceylon. This society aims at bringing Buddhism into close contact with Europe and its culture, for the needs of which this religion is held to be all-sufficing. An attempt has also been made simultaneously to take up new aims and graft them on to Burmese Buddhism, so as to give it a European cast. Thus, school-life has been put on a different footing, lectures are given to lay people, journals are published. The soul of the movement is a European, Mr. Allan B. MacGregor (his monastic name is Ananda Maitreya, or Metteya), who has gone over to Buddhism from Roman Catholicism. This movement dates from the year 1902. It was reorganized in 1903. One of the original points of the constitution had been to form a "Sangha of the West," carrying out missionary work in Europe and America. This plan was in 1903 given up as impracticable. But quite recently, in 1907, it has been taken up again, as a "Buddhist Society of Great Britain and Ireland" has been formed in London. Its scope is wider than a mere propaganda for Buddhism, comprising the promotion of a better knowledge of Buddhism and the study of Pâli and Sanskrit literature. But the publications issued so far show a strong missionary tendency. In Mandalay already in 1900 a society for promoting Buddhism was established. Its objects were : (1) To maintain the Buddhist monks in food, etc. ; (2) to promote the learning of Buddhist scriptures; (3) to start an Anglo-Vernacular Buddhist School; (4) to publish a monthly Buddhist journal; (5) to start a printing-press; (6) to look after the Buddhist monasteries, dagabas, inscriptions, etc.; (7) to train Buddhist monks in different languages, and send them abroad as missionaries. This programme expresses the needs which the modernized Buddhists in Burma feel at present.

### F. The Life of the People and Buddhism.

In Burma the life of the people is in every way connected with Buddhism.

So long as it existed as an independent kingdom, the influence of the monks extended even to the throne, and made itself widely felt there. Direct access to the King, by means of petitions and audiences, was granted to the higher spiritual functionaries. They were allowed—and they frequently made use of the privilege—to criticize the action of the Government when they considered it harmful to the people. They even possessed a jurisdiction of their own in contests with the laity. Every monastery had a certain inviolability, so that it could afford shelter to a criminal when pursued by justice, and in times of danger it was resorted to by the laity to guard special treasures. Thus the monkhood became an important political factor, which in a certain sense served as an intermediary between the despotic monarchy and its subjects.

Since the British annexation all this has ceased. Naturally, Buddhism did not willingly resign the temporal power, and the British rule has several times had to deal with insurrections (the last of these took place in 1897) which have been instigated and led by the monks. In such cases Gautama's disciples have not refrained from violent deeds and the shedding of blood. Although the political importance of the monks has now come to an end, the consideration in which they are held shows itself in many ways. The monks are treated with great reverence. If a layman enters a monastery to show them a mark of respect by his visit, or in order to discuss this or that matter with them, he must bow to the ground thrice before the monks, whether he is a distinguished person or a beggar. This bowing is accompanied with a reverential speech, addressed in the special form used by the Burmese in accosting persons of high rank. The monk is addressed with the title of Payah (Sir), whereas he addresses a layman as Tagah (supporter). The layman considers it a duty incumbent on him to look after the monastic buildings and their preservation, to provide the food and clothing of the monks, and to attend to their general welfare. They are not parsimonious in this respect. The clergy usually receive their share of the finest fruit and choicest vegetables.

The religious festivals are heartily shared in by the

people as a whole. The commonest of these are the four days of the lunar phases in each month, which the Singhalese also celebrate (see pp. 30 and 122). They then betake themselves in the early morning (the very zealous ones even go the night before) to a dagaba, present offerings to the monks, listen to the recitation of the sacred writings, and keep the day as a holiday. Some undertake the monastic rule of life for the day by spending it in reading or reciting pious passages, and in meditation; they take no food after the morning meal, and pay homage to the Buddha images. Especially during the Was season (middle of July to mid-October) the laity engage in all kinds of devotion on the four days of the month. At that time also wealthy families frequently invite the monks to their houses, so that they may instruct them in "the law," the teaching of Gautama; and in the presence of a large gathering of friends and acquaintances some important writing is read aloud, or an exhortation to good works (mostly the support of monasteries and dagabas) is delivered.

During the Was season no noisy entertainments must be given, especially there must be no *pwe*, those pantomimic dances so dear to the Burmese. On the contrary, the time should be spent devoutly and in meditation. The result of this is that the conclusion of the Was has the appearance of being a specially joyous festival, full of merriment and frolic. Those youths who have been spending a short time at the monastery have generally come to the end of their course of duties as monks, and naturally they return with redoubled pleasure to their homes and to the tide of secular life. At this time, also, the monks are drawn perforce into the current of worldly pleasures. They receive very handsome offerings and presents, and allow noisy, busy proceedings even within the monastery rooms sometimes.

Another noteworthy religious festival is that of the dagabas. Each dagaba has its own special day every year. All the people of the neighbourhood meet there for harmless amusement on the day, and celebrated dagabas draw visitors from long distances. There are some more festivals commemorating events from the Buddha legend, as the ascent into the Tuśita heaven to preach the law to his mother, or the attaining Buddhahood under the Bo-tree.

An essential part of all these festivals are the offerings to the monks. Their maintenance is the main element in Burmese piety. If the pious Burman can afford to do so, he builds a temple or dagaba at his own expense. That is the highest goal of his religious ambition. If that is not possible, he can at all events present images of the Buddha for the sanctuary, have pictures made, or pay for necessary repairs; he may give a bell or present the monks with clothing, food, all sorts of implements, and even articles of luxury. One must do something for the Buddhist community. The layman's point of view is that thereby merit is obtained, and a happy reincarnation at the close of this life, no less than the insuring of happiness and success in all sorts of human undertakings in this present world. There are also good works performed by laymen apart from those done to the monks, such as the quenching of the thirst of travellers by setting up vessels full of water or weak tea on the roads, or by building rest-houses in which the weary can find repose and shelter from the heat of the sun, or by saving animals from being killed, and taking them to a monastery to be cared for; but these things are of far inferior merit to the maintenance and care of monasteries. Characteristic of the spirit from which these deeds of piety spring is one of the commonest formulæ which the scholar learns in his early days, and repeats countless times when he makes offerings and at religious festivals:

"Awgatha, Awgatha, I worship with the body, with the mouth, and with the mind, with these three *kans.* The first, the second, the third; once, twice, until three times. The Lord, the precious one; the Law, the precious one; the Assembly, the precious one—these three precious things. I, the worshipper, most humbly, with fervid zeal, with clasped hands, pay reverence, give offerings, and with pious gaze bow me down. Thus by this worshipping I gain merit and increase in earnestness and purity of heart, and am freed from the Four States of Punishment; from the Three Evil Things, starvation, plague, and warfare; from the Eight Chambers of Hell; and from the Five Enemies. And at the end, when the last existence has come for me, may I pass into Nirvâṇa."[1]

There are numbers of such formulæ, longer or shorter as the case may be, ceaselessly repeated by the visitors to the sanctuaries, while they prostrate their bodies to the ground and raise their folded hands to

[1] Shway Yoe, "The Burman: his Life and Notions," p. 185 *et seq.* (London, 1896).

their foreheads. That also is a means for obtaining merit. Others use short formulæ which sound like spells, written for them on small pieces of paper or cloth (so-called prayer-flags), which they bring to the sanctuary together with flowers, and candles, or little oil-lamps.

But it is a very remarkable fact that, despite the strong current of Buddhist motive underlying the whole of the Burmese people's life, the real acting religious force is not Buddhist at all. On the contrary, we find here a factor dating from pre-Buddhist times, and which Buddhism—notwithstanding the powerful hold which it obtained over this people—has been entirely unable to supersede. It is the worship of the so-called *nat*. Who are the *nats?* The name is also applied to certain figures of the Buddhist mythology, namely, the *devas*, who inhabit the lower heavens. But that is merely an adaptation and transference. Originally the name applied to supernatural beings, who had no connection with Buddhism, but which sprung from ancient Burmese demon and nature worship.[1] There are evident signs in the cult of the present day to show that the *nat* on the one hand was the personification of certain forces of nature, and on the other hand it represents the spirit of the dead. The former case is shown in the connection of many

[1] Compare on the subject "The Thirty-seven Nats: a Phase of Spirit Worship in Burma," by Sir R. C. Temple (London, 1906); the same, "A Native Account of the Thirty-seven Nats," *Ind. Ant.*, vol. xxxv., p. 217 *et seq.* (1906). Also a review of the before-named works by Grierson, *Journal of the Royal Asiatic Society*, 1907, p. 238.

*nats* with specified localities or with trees and fruits; the latter is seen in the semi-historical allusions to many *nats* in the festival songs and all sorts of legends. There are innumerable *nats;* they are classified in thirty-seven different representatives, to each of which a special sacred hymn is dedicated. There is a house *nat*, a village *nat*, and together with them a number of the same kind of beings, who inhabit unspecified places in the desert, the roads, the rocks, the springs, or the streams. Most of the *nats* are of a dangerous nature; here and there, however, may be found a *nat* to whom one may apply for help. There are female as well as male *nats*. Miscreants who have been put to death, or persons who have met with a violent death, add to the number of *nats*. They are all under the rule of a *nat* King, the Thagya Min.

The worship of these beings is the real religion of by far the majority of the Burmese, who adhere to them with absolute, unalterable inward conviction. The testimony of those who are thoroughly acquainted with the life of the Burmese fully corroborates this fact. Only one such testimony is here quoted, that of Bishop Bigandet, who is universally acknowledged to be one of the best-informed scholars on this subject. He says:[1] "The Buddhism of the people has but little or no part in their daily life. In common life, from the day of birth to that of wedding, or even of death, all the customs and formulæ made use of by the Burmese originate with demon worship, and not with

[1] In a communication to J. G. Scott, the editor of the "Gazetteer of Upper Burma and the Shan States" (Rangoon, 1900), quoted in part i., vol. ii., p. 10.

Buddhism. If a misfortune befalls him, he attributes it to the *nat*; if he wishes to undertake an important matter, he tries to enlist the favour of the *nat*. Even the monks frequently give in to the influence of this strong undercurrent of animistic religion which underlies their Buddhist faith."

*Nat* worship occupies such an important place in the life of the ordinary Burmese that no one can overlook it, who has many dealings with this people. Every house has its *nat*. He is not a guardian spirit in the sense of specially concerning himself with the welfare of the inhabitants. But he has his established position in the house, and the inhabitants must see to it on their part that he is kept in good temper. The pillars of the house are bound round at the top with stuff made of the cotton-wool in which he loves to dwell. A vessel of holy water (which is reconsecrated monthly by formulæ used with twigs and leaves of certain trees) stands in the veranda, and the dwelling is often sprinkled with the water, to insure the protection of the *nat*. They bring him offerings, food, and fruit. They hang up cocoanuts and gay rags for him. The *nat* may be very dangerous to the stranger who comes heedlessly under the roof; he may frighten him into madness or bring an illness on him. Every village also has its *nat*, to whom a place of worship is erected at the entrance, close to the last huts. He has regular festivals in his honour, also special ones when a calamity has taken place, such as when an epidemic of cholera or smallpox has broken out in the place.

*Nat* festivals are characterized by wild dances and

the performance of remarkable songs. These are undertaken by women dressed up to represent the individual *nat*. Their performances frequently are of the nature of ballads, or represent scenes from the life of the *nat* during his earthly experience. Fireworks, cockfights, and wild music, are associated with these performances. The *nats* are frequently represented in pictures as gaily dressed puppets with swords and other weapons, and sometimes on horseback. They often figure on paper charms, and people have some of them tattooed on themselves. The superstitious practices connected with *nat* worship are innumerable. They are mostly performed by those women who dance at the *nat* festivals, and whose power to bring down curses, to exorcise illnesses, to call up the spirits of the dead, and to foretell the unknown, is blindly believed in.

So far is Buddhism from having obtained the mastery over this religion, that even the monks are dominated by it to an incredible extent. This is, naturally, the case mainly with the inmates of village monasteries in the interior of the country, especially in Upper Burma, whereas the superior type of monk in Rangoon expresses his dislike and contempt of the popular belief. In the country, however, they bind the pillars of the monasteries with cotton-wool for the temple *nat*, and the monks attend the *nat* festivals, especially during epidemics, in order to bring to bear their more powerful influence on the menacing spirit. The monks stand by the sick-bed or death-bed at the exorcising of the *nat*, they are the most popular tattooers and soothsayers, they decide which are lucky and unlucky days, and they interpret dreams.

A yet more complete intermixture of animistic and nature worship with Buddhism may be observed in the Shan States. This differs in many of its external features from the usual Burmese Buddhism; but it does not occupy a sufficiently important position for us to deal with it here, as we are only concerned with the main development of Buddhism.

## Chapter IV.—THE BUDDHISM OF SIAM

Siamese Buddhism is so similar to that of Ceylon and Burma in all its main features that it would be superfluous to describe it in detail. It would be merely repetition. On one special point, however, some closer attention is requisite, as it is peculiar to Siam.

This country still possesses a King of its own.[1] Wherever a Buddhist King has reigned he has always assumed a particular attitude. He is not the head of the Church, but he is its chief patron. From this arises a unique condition of affairs. The King himself is bound to render homage to the monks, so long as he does not rise above "the world," that is to say, enter the monkhood. Otherwise he is merely a layman. But the favour of Kings has a fundamental significance for the welfare of the monks. In reality they must rely upon him, and cannot afford to forgo his favour. Also, in his capacity of ruler he has a certain authoritative

[1] Cambodia also, in so far as it is independent of Siam (the northern, and, indeed, the most important, provinces of Cambodia are incorporated in Siam), nominally possesses a King of its own, but he is entirely under French control. The titular King of Cambodia stands in exactly the same relation to Buddhism as the King of Siam does in his country.

right over them. Both sides of the question are cleverly brought into harmony, and can be readily studied, in Siamese Buddhism.

There is a supreme official at the head of Siamese Buddhism, which has developed on the same hierarchical lines as it did in Burma; he is called the Sankharat. But he, as well as all the leading monks, who superintend large districts, must be nominated by the King. Besides this the King appoints one of the Princes of his own house to have an oversight of the conduct and habits of the monks. This official calls to account any monks guilty of serious misdemeanours. Such monks are then unfrocked and degraded to the position of laymen, and the punishment runs its course. Thus any elements dangerous to the State authority are held in check, and the clerical power is under control. On the other hand, however, the King shows marked deference (in all external appearance) to the Buddhist religion. He daily maintains a large number of monks at his personal expense; he builds temples and monasteries; he shows his reverence by bowing and raising of the hand to the head, although he assumes the special right of raising only one hand, whereas his subjects are all obliged to raise both hands folded together.

The most interesting act by which the Siamese King shows his reverence for the religion is the yearly visit to the temples for the purpose of presenting clothing to the monks.

In the middle of October—when the Was season comes to an end—it is customary in Siam for the laity to present monks' habits. For this purpose the King in person (occasionally he is represented by one of the Princes) visits a number of the monasteries at Bangkok, which are specially under his patronage. It is a gorgeous spectacle, as he generally goes in costly decorated barges (the travelling in Bangkok being more by water than by land). Princes, high officials, and a large retinue, accompany the Sovereign. He sits in his specially ornate barge under a canopy and the royal umbrella ; the clothing destined for presentation fills the boat. When he has landed at one of the monasteries, the King betakes himself in procession, accompanied with music, to the gateway of the principal temple hall. There he takes the clothing from the hands of the attendants, who have carried them so far ; he enters the hall and lays them on a table. This table is already laden with gifts, contributed in the name of the King. The King then lights the candles and incense, and bows thrice in act of worship, first before the Buddha images, then before the sacred books, and lastly before the assembled monks, belonging to the monastery, who have placed themselves in the background. He next renews to the Abbot the five vows which the Buddhist layman has to observe if he is in earnest about religion (see p. 21).

If it happen to be one of the sacred days of the month (Uposatha, Siamese: Ubosot, see p. 30), the King takes in addition the three vows belonging to the day: to eat no delicacy after midday, to attend no entertainment nor to use any scent, and to sleep on a low and simple bed. After taking these vows, the Prince announces to the monks his intention of presenting them with the above-mentioned gifts, whereupon the Abbot accepts them in the name of the monks, with suitable expressions of gratitude. When the King leaves the monastery, the monks recite a blessing, and he again bows to the Buddha, the sacred books, and the community. Besides the clothing presented, there are usually other gifts—vases, mats, furniture, and so forth.

Thus until the present day the custom has been maintained of the Buddhist religion outwardly ruling the highest authority in the State. The inner power of Buddhism in Siam has not been greater than in Ceylon and Burma. An unfathomable superstition, springing from various sources, has kept pace with this religion. Hinduism in particular has become closely interwoven with it. Chinese influences have also made themselves felt in many ways. The educational value of Buddhism for the people has therefore been remarkably limited, even in those countries where the "purer" Hînayâna is in vogue.

## Chapter V.—LAMAISM

Lamaism, that form of Buddhism which has developed in Tibet, and which takes its name from the title of the Tibetan monk, not only predominates in that country, but also in the smaller Himalayan States, Lâdak, Nepal, Bhotân, Sikkhim, as well as Mongolia, and it has branched out into Northern and Western China. It is a distinct, separate type of Buddhism, quite different from that of both the southern countries and of China, Japan, and Korea.

The reader will remember what has already been said

of the origin of Tibetan Buddhism (p. 71 *et seq.*); we have before us here that branch of the religion which preserved most of the Mahâyâna doctrine as it existed in India. It has disappeared from the banks of the Ganges and the Indus, but before it ceased to exist there it had taken new root in the wild mountain-tracts of the Himalayas, and thence again it had spread to the inaccessible plateau on the north. There the Mahâyâna Buddhism of India flowed into the blood of a people, robust, primitive, untouched by other influences, who eagerly absorbed and developed in a remarkable manner that fatal gift.

An entirely new atmosphere surrounds us in Lamaism. Similar to the contrast between the natural environment of the Irrawaddy and the snow-capped Himalayas is the contrast between the Buddhism which governs the north and that which rules in Ceylon and Farther India. *Here* the sun pours down on rice-fields and voluptuous forest or jungle thicket, palms and orchids, on naked or almost naked lithe brown human figures, childishly gay and joyous faces, decked with flowers. *There* rise wide, gloomy precipices, sinking into deep abysses; desolate plateaus, across which sweep raging storms; glaciers look down from the heights, the earth is rendered hard and unfruitful by rock; the faces of men are wild and forbidding—men who have to contend with the elements, broad, coarse figures, wrapped in skins and thick garments.

### A. The Sacred Buildings.

Even in the sacred buildings the different character is evident. The monasteries in Tibet rear themselves harshly and forbiddingly. They are solid buildings made of brick or quarry-stone; the walls are high and massive, with long rows of right-angled windows; the roof is usually flat. They have the look of fortresses when they are erected (as the Tibetans like to have them) on some picturesque eminence. Many of the lamaseries are huge places designed to accommodate several thousand monks. Then the monastery swells into a small town; it consists of a large number of solid buildings with streets and passages between them, a main building in the centre, and the whole enclosed within a massive wall. The monastic buildings are generally two-storied. A monastery usually contains a temple, which stands in the centre, surrounded by a courtyard; the living-rooms of the inmates are in the square surrounding it. A huge double door forms the main entrance. There are frequently open halls outside, standing somewhat apart, in which are placed prayer-wheels (cylinders) for the use of visitors. There are also not infrequently stûpas adorning the neighbourhood of the sacred buildings: the Tibetans call them *chorten*, the Sanskrit *chaitya*. Sometimes two such stûpas are connected with one another by a wall called *mendong*, in niches of which incense sticks may be lighted and other small offerings placed. If a stranger penetrates through the creaking gates into the courtyard, he must beware of the dogs belonging to the monastery, as they attack every intruder ferociously. The monks' rooms are simple and bare, larger and smaller cells side by side, with a veranda in front, running round the inner courtyard, generally on the upper story. The ground-floor, which has no outer windows, usually consists of dark storerooms.

The building for worship, which stands in the centre of the monastery courtyard, has a veranda in front of it, to which a short flight of steps gives access. Curtains which are drawn apart from the centre frequently hang over the entrance and make the light dim within. Already in the veranda we find several divinities, and as without some knowledge of the lamaistic gods further description would be rather unintelligible, we shall give a brief account of them before proceeding farther.

### B. The Lamaistic Gods.

While Southern Buddhism only admits images of the Buddha Gautama himself and some accompanying figures, no greater contrast can be afforded than that of Lamaism, which exhibits quite a bewildering crowd of deities. Sometimes they are figures from the ancient historical Buddhism ; sometimes Hindu gods which have crept into the Buddhist mythology ; then, again, a number of conceptions of the speculative fancy of Mahâyâna Buddhism ; yet again, other deities previously belonging to the ancient demon worship of the country and the Bon doctrine (see above, p. 72), local deities, individual guardian spirits, and so on : the whole weaves itself into a motley web which at first sight appears a hopeless tangle. For the sake of clearness we will separate into different classes the principal deities.

First there are the *Buddhas;* these are not indeed *the* Buddha, namely, Gautama. The conception of many other Buddhas, who lived in long past ages, a series of predecessors of the Prince Siddhârta, is, as we know, of early origin in Buddhism (see p. 45). The world stretches out through endless times, existing and passing away. Immense periods of time are classed together to form an epoch and to receive their special number of Buddhas. The last great world epoch saw twenty-eight Buddhas, including Gautama. But since the three most ancient ones were (according to legend) not in actual connection with Gautama, whereas all the others are said to have pointed on to him, those first three are not usually included in the series, thus leaving only twenty-four Buddhas as Gautama's predecessors. Amongst these the best known and most highly esteemed is Dîpamkara, the Light-bringer. Then, again, the six last forerunners of Gautama's are often represented with him in a group of seven. Another special group of Buddhas—older than the collection of seven—comprises five Buddhas, namely, the three last forerunners, Gautama himself, and the expected successor, the Buddha Maitrêya, who should arise when the five thousand years of Gautama should be accomplished.[1] This group of the five Buddhas plays an important rôle. The names as

[1] These five Buddhas are also common to Southern Buddhism; for instance, they are to be seen as statues at Anuradhapura at the Ruanweli Dagaba.

they follow in historical sequence are: Krakuchandra, Kanakamuni, Kâshiapa, Gautama and Maitrêya, (or, in Pâli, Kakusandha, Konagamana, Kassapa, Gotama, Metteyya). Through a special conception of Mahâyâna Buddhism, however, these five Buddhas have been promoted to a higher sphere. They were transitory appearances, whose historical representatives (such at least are supposed) when they entered Nirvâṇa at the close of their earthly career, ceased naturally to have an individual existence. These earthly appearances, however, are held to have sprung from a supernatural, imperishable nature. Thus each of these Buddhas is presupposed to be part of a "heavenly Buddha." Such heavenly Buddhas, therefore, are five, who are frequently called "the heavenly conquerors" (Jina). Among these five celestial prototypes of the historical Buddhas, the most conspicuous figure is the one corresponding to the historical Gautama. This is Amitâbha, (the boundless light), a Buddhist figure of the greatest popularity in the whole of Northern Buddhism.

When by means of these religious speculations as to celestial Buddhas stability was given to their transitory terrestrial appearance, so that the worship of the faithful could reach them, one could easily go a step further by placing above the five Buddhas the one supreme Buddha, as the ultimate origin—the Âdi-Buddha. In this way it became possible to combine the whole religious world of appearances into a unity.

From yet another quarter the number of forms of the Buddhas was augmented. Certain beings held in high esteem by the people, and practically of great importance, were raised to the position of celestial

Buddhas, as, for instance, a number of "medical" deities who were called "healing Buddhas." Other beings of universally high repute, whom they thought entitled to the highest rank, were on this account associated with the above-mentioned five heavenly Buddhas, in a little different representation. Thus to the figure of Amitâbha (the Buddha of endless light) was added another figure, Amitâyus (endless life).

Next to this class of the highest Buddhas comes that of the Bodhisattvas. As to their universal significance see p. 52 *et seq.* The Bodhisattvas serve as a further expansion of the above-outlined dogmatic speculation: thus to each of the five heavenly Buddhas, together with their five corresponding earthly ones, are added five Bodhisattvas, who are as spiritual "sons" or "reflexes" of the heavenly Buddhas. There is therefore a threefold series of five divine beings connected with one another, each heavenly Buddha having his supernatural reflex (a Bodhisattva) and his earthly counterpart, who has appeared in human form, or which should so appear in the case of Maitreya.

Among the Bodhisattvas, the most celebrated is Avalokita (Avalokiteśvara), the Bodhisattva who belongs to the trio comprising the historical Buddha Gautama and the heavenly Buddha Amitâbha. Avalokita is the divinity who is regularly reincarnate in the Dalai Lama of Lhassa. He is also tutelary deity of Tibet, and as such bears the complimentary title of Padmapâni (the lotos-handed). He is represented as friendly and compassionate, with the power to help all mankind. Avalokita has passed under a feminine guise (as Târâ, see p. 161) into Chinese Buddhism, and thence into Korean and Japanese (as Kwanyin or Kwannon).

Besides Avalokita, the most prominent Tibetan Bodhisattvas are Manjuśrî, the personification of wisdom; Samantabhadra, the divinity of religious ecstasy; and Vajrapâni, originally the Hindu god Indra, whose appearance as the wielder of the thunderbolt is held to be the highest exemplification of might.

A feminine counterpart of the Bodhisattvas is the so-called Târâ (star). There exist many Târâs, but they seem to be only different representations of that one which is a female transformation of the Bodhisattva Avalokita, and looked upon as his consort. The most conspicuous forms of the Târâ are the green and the white Târâ. It is said that the two wives of King Srong Tsan Gampo (*cf.* p. 71) were incarnations of the Târâ—the Nepalese Princess as the green Târâ, the Chinese as the white Târâ (the colours differentiating the variety of racial complexion). Another well-known Târâ is Marîchî, often represented with three faces and eight hands. One of the faces is that of a sow. The same animal carries sometimes the vehicle which she is riding upon or the lotos throne of her image. The number of the best-known incarnations of the Târâ is twenty-one; but she reincarnates again and again. The Mongols speak of the Emperor of Russia as an incarnation of the white Târâ.—A similar group of female deities are the Dâkkinîs. Their outfit is generally of a formidable kind—skulls, weapons, hand-drums, thunderbolts, and the like—their character dangerous (Waddell calls them "Furies"). They also incarnate in beings of the present day—one of them, for instance, in the Abbess of the Samding monastery in the Yamdok lake.

A third class of beings worshipped are the tutelary deities. They are looked on as being particularly clever at overcoming the noxious influence of demons. All Buddhas and Bodhisattvas have in themselves the power of exercising the functions of tutelary deities. As such they are depicted in a special outfit appropriate for the purpose. But there are also a number of supernatural beings, whose rôle is solely that of tutelary deities. These are the demon Princes. They are represented in the most dreadful and hideous way in order to demonstrate their capacity for terrifying or driving away demons. Skulls, decapitated heads and limbs, cups containing human flesh and blood, serpents and vipers, skins torn off, jaws with huge tusks in the act of mauling a human being, three or more eyes, several heads (some with animal, some with human faces), four or more arms holding weapons or implements of plunder in their hands—these are some of their characteristics. Each of these demon Princes has a consort, frequently represented with him; she is equally frightful and full of fury. The number of tutelary deities is amazingly great. All sorts of conceptions combine, emanating from both the North Indian type of Mahâyâna Buddhism as well as from the ancient Tibetan—Bon—religion, and intermingle with one another. From these tutelary deities there is in an ever-descending scale an innumerable horde of uncanny beings—nature spirits, such as serpent gods, a horse god, all sorts of figures out of Hindu mythology, some of a friendly and helpful character, but most of them images of terror.

Mention must also here be made of the Kings of the four cardinal points of the compass. They are held to be the guardians of the entrances to heaven, which rise from Mount Meru. The mountain is four-sided; on each side there dwells a guardian at the point where the heavenly region begins. The one on the east—Dhritarâśtra, King of the Gandharvas, a sort of angels—is white in colour, and holds a stringed instrument in his hands as his symbol. The one on the west—Virûpâkśa, King of the Nagas, the serpent gods—is red, and holds a *chorten* in his right and a serpent in his left hand. The guardian of the south is Virûdhaka, King of a class of demons called Khumbhanda. His colour is blue or green; he holds a sword. The one on the north, of yellow colour, is Vaiśravana (or Kubera), King of the Yakśas. He is represented with a flag in his right hand, and in the left an ichneumon with a jewel in its mouth. These watchers guard the heavens. But they also afford protection to the faithful, and are frequently portrayed and much revered.

Another much feared and courted of these lesser divinities is Yama, the judge of the dead. He sits in the centre of the regions of hell, of which there are eight hot and eight cold, not to mention four purgatories and countless minor adjoining hells. The King of Hell himself is compelled to endure as great sufferings as any of his victims. His consort is the terrible Lhamo, the tutelary deity of Lhassa. Yet another of these countless deities who must not be omitted is the very popular god of wealth, Jambhala, and the house god, or the god of the soil; for each house, each monastery, each temple, has its particular local divinity.

Another very large class of supernatural beings is that of the dangerous spirits. Among them are earlier gods belonging to the Bon religion, who in course of time have sunk to the position of spectres, also avenging spirits of those who have been murdered or ill-treated, star spirits, and various other fantastic creations. These spirits are so far included in the former class of divinities as they can be made serviceable to mankind by means of incantations.

Finally there are the saints who are worshipped. To these belong in the first place the most illustrious disciples of the Buddha, above all Maudgalyâyana and Śâriputra (his two favourite pupils), also Kâśyapa and Ânanda, and Upâli. Furthermore, there is a group of sixteen specially important apostles, the so-called Arhats, who are always represented together as "the sixteen strong holders of the doctrine."[1] Aśvaghoṣa, Nagarjuna, Atîśa, Tsongkapa, and other personalities well known in the history of Lamaism, are worshipped in this class. Also Padma Sambhava is found among these saints, but he plays a rôle less conspicuous than one should expect.

[1] In China it has become eighteen—the so-called Lohan. But in Korea and Japan there are still only sixteen, as there were in earlier Chinese Buddhism.

### C. The Inside of the Temples.

Now let us return to the temple and consider it more in detail. Already on the walls of the veranda and on both sides of the entrance we have noticed figures of the gods. There are pictures either painted on the walls or on a scroll of paper mounted on silk. All these gods have the character of tutelary deities. They belong to the class of demon Kings, and guard the sanctuary from enemies. Among them we find the four above-mentioned guardians of the mountain of the gods, two on each side of the entrance. There is also generally to be found on the wall of the veranda a large and characteristic painting of the so-called "wheel of life." It is a six-spoked wheel entwined with a demon figure, which rears its hideous head at the top. The six divisions between the spokes represent the six different regions in which one may find a new existence: The heavens, the Titans (a kind of semi-celestial beings), the man world, the animal world, the region of ghosts, the hells. The encompassing circle of the wheel is divided into twelve sections, each having a symbolic figure, representing the so-called twelve Nidânas, the causal nexus of reincarnation (see p. 13). Sometimes one sees all kinds of curious things hanging from the roof of the veranda, which are there to inspire reverence or fear in the minds of visitors. There are stuffed wild beasts, such as bears, buffaloes, apes, etc.

The inside of the temple is a square or quadrilateral room, of which the ceiling is usually supported by wooden pillars of a deep red colour. The walls are ornamented with numberless paintings, only in very small temples they are simply white. The wall paintings, crude in colour, represent mainly tutelary deities and saints. Some of the most gruesome demon Princes are kept veiled or hidden in a shrine. At the back wall the principal images are standing behind one or more altars. There are usually several statues in the centre, but there is no required uniformity in the matter of arrangement. Often the centre figure is the Buddha Gautama, with the Bodhisattva Avalokita on his left hand, and on the right hand Maitreya, the future Buddha. In other instances the historic Buddha is entirely absent; beside Avalokita stands the celestial Buddha Amitâbha, and the place of Maitreya is taken by the founder of the particular sect to which the temple belongs. There are also other forms of arrangement. The difference of representation between a Buddha and a Bodhisattva or a saint is generally not difficult to notice. The Buddha is represented in a simple manner: the head, with its singular tufts of hair, is uncovered, and has a lump on the top; the body is covered with a mantle, leaving the chest and a large part of the right arm bare. Almost always the Buddha is in a sitting posture, with feet crossed over one another.[1] The position of the hands (*mudrâ*) varies very much. A Bodhisattva is always quite differently portrayed. He is sumptuously adorned after the manner of an Indian Prince. The head is covered with a crown, the

[1] Only the Buddha of the future, Maitreya, is represented in the sitting position to which we Europeans are accustomed, with the feet hanging down.

ornaments coming down over the ears; he wears bracelets, and has chains on his breast; precious stones, either real or imitation, are worn in profusion. The hair is not shaved off, but bound in a knot on the top of the head. Some Bodhisattvas show several heads or arms. Avalokita especially is often represented with eleven heads, with four or many more ("thousand") arms. The saints, on the other hand, generally wear the normal monk's habit and a monk's cap.

Beside the central figures at the end of the hall, there are usually all sorts of other figures on either side. The images are generally made of wood or plaster gilded, less frequently of bronze. The centre of the hall is empty, so that the monks can assemble there for worship. But in front of the principal images there is a large altar. It generally consists of two stages of different levels. On the lower one offerings are placed—water, butter, rice, cakes, flowers, little lamps. On the higher stage are various objects. The most important of these are a small model of a *chorten*, a sacred manuscript, and the so-called *dorje*—a peculiar metal instrument, with a handle in the middle, at each end of which is fastened a bundle of four or eight birds' claws, tied together at the points. The *dorje* is the equivalent of the ancient thunderbolt of the Hindu god Indra. It is frequently used in lama worship for the exorcism of demons. There is besides on the altar a bell, a vessel full of holy water, a metal mirror, and a number of musical instruments.

The temple containing the images is called *lha*

*khang* (hall of the gods). Very large monasteries have more than one *lha khang*. Near the house of the gods is usually a large hall, where the monks assemble for the recitation of the sacred writings. This hall they call *du khang* (assembly hall). The common name of a monastery is *gompa*. Some very renowned places bear the title *ling*. If a monastery is organized more for study and doctrinal purposes, such an institution is called *choide*. The single colleges or schools of a *choide* are named *ta ts'ang*.

### D. The Lamaistic Monkhood.

The influential position held by the monks in Tibet, the manifold advantages connected with its status, the superstitious value set on its efficacy, not to mention a certain compulsion exercised on the laity by the clergy—all these things combine to draw a large number of laymen into the monastic Orders. Almost without exception, those who intend to become monks enter the monastery as children. It is customary in many parts of Tibet, and the Church keeps watch over the matter, for every family under ordinary circumstances to devote at least one son to the monkhood, usually the firstborn. The child selected for this purpose spends the first few years in the paternal home. But he is handed over to the monastery when he is about eight or nine years old. He must be healthy and without deformity; some monasteries, even, take only children out of families of some rank and possession. The child on first entering the monastery is merely a scholar. He is entrusted to the care of a monk who becomes his teacher (*gergän*), who instructs him in reading and writing Tibetan, and with whom he commits to memory important formulæ, prayers, short writings, besides performing a number of minor duties and ceremonies in the temple. This first course of instruction lasts for three or four years. During this time the child wears ordinary secular clothing; a tuft of his hair is cut off symbolically, but the head is not clean-shaven. As such a scholar the boy has begun the course of a *dâpa*, the general appellation for all ecclesiastic personages.

When the teacher considers his pupil sufficiently trained, he is promoted to the position of *genyen*, or novice. For this promotion the boy and his teacher apply to the Abbot, bringing some presents with them. The Abbot thoroughly interrogates the boy as to his character, health, freedom, family, and personal determination to enter the monkhood. The aspirant is also examined on what he has learnt. If all is satisfactory, his name is entered in the register of the monastery. The *genyen* wears the monastic habit, though he has as yet no share in worship and monastic duties, and his head is not completely shaven, one tuft remaining in the centre of the crown. The next promotion is the novice's admission as *getsul*, or junior monk. This is the entrance into the community, though not as a full monk. The function must be performed by a higher lama, who is looked upon as an incarnation of a deity, and a chapter has to be assembled. The remaining tuft of hair is cut off from the head of the candidate; he receives his monastic name, and promises obedience to all rules and precepts. The ordination takes place at a larger monastery, and generally a number of novices unite in it. Of course they have to pay some reward to the higher lama who presides at the ceremony. The junior monk possesses the outfit of a regular monk. He is also entitled now to take part in the general service and recitation with the other monks.

If a *getsul* is strenuous and wants to reach higher aims, he has to pass one further stage, which makes him a full monk, *gelong*. For this purpose he must give himself to studies in one of the most renowned lamaseries at Lhasa or Tashi Lhumpo. The course of learning is not an easy task. It includes much memorizing as well as getting familiar with usual explanations and with the subjects of disputations. A great many technical terms must be known, and the mode of chanting when reading the sacred books must be practised. When the *getsul* has shown himself qualified to become a *gelong* by passing the necessary examinations, he applies for the ordination to the head lama of the monastery where he is studying. The ordination is similar to the Upasampada ordination of the Southern Buddhists. A *gelong* must be at least fully twenty-five years of age.

The term "lama," which Europeans use to designate all Tibetan monks, is in Tibet limited to ecclesiastics of very high standing, heads of a monastery or monks in a specially honourable position. "Lama" means "the superior one" (see p. 73).

Women are allowed to embrace the monastic life as well as man, though their position is much inferior.

Their convents are styled *ani gompa* or *tsunpo*. The general appearance of the nun resembles that of the monk; the head is shaven, and no ornaments are allowed. In Central and Eastern Tibet nunneries are not uncommon, and among the most noteworthy places of pilgrimages is the Samding monastery of nuns as well as monks. In Western Tibet nuns are few.

The regular course of training is not by all monks followed up, some being hampered by want of mental faculties, others by want of means. There are many monks who remain simple *genyens* through all their life; others stop at the stage of *getsul*. It happens that a monk disagreeing with his monastery for personal reasons runs away from it, and seeks admittance in some smaller place, where the regulations are not so strict, or he becomes a monk on his own account, wherever he finds an opening in consequence of the superstition of the people. An instance of such a "run-away lama" is found in Huc and Gabet's "Travels" (vol. i., p. 20). Their companion, Samdad Chiemba, was a novice, who "had escaped from his lamasery in order to avoid the too frequent and too severe corrections of the master under whom he was more immediately placed." This man afterwards had not returned to any monastery. Cases of a similar kind are not rare.

The clothing of the monks of Tibet, in consequence of the climate, is much warmer than that in southern lands. They wear an under-garment, stockings, foot-gear, trousers, but always over these (when in full dress) the three prescribed garments of the earliest times: the loin-cloth, held up by a girdle; an upper garment with sleeves; and over that the wide mantle which covers the left shoulder, but leaves the right shoulder bare, being passed under the right arm. The colour of their clothing is either orange or red, according to the sect to which they belong. On festive occasions the superior authorities, such as Abbots and Directors, wear very beautiful, highly ornamented robes and many decorations. The difference in outward appearance between a high church dignitary at worship and a plain village lama is, indeed, not less than between some Catholic Archbishop celebrating Mass and a simple mendicant friar. The lama's fine robes are of silk, although it is contrary to the early regulation; only ordinary clothing is made of woollen material.

The headgear is very varied, and has special meaning; the different sects are distinguished from one another by its shape and colour. The principal groups of sects are called Red-cap, Yellow-cap, Black-cap. The shapes are of North Indian, or Chinese, or Mongolian origin. Many of them have lappets hanging from the back and sides, so as to protect the back of the head and the ears. Others resemble a Catholic Bishop's mitre. The fantastic shape of the cap often heightens the artistic effect of the monastic dress.

One or more amulet boxes, a case for pen and ink, a small flask for holy water, a rosary consisting of 108 beads, and a prayer cylinder, complete the equipment of a Tibetan monk.

The *daily occupation* of the monk is of a wholly different character from that of Southern Buddhism, because Lamaism has regular united duties of worship, whereas the duty of the daily begging walk has been given up. The monk has to rise early and begin the day with prayer. The first assembly for worship in the temple must take place before sunrise. The summons to it is ringing of bells and blasts of shell trumpets. After everyone has performed his ablutions, they all meet at the entrance to the temple, and enter together, taking their places on the mats in the centre. The worship opens by a united recitation of prayers and invocations, after which the monks have their morning tea handed round to them by the novices. Next there are various long liturgies, either recited by one or by all. These liturgies are prize songs in honour of certain Buddhas, Bodhisattvas, or saints, and invocations of powerful tutelary deities. They include a very important ceremony, which is enacted daily in the large monasteries, namely, the presentation of the *maṇḍala* offering. Gifts (consisting of a few grains of rice) for the entire universe, according to the conception of the Buddhist cosmogony, are placed in special order on a board in the centre of which there rises a sort of pagoda of rice, which is meant to symbolize Mount Meru, the centre of the universe. While for each individual part and division of the world (of which there are altogether thirty-eight) the gifts are laid on the tray within a sacred circle, a short formula of presentation is spoken. The early service lasts rather a long time, and is interrupted by the handing of tea. At the close the monks retire to their cells.

It is expected that the monks should invoke their individual guardian spirits in their cells, and also specially celebrate the sunrise with appropriate prayers.

At nine o'clock the second service takes place; this is mainly devoted to the tutelary deities (the demon Princes). A third general service is held at midday, a fourth about three o'clock in the afternoon, a fifth in the evening, about six or seven o'clock. But not all the monasteries are sufficiently austere to observe all these times of worship; many of them are satisfied with four, or even three, services. They are not so strict, either, as to require the attendance of every monk at every service; the older and more respected monks can absent themselves, and they often find an excuse for so doing.

During all the services tea is handed round by the novices. Larger meals take place three times a day—the first after early service, the second at midday, and the third in the evening, after the last service. Meat is not forbidden to the ordinary monks, but is eaten whenever opportunity offers, especially the flesh of the yak, the well-known Tibetan ox.[1] Mutton also they like, but not goat's flesh. Birds and fish are altogether prohibited in many sects. Only lamas who are ambitious of a reputation for special sanctity give up the use of meat entirely. In Lamaism no account is taken of abstinence from meals after midday.

Besides the usual acts of worship, there are a

[1] Waddell, "Lhasa and its Mysteries," third edition, p. 327: "We passed the village of Cheri, containing a large slaughter-house, where dozens of sheep and yak-oxen are slaughtered daily for the consumption chiefly of the 9,000 monks of Däpung." See also pp. 334, 374.

number of extra ones for special festivals, and for laymen who for some cause or other desire a special service. All these religious observances are generally composed of prayers or invocations, and of the offering of gifts, such as rice, water, cakes, flowers, incense, lamps, or meat, accompanied by the recitation of blessing formulæ and noisy music. Many of the services ordered by laymen take place in the temples, but others also in their houses. The simplest ceremony performed by the monk for the layman is reading aloud the sacred writings in their houses. The sacred word is considered so efficacious that the mere recital of texts averts danger and banishes demons. Hence the monks are often summoned by laymen for this purpose, and naturally it is done for money or money's worth.

Such are the religious occupations of the monk; but there are secular ones also. Most of the monasteries, even when they are not very large, entail all sorts of housework, and duties connected with the administration and organization of the establishment. In important monasteries there are regular posts which are assigned yearly to individual monks, such as the post of treasurer, steward, master of ceremonies, entertainer of guests, custodian of the water-supply, secretary, and so on. Moreover, the monks engage in all sorts of secular undertakings, which have no connection with the monastery. Few things, indeed, take place in Tibet in which a monk has not some part, and very often it is no creditable one. They occupy themselves a great deal with business and trade, are sharp money-lenders, and know well how to make a profit for themselves in anything.

All the larger monasteries are rich. They possess much land; part of it they let, and part of it they get laymen to cultivate for them. Much wealth flows into the monastery also by freewill offerings, by the gifts of visitors, by the sale of countless charms, pictures, and horoscopes, made by the monks. Once or twice a year a number of the monks go on pilgrimage, and visit villages to beg alms for the monastery, especially corn, butter, meat, and live-stock. This usually takes place at harvest-time. The revenue of a lamasery is not personal property of the monks, but is used for general purposes, keeping the place in good state, supplying the temple necessities, and providing other things for the community. The inmates have to support themselves as to their personal wants by their own earnings.

In the more prominent monasteries a strict supervision is kept over the young monks and novices. Transgressions of monastic rules must be notified by whoever makes the discovery. There is a special judicial functionary for such cases, to whom selected monks are subordinate to act as administrators of punishment. Severe misdemeanours, such as murder, theft, or sacrilege, are severely dealt with by corporal punishment, which may even cause death. Slighter offences entail a small number of stripes or certain acts of penance. But many flagrant sins go unpunished, because they are so common. In this connection mention must specially be made of the sins of intemperance and unchastity. Indulgence in strong drink is only punished when carried to the greatest excess. No one sees any harm in drinking the ordinary Tibetan beer, when done in moderation. But above all else it has proved impossible in Lamaism to enforce the law of chastity. It is only the reformed sect of the Gelugpa which still enforces the oath on its adherents. None of the other communities require chastity in their associates. Whoever observes it does so at his own pleasure, and enjoys special credit for it. But many live habitually with women, without any objection being raised as to a forbidden thing. The law of chastity is violated more or less in secret even by many monks of the strict Gelugpa sect.

There are also hermits in Lamaism, and they are not rare. Their appearance is not monkish; they allow the hair and beard to grow. Their line of life is sometimes ascetic in the highest degree. They occupy themselves mostly in repeating the spell of their tutelary deity innumerable times. One may find recluses who are shut up in the dark of a cave or hole for many years. They live by charity and by support of a monastery to which they are attached (*cf.* P. Landon, "Lhasa," third edition, p. 309; Waddell, "Lhasa and its Mysteries," pp. 237-241). The corpses of monks and hermits are burned, whilst dead bodies of the common people usually are thrown to be devoured by dogs, vultures, and other animals.

### E. The Sacred Writings.

Lamaism possesses its canon in the Tibetan language. Many of the books are accurate translations from the ancient Indian texts, almost all prepared from

Sanskrit, the language of the Mahâyâna school; some others are of Tibetan origin, also some are translated from Chinese. The canon bears the name of Kanjur (spelt Bkah-gyur, the translated teaching). But alongside it there is also a very important collection of universally accepted commentaries of the sacred text called Tanjur (Bstan-gyur). The sacred canon is either printed or copied. The written copies are the most valuable; they are often embellished with clever and costly illuminations, the capital letters are in gold or silver, and in the margin there are bright and pretty miniatures. Their art of printing is primitive, similar to the Chinese. The prints are drawn from wood-blocks, carved with the text. Whether they are printed or written, they still retain the form of the ancient Indian palm-leaf manuscripts, each leaf being about three times as broad as it is high, with writing on both sides, and the leaves unattached, the whole set belonging to one section being enclosed between two wooden covers. The whole Kanjur consists of 108 such volumes. The number 108, which we have already come across in the rosary and in the divisions of the sole of Buddha's foot, has in Buddhism a special significance. Some students have thought it might be derived from a purely mathematical calculation—$1 \times 2 \times 2 \times 3 \times 3 \times 3 = 108$.[1] It is subdivided like the southern canon into three parts: Vinaya (Dulva), Sûtra (Dô), and Abidharma (Chosnonpa). The canon of the accompanying commentary consists

[1] Alabaster, "The Wheel of the Law," p. 290. For another calculation ($12 \times 9$) see J. C. Oman, "The Mystics, Ascetics, and Saints of India" (London, 1903), p. 40.

of 225 volumes. Besides the elucidations of the sacred text, it contains also many works on the art of exorcism, as well as some treatises of a more philosophical, rhetorical, and grammatical nature.

The sacred writings are most highly prized in Lamaism; they receive almost divine honours. They are carried with extraordinary care, they have their special room in the temples, and have incense, candles, and little lamps, offered to them. It would appear rude and godless if anyone let a leaf of it drop on the floor, and were to touch it with his foot.

### F. The Sects.

Lamaism has split up into a number of divisions. These were called into existence by noted teachers, who from time to time attempted by reforms to check the extravagant developments of this exuberant religion. None of the reforms attained any general supremacy, and the schism grew always greater. The first of these attempted reforms was that of Atîśa (see p. 73). This was called the Kadampa school, and received another reformer in the person of the celebrated Tsong Kapa, from whose time it was known as Gelugpa. This sect is by far the strongest and most noted in Tibet. Beside it may be mentioned a few other divisions, such as the Kargyupa, called into existence by a lama of the eleventh century, and the Saskyapa, which rose in the same century. Numerous subdivisions have sprung from these main ones. There are also monasteries which from the earliest times have held aloof from these reforms. They are called Ningmapa.

The points in which these sects differ from one another are sometimes matters of dogma, sometimes of practice, sometimes, again, of the acceptance of a certain set of saints, who are held to be the chain of tradition of the true doctrine, and the worship of special tutelary deities.

1. The Gelugpa sect gives special reverence to its founder Tsong Kapa, whom they rank higher than the founder of Lamaism, Padma Sambhava, and than the first ancient reformer Atîśa. In the temples Tsong Kapa usually has the central place of honour at the back, between a Buddha and a Bodhisattva. Tsong Kapa, who is held to have received the doctrine by direct transmission from Atîśa, and thereby from the principal teachers of the Indian Mahâyâna, strove to reinstate the original stern rules of life by means of discipline, such as that their clothing should be made from rags sewn together, their food be obtained by begging, a strict retirement be observed during the Was season, earnestness in meditation, and so on. On the other hand, he established an ornate and strictly regulated ritual. Perhaps this last fact is due to his having come in contact with Roman Catholic Christendom. Tsong Kapa came originally from North-West China (he was born at Kumbum, a celebrated monastery on the Chinese frontier), and lived from 1356 to 1418, in a period, therefore, when Roman Catholic missions had already penetrated Central Asia and China for some considerable time. The austerity of life enjoined by the founder was soon much modified in the sect, but it still preserves a stricter discipline in the matter of

celibacy, which is peculiar to this sect. The stamp set on ritual observances has won a permanent hold, and has also spread to other sects.

The Gelugpa monks hold as their presiding celestial Buddha, or Âdi-Buddha, the Buddha Vajradhara, a metamorphosis of the god Indra. The origin of their special doctrine and observances is bound up with the Bodhisattva Maitrêya, the coming Buddha, who is said to have specially inspired their teachers. But they also consider themselves closely allied to the Bodhisattva Manjuśrî. The Gelugpa monks received from their founder a special form of headgear, of an orange colour. Also he ordered the outer garment to be yellow, whereas at that time a dark red colour was universally worn for caps and clothing. Thus yellow has continued to be the distinguishing colour of the Gelugpa sect down to the present day.

2. The Kargyupa lamas worship the same Âdi-Buddha as the foregoing sect. But they place themselves in a different attitude towards him, inasmuch as they attribute their doctrinal tradition as coming direct from him, and not through Maitrêya or any other Bodhisattva. Its founder was a lama called Marpa, but their most honoured saint is the pupil of this Marpa, the well-known poet and ascetic, Milaraspa. He is specially renowned as the exorcist of demons. On the wall of every large monastery belonging to this sect there is a portrait of him, dressed as an Indian monk, in the attitude of adjuration, and surrounded by all sorts of cheerful scenes taken from the legends about his life. The Kargyupas originally distinguished themselves by performing the

work of meditation outside the monastery, in the retirement of some cave or wilderness. They had also their special methods of meditation, but in course of time they renounced the hermit attitude.

3. The Saskyapa sect worships as its special patron the Bodhisattva Manjuśrî. From him was handed down to their adherents in direct line, beginning with some Northern Indian sages, their special tradition. It consists mainly in forms of incantation. The Saskyapa sect is stronger than any other in the matter of magic, and thereby won a predominant influence in the earlier centuries, which has waned very much of late. The Saskyapa monks wear red hoods and upper garments.

4. The Ningmapa sect. This is the original form of Lamaism, which has not recognized any subsequent reform. Naturally, their greatest saint is the founder of Lamaism, Padma Sambhava, and beside him there are a number of his disciples. The Ningmapa monks consider Samantabhadra as the Âdi-Buddha. The Ningmapa have retained more of the ancient Tibetan Bon religion than any other sect. Its adherents wear red caps and red clothing. Some of their special subdivisions, who hold closely to the old Bon tradition, are recognizable by a black headdress.

Each of these sects has a special kind of attitude for meditation, which has a name of its own; each of them also has a special tantric formula by which it is distinguishable. As regards the subordinate sects, at least two must be mentioned—the Karmapa and the Dugpa schools (two divisions of the Kargyupa sect), which possess a certain importance of their own.

The lamas reckon altogether eighteen different sects in their religion; but possibly this is a conventional number adopted in imitation of the eighteen ancient Indian sects (see p. 39).

### G. The Hierarchy.

The most noticeable feature of Lamaism, and which in past times has called special attention to it, is the hierarchical character of the monkhood, culminating in the person of the Dalai Lama of Lhasa. The most important historical dates of the rise of this hierarchy have been already given (p. 74 *et seq.*). We will at this point merely glance at the whole system as it appears at the present time.

In the hierarchical system there are two primary divisions. The minor includes the different ecclesiastical degrees; the higher contains the different degrees of incarnations of celestial beings.

The grades of ecclesiastical position start with that of the junior monk (*getsul*); then comes the full monk (*gelong*); then the Abbot (*khanpo*), who is superintendent of a monastery. The monks of a large monastery hold different degrees of rank from one another, according to more or less honourable posts assigned to them. There are also certain grades due to the amount of learning shown at their examinations and in public disputation. The two highest degrees of this kind are Geshe and Rabjampa. Those who win such a diploma are entitled to the highest Church offices. Besides there are some honorary titles bestowed on able men by the Grand

Lamas. Such is the title of Choje, of Lotsava, and of Pandita.

Those who are conspicuous among such graduates, or who are specially distinguished Abbots, are promoted to larger monasteries, and have the right of visitation of subordinate monasteries.

But what is quite peculiar to the Lamaistic Church is the theory of rank founded on the principle of reincarnation.

It is held that saintly persons who have died are reincorporate in certain lamas. The lowest grade of this kind is represented by those who are said to be the reincarnation of an earlier lama teacher as saint. Above this degree are the Julku (or in Mongolian *Khutuktu*), who are supposed to be the reincarnation of old Indian Buddhist saints. At the top there are those Lamas, in whom a Bodhisattva is reincarnate. Amongst these the most noted is the Dalai Lama at Lhasa.

The method by which, on the death of such an incarnation, his successor is determined is highly interesting. It is worked out with peculiar elaboration in the case of the Dalai Lama at Lhasa.

It is held that the celestial being who was incorporate in the ecclesiastical dignitary—in the case of the Dalai Lama it is the Bodhisattva Avalokita—becomes reincarnate at least forty-nine days after his death. Therefore inquiry is made throughout the whole of Tibet as to the birth of all children about that date, which took place with remarkable accompanying signs. Such marvels are easily to be heard of from one direction or another. Naturally, corroborate proofs are required. Those supplied are often astronomical phenomena, which are magnified by the eye of superstition. Or there may be some phenomenon in a tank or stream, an unexplained light (St. Elmo's fire), a special thunderclap, or a peculiar mark on the body of a child. Again, it may be averred that shortly after birth the child was found seated with its legs crossed in the Buddha's attitude of meditation, and when a rosary was placed in its hands the child appeared to be silently reciting the appointed prayers. The more remarkable the signs adduced about the child, the better. There are always a large number of aspirants; but at once a small selection is made from them, governed by certain practical considerations.[1] These have next to undergo a remarkable test. A number of the possessions of the deceased Dalai Lama are placed or laid before them, such as a picture of the Buddha which he particularly prized, a bell, a hand-drum, and an accurate imitation of each beside it. The child must now seize the original articles, and thus show that he has the indwelling Bodhisattva by his recognition of the genuine things. From the children who have passed this test successfully one is further distinguished by means of lots. Amid great pomp in the chief

[1] They do not, for instance, willingly select one from a very distinguished family, for fear of the relatives obtaining too influential a position by means of the child. They prefer to make the selection from the family of a poor peasant, who has no influence whatever. The neighbourhood, also, has a somewhat determining influence on the selection, those districts adjacent to the Chinese border being considered the most eligible.

sanctuary of Mount Potala at Lhasa, one name is drawn forth from a golden vase, in which all the names (sealed up) had been placed, and this is accepted as the right one. Besides the highest lama dignitaries, several representatives of the Chinese Emperor, and especially the Governor of Lhasa, the Amban, must take part in all these required measures and performances; and it is the Amban who draws the lot from the urn. Moreover, the Chinese Emperor must be accurately informed beforehand of every detail, and must give his consent. Thus the subordination of the Dalai Lama to Pekin is demonstrated.

The child is conducted with his parents to the appointed place and suitably brought up; they have a house and maintenance provided for them, and receive a high title. The Dalai Lama only becomes independent at the age of eighteen; until then he is under the "Regent," a high lama who is selected from one of the four great monasteries in Lhasa, Tengyai Ling, Kundai Ling, Tsemchog Ling, Tsamo Ling.

After the Dalai Lama the most influential incarnations of Bodhisattvas are the Grand Lama of the monastery of Tashi Lhumpo, near Shigatze, in Western Tibet, the so-called Panchen Erdeni; the Mongolian Grand Lama at Urga, who is a reincarnation of the famous historiographer Târanâtha (canonized as Jetsun Dampa); the Chief Lama of the Saskya sect; and the Grand Lama of Bhotan. It is worthy of notice that among the celebrated reincarnations of Lamaism a woman is to be found. This is the

Abbess of a large nunnery (with which also a monastery is connected) at Samding, on the shore of the sacred Yamdok Lake, to the south of Lhasa. She is held to be the incarnation of an Indian goddess, Vajra Varâhî, the "diamond sow" (in Tibetan, Dorje Phagmo).

The number of monasteries in Tibet is over 3,100, the largest of which contain as many as 10,000 monks. "The House of the Lord" (Jowo Khang or Jo Khang) at Lhasa far surpasses all others both in importance and in sanctity. It is the temple of the Dalai Lama. The entire sacred residence at Lhasa bears the name of Potala. It is an imposing height overlooking the green plains, rising above the city and entirely covered with the lofty, majestic pile of Tibetan monastic buildings, whose noble walls, built of blocks of granite and painted white and red, are broken by countless long rows of windows, with broad zigzag staircases and flat roofs, a combination which, to the European eye, has a very picturesque and attractive appearance. Above the flat roofs of the other buildings tower the gilded Chinese-shaped roofs of the Jo Khang, the temple of the Dalai Lama. This greatest of all the sanctuaries of the Asiatic religious world lies apart from other buildings on the sacred mount. To it belongs (in the strictest sense of the word) the name of Lhasa (dwelling-place of the gods). In the Jo Khang is the celebrated highly gilt image of Buddha Gautama, which was brought hither from Pekin by the Chinese Princess who became the consort of Srong Tsang Gampo in the seventh century A.D. It had been sent as a present to the Chinese Emperor in bygone times from India. For the first time since centuries—if indeed ever—the gaze of Europeans rested on it when the British expedition of 1903-04 entered Lhasa. The whole place, which had always hitherto been considered sacred and inaccessible by strangers, is now well known.

Tashi Lhumpo, the temple of Panchen Erdeni, is hardly less important than that of Lhasa. Others of the noted temples of Central Tibet are Galdan (in which Tsong Kapa is said to be buried), to the east of Lhasa; Daipung and Serra, to the west and north of the capital; Saskya (the birthplace of the sect of that name), in the south-west of Shigatze, famous for its unique library.

### H. The People and Religion.

How is it with the people over whom the monkish hierarchy has cast this network?

There is no doubt as to the fact that Buddhism raised the people of Tibet from a condition of savagery and barbarity to a somewhat higher level. The hordes of ignorant and uneducated people of ancient Tibet received an intellectual cohesion both with one another and with the outer world (with India and China); they attained a historical continuity; they also received a certain individual education on the technical and industrial side as well as on the spiritual. Indian civilization penetrated into the country, and drew the primitive mountain races into its school, taught them to build temples and to make all sorts of implements, reduced their language to writing (adapted from Sanskrit), settled them into towns, and developed commerce. Even their moral consciousness was changed by contact with the moral ideals of the Buddha Gautama. The many instances of kindliness and good behaviour which the traveller to-day experiences at the hands of the simple Tibetan people, as long as he behaves reasonably and causes no unusual disturbance, are perhaps due in part to the influence of Buddhism, although we must be cautious in drawing such inferences, because we have no information as to the Tibetan character previous to the coming of Buddhism. At all events, the whole moral condition of the country at the present time is coloured by Buddhism. It has in many respects given this people its poise and its backbone. But how far has it proved able to continue to raise it during the ten or eleven centuries of its supremacy?

Of the higher Buddhist conceptions, one only has taken hold of and soaked into the Tibetan people, that of future recompense. The belief in the reincarnation of the soul, corresponding with the moral value of the previous existence, is everywhere current, and explains the sufferings and fatal events. It should be noticed that it is really a belief in the transmigration of the *soul*. The metaphysical subtleties peculiar to original Buddhism (that there is no actual soul) are as little understood in popular Lamaism as in the popular Buddhism of any other country. The soul migrates. The limit of its wandering is within the six divisions of the world: these are the heavens; the dwellings of supernatural, semi-celestial beings; human life; the animal world; the existence of certain haunting ghosts; and lastly the hells—each of these classes containing numbers of different lots. The greatest importance attaches to the reincarnation of the soul in heavens or hells. The different heavens of the Buddhist system of doctrine (the six *dêva* heavens, the sixteen Brahma heavens, and the four highest heavens of void, above which later fancy placed the heaven of the five superior Buddhas and the heaven of the Âdi-Buddha) are made one in the popular imagination, and are usually represented simply as the *Paradise of Amitâbha.* The hells are depicted with fearful horrors both by word and brush, especially the eight great hot hells and the eight great cold hells. The desire to save the soul from hell, and to lead it into Paradise, is the one great lever of Lama piety. The other lever—and a much more potent one—is the dread of *evil spirits.*

The terror of dangerous and dreadful spirits rules to an astonishing extent. It is undoubtedly connected with the awe-inspiring powers of nature which surround the Tibetans. Those gloomy mountain ravines and desolate peaks, those waste mysterious plateaus and morasses, those snowy summits and glaciers, those stony wastes, those icy and terribly severe tempests, landslips, avalanches, thunderstorms, and earthquakes, the last of which are of frequent occurrence in Eastern Tibet—such things are a fruitful soil for a superstitious imagination. And Buddhism simply accepted and accentuated this tendency. It came provided with a powerful equipment of deities, charms, and methods of exorcism, of the Mahâyâna doctrine from Northern India, and this equipment so completely coalesced with the existing superstitions of Tibet that it is difficult to know which was the conqueror and which the conquered.

Almost everything that an ordinary man asks of Lamaism is a charm as a help against the dread powers. The commonest and most widespread charm is that of the word. It is made to act in many ways which can here only be touched upon.

The reading of parts from the sacred canon is the simplest method of making use of the charm of the word. For that purpose the monks (the only people who can read) are bidden to private houses. All portions of the sacred writings are equally efficacious, but not every portion is suitable for every occasion. The monk understands this rule, and acts accordingly. The magic power is concentrated in certain sacred formulæ, which are to be repeated again and again. Of these the best known is the celebrated 'Om! mani padme, hûm!" literally translated "Om! the jewel in the lotos, hûm!" (the first and last words are interjections). This formula is the special word of consecration of the Bodhisattva Avalokita (Padmapâni), who rules the Western Paradise. The repetition of this phrase not only secures the help of this powerful Bodhisattva for all possible earthly requirements, but also assists the industrious suppliant to enter that Paradise. The formula is therefore praised as containing all happiness, knowledge, and capacity. It is adorned with all sorts of mystic additions and interpretations; the six syllables represent the six divisions of the world, and each has its special appointed colour, etc. Besides this best-known formula there are many other similar ones. But one must be careful as to their right application. For not merely has each its particular divinity, but the kind of rosary to be used in prayer, for instance, is not the same for one as for another. Some require, in order that the spell may be efficacious, that the beads be made of human bones, others that they be of coral, and others something else.

The sacred formulæ are not only spoken; they are efficacious also when written. Hence the extraordinary numbers of charm papers, the so-called *mantras* or *dhâranîs* of Lamaism. The *dhâranî* proper consists of sets of Tibetan words connected with Sanskrit syllables, and is not meant to be uttered, but only written. In a wider sense the *dhâranî* is a longer treatise of mystical meaning. The *mantra* is shorter, sometimes only a series of incoherent syllables. The *mantras* and *dhâranîs* are totally incomprehensible to the common people, but they are firmly believed in as agencies of supernatural power. Such sayings are attached to walls or are carried on the person. In case of illness the person swallows such a charm, either by itself or mixed with some other ingredients. They have them reflected in a sacred mirror, which is commonly to be found in a temple; then the mirror is diligently washed, and the patient drinks the water which has been used for the purpose, and which is supposed to have absorbed the spirit of the formula. The *dhâranîs* which are worn are secreted in amulets, together with a few threads or rags of the garment of a holy man, a few grains of rice from some big offering, or other objects worthy of reverence. Such amulet boxes are to be seen on every Tibetan. They hang from the neck or girdle, and are most carefully treasured.

Another method to obtain the protection of the charms is to write them on rags of cloth, and hang them up as flags to flutter in the wind. These so-called prayer-flags are extremely common in Lamaism, from the most abject one to the most costly one, printed on silk, which contains long and elaborate exorcisms. At the entrance of every lamasery, in the neighbourhood of a *chorten*, in temples, on altars, also on the roofs of dwelling-houses, by the roadside —everywhere, in fact—one comes across these prayer-flags.

The most singular way, however, of making use of the word as a charm is the *prayer-cylinder* (incorrectly called prayer-wheel or prayer-mill). The sacred formula (or a number of them) is printed on a long strip of paper rolled round the cylinder, which is enclosed in a box, and by means of a stick, which is the axle on which it revolves, it is fastened to a handle or in a case. Every turn of the cylinder sets the word in motion, and makes its wholesome influence operative. The Tibetans carry such prayer-cylinders in their hands, and swing them mechanically while they are talking or doing anything else; they are certain that by so doing they accumulate merit, and place themselves under the protection of the sacred word. Indeed, they have gone so far as to enlist the services of nature for this purpose, getting the cylinders set in motion by the wind or the flowing of a brook. It is even by means of such utterly impersonal and lifeless action that a blessing may be won from the word for the benefit of the owner of the instrument. The cult of the word could hardly go farther than this.

The sacred *symbols* are very closely allied to the sacred word. Lamaism owns a great many of them; some are thoroughly Buddhist. Thus, the *svastika*, which has been called the Buddhist cross, appears to have been a very ancient symbol, merely adopted by Buddhism. This is its correct form, 卍; the adherents of the old Bon religion have reversed it, so as to make it their own, 卐. Another ancient Buddhist symbol is the wheel, in pre-Buddhist times the symbol of authority of a great monarch. It was then applied to Gautama, the spiritual ruler of the world, and in the rolling of the wheel was typified the spread of his teaching. The wheel has frequently six spokes, sometimes eight, sometimes an immense number ("thousand"). The third common symbol of Buddhism is the lotos-blossom. This beautiful flower, owing to its fine form, to the purity of its blossoms, and to its growth out of the obscure depths of the water (symbol of the supernatural, which does not spring from the nourishing soil of the earth), has attracted attention, and thus become a much-used illustration of the "pure doctrine." Besides these popular symbols there is a number of special ones, which cannot be enumerated here. The tiger, dragon, phœnix, and bat, are symbolical animals, all drawn from a Chinese source. Such symbols are often printed on the charm to render it the more efficacious. One sees them in the temples, and on the implements for offerings, where they are used not merely for their decorative value, but because the sacred symbols are of miraculous power and add their influence to the great task of keeping in control the demons.

Mention must be made in this connection of the singular efficacy which Lamaism attributes to certain positions of the fingers and hands. The reciting of magical incantations has to be combined with a particular attitude in sitting and position of the fingers and hands. The result attached to the pose of the hands is derived from the various ways of *mudrâ* in which the Buddha is represented (see p. 133). Attitudes of the Buddha, originally the simple artistic expression of certain situations, were reduced to a system, each having a special significance. From this followed the idea of a certain supernatural power peculiar to certain attitudes, and therefrom was constructed a regular doctrine as to the poses of fingers and hands, which must accompany the recital of banning or blessing formulæ.

All these means of supernatural power—the sacred word, the symbols, the attitudes—show their full value in combination with the offerings. Lamaism has an abundance of offerings, from the simplest to the most elaborate. In reality, everything is capable of being made an offering. The simplest gifts are flowers and incense. The regular daily offering on the temple altars are water, rice, fruit, cakes, and lamps or lights. Fruits and cakes are frequently artificially imitated in wood, so as not to require daily renewal. But apart from this, the layman is at liberty to bring, as an offering for some special purpose, whatever seems to him valuable or calculated to propitiate the divinity. A certain offering which every layman is bound to bring at least once yearly (whilst the monks present it twice a month for themselves) is the offering for the whole circle of gods and demons. Here are to be met plain indications of the bloody sacrifices of past times; thus for certain deities there are so-called skull-cups set out, whose contents are at the present day weak tea, but formerly they were, doubtless, human blood. Meat is also included in these offerings. Many of the offerings are destroyed (burnt); others are eaten by the lamas, of which a small piece is always left and thrown outside the temple for the "hungry ghosts," the inhabitants of a special quarter of the universe. Valuable goods brought as offerings by laymen are kept as the property of the lamasery. The offerings are presented in an elaborate ritual, and with the accompaniment of loud music. The special gifts by which laymen attempt to obtain some favour or dispensation are numberless. The most dangerous demons receive gifts only in the evening, after sunset or during the night. Great offerings are accompanied by processions, religious dances, and performances. In all these matters Buddhism has united with the ancient Tibetan ideas and customs belonging to the Bon religion, and openly flaunts a thousand features which are thoroughly alien and antagonistic to its original character.

The bulk of the population is, owing to the above-described practices, entirely in the hands of the monks. But there is one limitation to this. It is not the monks only who are concerned in this; there also exists a large class of wizards. They are laymen, but keep up a friendly connection with the lamaseries, in what might be termed "business relations." They are consulted and urged to undertake magic, and they often exert a strong influence even over the monks. They bear the honourable title of "defenders of the faith," and at their head is a most venerable person called the Nächung, who is consulted on all obviously important matters. He resides at Lhasa, and is connected with the large Daipung monastery. Another magician of similar influence in Lhasa is the Karmashar (*cf.* Waddell, "Lhasa and its Mysteries," pp. 380-386). But side by side with these wizards we see lamas active in the same line. A well-known phrase is: "Without a lama in front there is no admission to the deity." This phrase, indeed, expresses the universal feeling. Buddhism is a religion which, in its original form, seems less than any other to require priestly intervention, and which puts every man on his own responsibility; yet it has become here the most striking example of priestly domination and patronage: the people endure a priestly tyranny beyond that endured in any other place on earth. The most remarkable proof of this condition of affairs is the crowd of pilgrims which ceaselessly streams into Lhasa from all parts of the wide lama territory, in order to worship the head of the monastic system in the person of the Dalai Lama. Those scenes, which may be watched daily under the golden roof of the Jo Khang at Lhasa, show plainly the despotic rule of Buddhism in Tibet. The divine child (for usually it is a mere child, as few of the Dalai Lamas attain manhood) sits on a platform overshadowed by the baldachino, with a kind of sceptre in his hand, from which are suspended gay ribbons, thousands of devotees in front of him, who are slowly led past his throne with folded hands, and, during the brief pause they make in front of him, prostrate themselves on the ground, and strike the edge of the platform with their foreheads, rapidly murmuring prayers, and the wishes of their hearts; while the object of their homage touches the heads of the pilgrims with the ribbons of his sceptre, in token of blessing and of acceptance of their prayers. A crowd of satellites surrounds this Bodhisattva in human form, the most illustrious of whom are credited by the people with supernatural powers, such as being able to fly through the air and to descend into the hidden parts of the world, to render themselves invisible, and to live without food. Above this whole galaxy of the human monkhood the faithful beholds the celestial crowd, who are their unseen allies. At the other side arise the dreadful, horrible, bloodthirsty, dread powers, full of terrible strength, but held in check by the monkhood. In the midst of them the poor, ignorant herd of human beings crouches timidly and reverently, watching terror-stricken the evil ones, and imploring succour from the wonder-working helpers, with prayers, gifts, and charms. The Lamaism of Tibet has held the people in this condition for centuries past.

The monks are the rulers. Their lamaseries are fortresses dominating the country, and like fortresses they possess, hidden within their walls, arms and ammunition, which the lama well knows to use when occasion arises. The history of the lamas is a very warlike one from the earliest times down to the recent defence of the citadel temple of Gyantse against the British expedition. But worse than their outwardly warlike attitude, and than all the blood shed in war with the Chinese or the British, is the silent war perpetually carried on against the highest interests of their own nation. All the valuable products of the country the lamas absorb for their own use, from the gold, silver, and jewels, down to the little bits of butter brought by the very poor. They have barred the way to every form of commerce. They are doctors, chemists, painters, tradesmen, money-lenders, and beggars who take no refusal, besides being priests, prophets, and wizards. What they may not themselves undertake, such as the superintendence of their large properties and all sorts of handicrafts, they compel laymen to do for them, and these become little else than serfs to them. In every respect they are on an elevated and more sheltered plane than others. Whoever steals anything from a lama, or murders one, incurs a penalty five- or tenfold greater than is exacted in other cases. Nevertheless the people not only endure this extraordinary and burdensome yoke, but it gains ever new ascendancy from the people themselves, and has its roots in them, in the obscure depth of the soul of the individual, which no scientific investigation will ever fully explain.

## Chapter VI.—CHINESE BUDDHISM

The position of Buddhism in China is usually considered to be a peculiar one, as it shares the supremacy of that country in the matter of religion with Taoism and Confucianism. One often meets the remark, therefore, that it is a conspicuous anomaly for the Chinese to be capable of combining three religions in his own person. Yet if one considers the fact more carefully, it appears simpler and more natural than it does at first sight. There is no essential difference in China from other Buddhist countries; we find alongside of Buddhism the old pre-Buddhist religion of the country, only this native religion assumed a different attitude towards the foreign import from that of other countries, namely, one of aloofness, whereby it prevented Buddhism from penetrating (to any large extent) amongst the bulk of the population. Even before the advent of Buddhism this indigenous religion had split up into two currents[1]—an inferior one, which became prevalent amongst the masses, so-called Taoism; and another held by the governing and educated class, which may be most fitly called the State religion.[2] Both these currents, however, were

[1] In fact, there were more than these two, but the others did not become so prominent. Ssŭ Ma Tan, the father of the great historian Ssŭ Ma Ch'ien, mentions *six* main divisions of the ancient speculative life.

[2] It should not be called Confucianism, as the teaching of Confucius is a moral system, and has little to do with religion. To Confucius the backbone of morality was the old history of his country and its great examples.

closely allied to one another, and cannot be called two different religions. When Buddhism came into contact with them, it was unable to gain the ascendancy which it had won in southern countries and in Tibet. Here Buddhism had stronger organization to encounter. It therefore adopted a more modest manner towards them. It could not win the people as a whole, but it succeeded in getting a foothold by means of monasteries and monks, a corporate existence. The laity borrowed from it various motives and conceptions at their discretion, which could be combined with their own indigenous religion; but they are not governed by genuine Buddhism, however closely they may be outwardly joined to it.

## A. The Monasteries.

The majority of Buddhist monasteries in China lie outside the cities, in the open country. Even the town monasteries (which for the most part are decadent and of less reputation) are built, whenever it is possible, apart from other habitations. They like to have them surrounded by trees. Even where a monastery happens to be situated in the midst of fields in cultivatod plains, there are many trees planted in its vicinity. But the ideal position for a monastery is on a wooded height. All the most noted places of Buddhist worship in China are in such positions, and a usual term for the temple is, therefore, *shan* (mountain), a term sometimes even applied to a sanctuary, when there is no hill or height whatever in its neighbourhood. Two motives are combined in this predilection for wooded heights. For one thing, it is a very ancient Buddhist order, which directs the monk to seek the seclusion of uncultivated regions, and that, in China, is synonymous with wood and mountain. Then also, in China, Buddhism unquestionably possesses a great number of such heights which were before its time considered sacred by the people. By occupying them Buddhism turned the existing veneration to its own advantage. Even to-day the tradition is firmly established in many such localities that Taoist authorities had dwelt there before the advent of the Buddhists; or legends exist about nature demons (dragons), which were conquered after stubborn combats with the monks.

The forest in the neighbourhood of the monastery had also its practical value, as the wood was always required for household repairs and for new buildings The position of the monastery in the midst of lofty venerable trees, which spread a green shade over the sanctuary, rarely fails to impress even the European. The charm of the landscape is often enhanced by the presence of water, to which the monks gladly turn. Amongst the flowers and herbs a clear brook murmurs under shrubs and trees; or a waterfall gushes from a cliff; or a spring sparkles in a dusky grotto, around which all sorts of legends group themselves. The banks and islands are equally favourite places of Buddhist settlements.

Here a word may be said about the *names* of the Buddhist sanctuaries as distinguished from the non-Buddhist temples. The exact and accurate expression for a Buddhist monastery is *ssŭ.* In order to make the word more recognizable in speaking (the sound *ssŭ* has many meanings), it is lengthened out into *ho shang ssŭ* (the monks' monastery) or *ssŭ yüen* (monastery court). A Taoist monastery would never be designated a *ssŭ* (they are mostly called *kung* or *kuan*), nor would the temple of a town or village, if it belonged to the State religion. Small Buddhist monasteries, or more frequently convents, bear the name of *an.* Single halls of a monastery are called *tien*, but that is also the name for small temples attached to larger ones. Single chapels by the roadside are called *ko.*

Although the Buddhist monasteries differ very much in size and importance, in essentials they are all modelled on one plan. The whole monastery precincts are enclosed by a wall, and within it the different kinds of buildings are kept quite distinct. The dwelling-rooms of the monks and all apartments pertaining to them are clearly separated from the halls for worship. The former buildings enclose the four sides, a quadrangle of ordinary two-storied houses. Within the courtyard are the temple buildings, each separated from the other. In some well-endowed monasteries there are three such temple halls. The first is an entrance-hall, called the Hall of the Four Great Kings of Heaven. Here rule the divine watchers and guardians of the monastery. Behind it is the principal hall, with the most important images of the gods, usually called the Precious Hall of the Great Hero—the Buddha (*ta hsiung pao tien*). Still farther back is the so-called Hall of the Law (*fa tang*), frequently adjoining the Abbot's dwelling-house, and for that reason also named *fang chang*, which is the Abbot's own title. Each of the three halls is separated from the other by a small courtyard, and frequently you ascend slightly from one to the other, so that the hall of the law with its basement stands at the highest level. But the central hall is the largest, and its roof projects, as a rule, above the other buildings.

The monastery buildings which enclose these central halls at right angles contain mainly the monks' cells, besides several guest-rooms, store-rooms, kitchens, one common dining-hall, one reception-room for large festivals, and also various unimportant shrines for worship. Outside the actual monastery quadrangle stands an isolated tower, in which hangs the principal bell of the monastery.

In smaller monasteries this plan is usually so far condensed that you enter through a gate, which serves as shrine for the tutelary gods, into the right-angled courtyard, on the right and left sides of which are the buildings which compose the monks' rooms. The back building of the courtyard is the temple hall, in which are the images of the gods, frequently in two stories.

Very large monasteries possess more than three buildings for worship. They show two entrance-halls, containing tutelary gods, and besides the above-mentioned places for worship a special building for meditation—the so-called *ch'an t'ang*—also various single rooms for saints and some very popular gods, a hall for the ordination of monks, a library for the sacred canon, and a house with urns containing the ashes of cremated monks or Abbots. There may be many other rooms of less importance. In addition there are several large-sized kitchens, as well as a large dining-room and one or two smaller ones, various store-rooms, washhouses, and lavatories. There is a special house for sick or very old monks; cowhouses in which are the monastery herds, and also the beasts brought to be taken care of; buildings for lay workers, servants, craftsmen, who occasionally have their families living with them: all these buildings, together with the many cells of the monks, small gardens and courtyards before the individual cottages, not infrequently give to a monastery the appearance of a village in itself. In front of the entrance of such important monasteries may be seen a pond covered with lotos-blossoms, in which fish and tortoises are kept. Large and richly decorated archways span the road before the monastery is reached, and a number of pavilions are passed, destined either for pilgrims to rest in, or as penthouses to shelter tablets inscribed with a summary of the history of the monastery, or an imperial decree conferring some benefit on it.

The building material mainly used for them is wood, although the foundations and such parts of the building as have to bear great weight are of stone, as also the encompassing walls. Stone also serves for steps, balustrades, pavements of courts and passages; but the main part of the building is of wood. Pillars play an important part in construction. All buildings are so constructed that the inner walls should form a sheltered corridor from the rain; this is done by means of overhanging eaves, and the overhanging part of the roof is therefore supported by pillars. This is also the case with the roofs of temples. The pillars are almost invariably made of wood, and some are of enormous height; only the bases are frequently made of stone.

The style of architecture is the ordinary Chinese one. The curved roofs form the chief decoration, with the twofold and threefold grouping. The interior of the rooms shows no profusion of luxury or art. Wall-painting is very rare. The floor consists of well-trodden earth, or wooden planks, or very rarely stone pavement, in which are embedded characteristic Buddhist symbols, such as the lotos blossom.

On the whole the monasteries are kept clean and tidy; naturally, one is comparing them with an Asiatic standard. In the courts and small entrance-gardens there are frequently some nice trees and flowers planted, which give a very pleasant impression.

### B. The Temple Gods.

Chinese Buddhism has not such a number of gods as Lamaism. Although the figures in the temples are numerous enough to mislead Europeans at first sight (and it is not easy to obtain from the ordinary monks accurate information about them individually), still, in time one learns to discriminate among them with a fair amount of accuracy. They may be divided into four classes: (1) Buddhas, (2) Bodhisattvas, (3) saints and patriarchs, (4) tutelary deities.

Amongst the Buddhas, the historic Buddha[1] Gautama, or, as the Chinese more frequently call him, Śâkyamuni (Shih-chia-mu-ni), is the first to be mentioned. He is generally represented seated in the attitude of meditation, while the seat is formed of a lotos-blossom. The eyes are almost covered by the lids, only showing through a narrow slit, but this must not be mistaken for a representation of the Mongolian type of eye. On the contrary, all the higher divinities, Buddhas and Bodhisattvas, resemble the Indian races in feature. The half-closed eyes are part of the act of meditation. The head is usually ornamented with tufts of hair dyed blue, from the centre of which comes a projection (as in Southern Buddhism). There is another projection on the forehead between the eyes (the *ûrnâ* of Southern Buddhism), which is often ornamented with a jewel. The ears are large, and the lobes hang down almost to the shoulder. A simple garment enfolds the body, leaving the neck and chest exposed, but both shoulders, arms, and the rest of the body, are concealed. The hands lie in the lap on the upturned soles of the feet. With a few slight differences, the figure is a replica of that portrayed in Southern Buddhism.

The background of the Buddha (as also of other figures) is frequently in the shape of a nimbus. The nimbus, originally a mass of light, which emanated from the light-giving gods, and which was already known in the Alexandrian epoch of the Grecian

[1] The Chinese equivalent for Buddha is Fo, which formerly was pronounced Bud, the transcription of the first syllable of the name Buddha.

Empire, was adopted alike by Buddhism and Christianity. It is also to be found in Southern Buddhism and in Lamaism. There is a distinction between the large and the small nimbus. The large nimbus is usually represented in Chinese Buddhism by an ornamental screen, behind the whole figure of the god, extending considerably above it and running up to a point at the top, so that the shape of the whole has a resemblance to the leaf of the holy Bo-tree, which presumably must have been the model for it. This nimbus is generally made of wood, gilded, painted, and ornamented with carving. The small nimbus is frequently found in combination with it, surrounding the head only. It resembles the Roman Catholic halo, circular as a rule, but occasionally with undulating, flame-like rays. The Chinese name of the nimbus is *hao kuang* (hair rays).

The historic Buddha is also to be found in a standing position. He is besides represented as a little child, when he spoke at the time of his birth, with one hand pointing heavenward and the other earthward: "Now, for the last time, I am reincarnate. Among all the dwellers in heaven and earth to me is due the greatest honour." He is also represented as the ascetic Gautama, a middle-aged man, the face surrounded by a shaggy beard, the hair unkempt, the body wrapped in rags, one knee bent to the ground. This is a rare figure, seen sometimes in Western and Northern China. One more frequently notices the Buddha entering Nirvâṇa, whom we mentioned in Southern Buddhism. In China, however, he is called the Sleeping Buddha (Shui-fo), and is not only wrapped up in coverings, but also may be found lying in a genuine Chinese bed, in which the marble figure (this is as the present writer saw it) has a most extraordinary appearance. Besides the historic Buddha, one sees in Chinese temples also some of those other Buddhas of the Mahâyâna creed, which we have already mentioned in connection with Lamaism. From the large number of old-time human Buddhas speculation has selected five, who (as in Lamaism) were coordinated with their five heavenly Buddhas in eternal correspondence, and also with their five Bodhisattvas as mediating representatives of these celestial Buddhas. The best known of the celestial Buddhas is Amitâbha, now called by the Chinese O-mi-to-fo. He is so universally popular that his name occurs in numberless formulæ of prayer and of greeting. He is honoured above all as ruler of the Western Paradise, which Chinese believers have an ardent hope of entering. Amitâbha is often represented standing with unusually long arms hanging down, named Chieh-yin-fo, the Buddha who receives and guides—viz., into the Paradise. Two other very common celestial Buddhas are Vairochana (whom the Chinese call Pi-lu-fo) and Loshanâ (Lo-shih-fo).

All these images of Buddhas are represented in a similar way to those of the historic Buddha, except that the two last always have their own *mudrâ*: Pi-lu-fo lays both his hands together in the centre of the chest, so that the index fingers point upwards; Lo-shih-fo raises the left hand midway and joins the tips of the thumb and middle finger, while the right hand rests in his lap.

Chinese Buddhism does not include in this group Maitrêya (Chinese, Mi-le-fo), the Buddha of the future—at all events, not in the large images of the temples. He has received the special rôle of tutelary deity, and is always represented in a quite peculiar way, a fat laughing figure cowering on the ground, so that the left leg lies crosswise in front of the body. The right hand holds either a rosary or a lotos-bud; the left encircles the mouth of a bag, the so-called bag of the five lucky gifts. The head is entirely shaven; the lobes of the ears reach the shoulders. The wide mantle, which is his only garment, is thrown back, displaying shoulders, breast, and belly.

In Western China one of the old human Buddhas may frequently be met with—namely, the Buddha Dîpamkara. His name, the Shining One, is translated into Chinese Jan-têng-fo. This Buddha is generally covered with a number of little oil-lamps, which burn in his honour; they usually number 108, a number of special sacred significance (see p. 178).

Among the Chinese *Bodhisattvas* the most important figure is Kwanyin. She is the Indo-Tibetan Avalokita, translated into the Chinese and feminine form. In older times this Bodhisattva was also honoured in China as a male figure, of which traces may still be found here and there. Later, under what influence is not quite evident, the form changed into the female. A legend makes her the daughter of an old King of the seventh century B.C.,[1] who, by the heroic accomplishment of a nun's duties

[1] According to Chinese reckoning, the Buddha Gautama lived in the tenth century B.C., and so she belongs already to his epoch.

and by martyrdom, had attained the position of a Bodhisattva. In her is concentrated all that a pious fancy attributes to womanhood, and which it seeks in womanhood. She is gentleness and helpfulness personified, especially watching those engaged in perilous callings, such as sailors; the patroness of women in all their concerns, especially invoked in cases of childlessness and danger at birth; and showing a variety of forms and images unlike that of any other deity in Chinese Buddhism.

Besides Kwanyin, four other Bodhisattvas stand out prominently. First there is Ta-shih-chi (the Indian Mahâsthâma or Mahâsthâmaprâpta). Together with Kwanyin he has his place in the western Paradise, ruled by Amitâbha, and therefore with her he is the regular companion of this Buddha. All three (Amitâbha in the middle, Kwanyin on the left—the place of honour in Chinese etiquette—and Ta-shih-chi on the right) are often placed beside one another as "the three holy ones of the western region" (*hsi fang san shêng*). Two other noted Bodhisattvas are Wen-shu and P'u-hsien (corresponding to the Indian names Manjuśrî and Samantabhadra). The former usually rides on a lion, the latter on an elephant; they often appear as a triad with Kwanyin in the middle. The fourth well-known Bodhisattva is Ti-tsang. He is the ruler of Hades, and as such he is much revered by the people. Under him are twelve Kings of hell, the executioners of all the hellish pains and horrors, from which, however, the good-natured Bodhisattva, if assiduously worshipped, can deliver people.

The third class of the higher beings are the *saints*. These are the ancient disciples of the Buddha Gautama. Their Chinese name is Lo-han (the Indian Arhat or Arhant). The most important ones are Gautama's two favourite disciples. But in Chinese Buddhism it is not Maudgalyâyana and Śariputra who take these places (as we find it in Southern Buddhism), but Ânanda and Kâśyapa. These two are represented on each side of the Buddha Gautama, Ânanda as a younger man, and Kâśyapa as an older one, both in an attitude of reverence with folded hands. Another group of Buddha disciples are the so-called eighteen Lo-han. In the older monasteries you sometimes find the original number of sixteen. They are legendary beings with a historic background.[1] Their significance is as guardians of Gautama's doctrine. A larger circle was formed of the 500 Lo-han, who are only to be seen in a few temples, occupying a whole room to themselves. Among these 500 may be noticed not only several Chinese Emperors who favoured Buddhism, like K'ang-hsi and Ch'ien-lung, but in temples at Canton and Hangchow even the illustrious European traveller of the thirteenth century, Marco Polo, is included amongst these guardians of the Buddhist faith.[2]

[1] One of these Lo-han has an appearance quite similar to the one described above as Maitrêyas. He is an incarnation of this Bodhisattva, and has been added to the old number of sixteen only in more modern times. He is called "Pu-tai-ho-shang" (the monk with the calico bag), in Japan "Hotai."

[2] In Yule's "Marco Polo," third edition, vol. i., p. 76 of the Introduction, this statement is denied (at least for Canton), on

Next to the Lo-han are the *patriarchs.* Of their whole number only one has gained universal reverence, viz., Bodhidharma, who transferred the seat of the patriarchate from India to China (see p. 80). He is always given quite un-Chinese, with a large beard, and with such peculiar features that it seems probable that some authentic tradition has been handed down as to his portrait. His name is transcribed Po-ti-ta-mo. He is generally called Ta-mo tsu-shih, as tsu-shih is the Chinese name for the patriarch. Here and there a Chinese temple contains all the six patriarchs, Ta-mo together with his five followers. Three of them receive special consideration in some very decayed monasteries on the Yangtze, north of Kiukiang, where these esteemed teachers lived.

Lastly the *tutelary gods.* There are the four great heavenly guardians whom we already know from Lamaism (see p. 163); Wei-to (transcription of Veda), a warlike, fierce figure, with a sword in its hands, which sometimes rests crosswise above the arms put together in prayer; also Fan-t'ien wang (Brahma) and Ti-shih (Indra); besides these there are frequently a multitude of twenty or twenty-four *devas.* All these tutelary deities are of Indian origin. Besides these are noticed some purely Chinese tutelary gods, the so-called *chia-lan,* amongst whom the most prominent is the Chinese war-god, Kwanti, originally a brave general of the third century A.D.; at the close of the sixteenth

---

the authority of Mr. Wylie. But the present writer, by personal observation and inquiry, has proved that it is correct in Hangchow as well as in Canton.

century he was promoted to be a god, and, owing to his great popularity, made his way from the State religion into the Buddhist temples. There are others also of these *chia-lan* who are not genuinely Buddhistic, as, for instance, Confucius, Wenchang, and the so-called "kitchen-god," who indeed is not to be found in the temple rooms, but is standing in almost every monastery kitchen; its origin is in Taoism (Tsao-chün).[1]

The images of the gods are usually made from wood or clay, gilded or painted; specially costly ones are bronze or marble. When the craftsmen have finished their work, the image is vivified by a special solemn rite, and is raised to the actual godship. As a rule there is a small hole in the back of the image, through which some animal—a snake, a cat, a frog, or a centipede—is inserted into the hollows inside, and the opening is closed. The soul of the creature gives the impetus of life to the dead image. Afterwards the pupil of the eye is painted in, and thereby the deity has taken full possession of the image. This act is called *k'ai kuang*, the opening of eyelight.

The arrangement of the sacred images in the temples is fairly uniform.

In the entrance-hall, on the right and left hand side, stand two of the four great heavenly Kings, usually immense figures 10 or 12 feet in height.

[1] In the pilgrim I-Tsing's travels mention is made also of an Indian kitchen-god, who later on was worshipped in China. (See Takakusu's translation of I-Tsing, p. 38.) But this god (Mahâkâla) seems not to be connected with the modern Buddhist deity.

Each has its own colour, but they vary occasionally. Generally the guardian of the North (Chinese, To-wen), who holds a pearl and a snake, is black; that of the West (Kuang-mu), holding a sword, is white; the guardian of the South (Tsêng-chang), holding in his hand an umbrella, is red; that of the East (Ch'ih-kuo), holding a guitar, is blue. In the centre of the entrance-hall stand two figures, one looking outwards, Mi-le, one looking inwards, Wei-to. One sometimes sees in this hall also an image of Kwanti, the god of war.

In the principal hall (*ta hsiung pao tien*) a Buddha or group of Buddhas occupies the centre behind the principal altar. These central figures are usually very large and imposing. When it is a single figure, it must be the historic Buddha Gautama, before whom, in that case, stand his disciples Ânanda and Kâśyapa. But frequently one finds three Buddha figures in the centre of the hall. When first asked about them by the stranger, the monks call them Fo, Fa, and Shêng—that is, Buddha, the doctrine, and the community. More accurately they are the Buddhas Vairochana (Pi-lu-fo), Loshanâ (Lo-shih-fo), and Śâkyamuni (Shi-chia-fo). These three form the so-called Trikâya, or threefold embodiment (*cf.* Eitel "Sanskrit-Chinese Dictionary," p. 178 *et seq.*). Another very usual trio is Śâkyamuni, Amitâbha, and Yo-shih-fo (Vaidûrya Buddha), the Buddha of healing.[1] Various other combinations of grouping may

[1] Nowhere does one find in the temples a trio of the "Buddha of the present, the past, and future." The Buddha of the future, Mi-le, never stands among the large figures in the centre of the principal hall.

still be found here and there. So the temples on the island of Pu-t'o, a sacred locality of great renown, generally have the picture of Kwanyin in the centre of the principal hall, because the island is specially dedicated to that goddess. Although Kwanyin is only a Bodhisattva, even the highest Buddha must there give place to her. In front of the great central figures on the altar-table stands a row of smaller Bodhisattvas of importance, the three sacred ones of the western Paradise, a Mi-le and others. On the back side of the screen in front of which the gods are enthroned, turned towards the inner door of the principal hall, there is usually a representation of Kwanyin. P'u-hsien and Wen-shu stand on either side of it. Along the two side-walls are the baroque figures of the eighteen Lo-han seated on a broad shelf against the wall, sometimes increased in number by twenty *devas*. Against the back-wall, on each side of the inner door, there is usually a figure of Bodhidharma on the left, and one or more tutelary deities (*chia-lan*), on the right.

The hall of the law (*fa tang*) contains no great images. It is set apart for the reading aloud and explanation of the sacred text to the monks. It is true that there are smaller statues set out on the platform from which the teacher is wont to address the monks—for instance, Amitâbha or Yo-shih-fo or others. The hall for meditation also contains only smaller images of different Buddhas or Bodhisattvas.

The arrangement of the many chapels which in important monasteries are dedicated to the most diverse deities (especially to Kwanyin and Ti-tsang), or to some patriarchs and famous teachers, cannot here be dealt with in detail.

The sanctuaries are provided with gaily embroidered altar-clothes, with long silk banners, attached below with brass fittings, with wooden tablets gorgeously inscribed in gold. On the altar are candlesticks, incense-burners, dishes for offerings, flowers, and artificial fruits; you never miss a few specimens of the famous "wooden fish," a much-used instrument on which to beat when prayers or texts are being recited. Although it can now hardly be recognized, this was originally representative of a fish, of which the head and tail are bent together, while the inside is hollowed out and a broad opening is left in the centre.[1] A blow on this peculiar instrument made with a knocker gives an empty, resonant sound, which is repeated by the reciter with great swiftness and regularity. Low round footstools made of straw are used by the monks for kneeling during worship.

[1] It would be worth while to clear up the origin of the use of the fish in Buddhist cult, especially as the fish is also an ancient Christian symbol. The Chinese monks generally explain it by saying that the fish is a symbol of watchfulness, as the fish never closes its eyes, nor does it require rest (*cf.* the Japanese discourse on "Infinite Vision," translated by J. M. James in Trans. of the As. Soc. of Japan, vol. vii., part iv., p. 274). A Japanese (and Chinese) legend relates that a wicked monk after death was changed into a water-plant, which had to grow under water. An Abbot discovered, from some dismal groaning in the water, the fact, and received the instruction that the unfortunate monk could be saved from his punishment if the wood of that plant would be used to make an instrument to be beaten when the holy word was recited. So the wooden fish was made.

### C. The Monks.

The monastic communities are mainly recruited from the ranks of children who are designated for this life by their parents in early youth, and are brought by them to the monastery. Only comparatively few monasteries have any important influx of grown men. Not infrequently the children destined for the monastic life by their parents are given in exchange for a money indemnification.[1] Otherwise a child may be vowed at a time of illness or in fear of death. The little ones are sent away to the monasteries, even at the age of one or two, and are entirely brought up there. Each one receives his special foster-father and teacher from the ranks of the monks. From about the seventh year they begin to be initiated into what they will have to know and to do later as monks. They learn to read extracts from important writings, and to repeat them by heart. They take part in worship, and make themselves acquainted with all the externals of religion. So they grow up with a practical knowledge of a monk's work, and accept it from childhood up as their destined career. The monastic habit, also, is worn by them from the beginning, and their heads are completely shaved.

When they have reached the age of twenty (so at least runs the rule, though it is not always strictly adhered to), they are formally admitted to the monastic

[1] In cases which were personally known to me, twenty-five Mexican dollars were paid for a child, of which the value at that time was about forty shillings. A similar statement is given in Milne's "Life in China," p. 132.

life. Then they undergo three ceremonies, each of which has its peculiar significance, and ought, indeed, to be separated from the others by a longer space of time, but which for practical reasons are despatched in the course of a few days. The first of these ceremonies is the formal reception into the noviciate; the second is the full reception as monk; to these is added in China a third festivity, at which are undertaken the duties and commands of the way which leads to the rank of Bodhisattva.

The two first ceremonies are simple, and resemble those mentioned in connection with Southern Buddhism (pp. 96, 100 *et seq.*). The third is more exacting and more complicated—the initiation of a future Bodhisattva. The monks undertake a number of duties and obligations which spring from the teaching of the Mahâyâna school. A remarkable ceremony has therefore come into vogue, which bears witness to the ascetic endurance and force of will of the monks. One of the old works on the duties of monks says: "A Bodhisattva must be capable of giving up his body, his flesh, his hands, and his feet, to tigers, wolves, lions, and every kind of ravenous monsters." It is therefore the practice, in China, that the monk at his last consecration should receive a number of wounds by branding, as a sign of his capacity to endure hard sufferings and to sacrifice himself. This branding on the clean-shaven head is the predominating sign of the Bodhisattva consecration. The branding is truly painful. Three, nine, twelve, or even eighteen places (according to the zeal shown by the candidate) have small cylindrical-shaped pieces of charcoal stuck on them by an adhesive substance made from fruits; these are set alight and allowed to glow till the gum melts and burns deeply into the flesh. While this takes place the aspirant, with uplifted hands, must ceaselessly cry "Omito" (Amitâbha), which doubtless often becomes a cry of anguish. An assistant monk holds the head of the branded man, and presses his thumbs firmly into the temples, which lessens the pain. The scars of the branding remain for ever.

The right to give ordination is only possessed by certain noted monasteries, who have obtained it by imperial decree. But in neighbourhoods where there are few candidates and several larger monasteries it does not take place every year in the same monastery. The monks get a diploma at their initiation, of which there are three kinds—viz., that of a novice, of a full monk, and of a Bodhisattva. The novices are styled *shami* (Sanskrit *śramanera*), the full monks *shamên* (*śramana*), or *hoshang*.[1] Another honourable appellation of the monk is *fa-shih* (teacher of the law), which in its Japanese pronunciation (*bo-si*) gave origin to the well-known term *bonze*. (Other scholars derive it from the Burmese *Hpongyi*, but with less evidence.) The monk gives up his former lay name, and receives a religious one, the *fa-ming* or *fa-hao*, also spoken of as *tu hui* (ordination name).

According to the monastic rules, a monk's duties are very arduous, but how far they are actually performed is quite another question.

[1] On the derivation of *hoshang*, *cf.* Takakusu's edition of I-Tsing's "Record of the Buddhist Religion," p. 118.

The most conspicuous daily task is participation in devotional exercises. There were originally six appointed times of devotion for the inhabitants of monasteries — early at sunrise, between eight and nine, between eleven and twelve, at three in the afternoon, and at seven and at nine in the evening. These generally contract to three times daily—one early, one midday, and one at evening worship. The usual form consists in a list of invocations, praises, and recitation of weighty chapters from the sacred writings. These are sometimes murmured, sometimes chanted like a psalm in a more distinct melody. The whole course of worship is accompanied by a continuous playing of all sorts of instruments, such as the "wooden fish," bells small and large, drums, cymbals, and tambourines. Each monk has his appointed place in which to stand or kneel. They are arranged in two divisions, which in many parts of the service face one another, and at other times all face towards the altar. A monk who officiates before the altar, between the two divisions, conducts the ceremony. There is frequently a sacrifice connected with the worship; the usual one only consists in rice and tea. The conductor of the service divides the gifts—with mystic waving of the fingers—between the powers which are being worshipped. A procession usually marks the close of the service.

Festivals naturally have their own ceremonials. Chinese Buddhism knows the old Uposatha days, and calls them fast-days (*chai-jï*). They are the eighth, the fourteenth, the twenty-second, and the twenty-eighth days of the month. But as the middle and the end of the month are often marked by two fast-days (the fourteenth and fifteenth, as well as the twenty-eighth and twenty-ninth or the twenty-ninth and thirtieth), the whole number is then six. Besides these the Buddhist calendar contains a large number of festivals, birthdays of all the Buddhas, Bodhisattvas, and saints, days to commemorate the death of certain persons connected with the history of the individual monastery, special days for the honouring of the *devas*, festivals of the sun and the moon, festivals to pray for good weather or rain or snow; then the universal Chinese festivals—the birthday of the Emperor and Empress, the festivals of the beginning of summer, of the "hungry ghosts," of the end of summer, of the beginning of winter, of the end of winter, of New Year, etc. All these occasions have their appropriate ritual. Besides these, every kind of wish or petition of the laity is brought to the monks. Harvest anxieties, domestic joys and sorrows, illness and death, all alike require prayers or ceremonial dealings at the hands of the monks.

Whilst Chinese Buddhism, by honouring and invoking all kinds of spiritual beings, has entirely departed from the line of its founder, it on the other hand still preserves a certain continuity with the old doctrine by the *Duty of Meditation.* There are schools and monasteries in which meditation is held to be of such importance that an appointed time is allotted to it every day. Those who meditate betake themselves to the Hall of Meditation, and in a certain prescribed attitude exercise their minds on the problem of abstraction. But almost everywhere, where meditation is still practised, it has changed into a lifeless and formal thing. This is especially evident where these meditations are worked out in company, as is customary in some monasteries, which boast of old tradition with regard to this rite. They differentiate between sedentary or ambulatory meditation. They are merely external exercises, carried out in prescibed order. All sit down in a fixed attitude; for a few moments there is absolute silence; then a pious formula is uttered by all at the same time; after that—at a given signal—all spring up and walk round a table (by ranks) which stands in the centre of the hall, covered with images of the gods. The walk becomes more and more rapid, till it is a run; a superintendent stands by with a sort of lash and drives on the dilatory ones; suddenly a bell sounds and each returns to his place and sits quietly down. In many monasteries meditation has been entirely discontinued, and replaced by the recitation of pious formulæ. How much or how little of this is practised by the individual monk is left entirely to his own discretion.

Besides the religious obligations, however, there are many other duties. The whole monastic community—a body of thirty or forty individuals even in a moderate-sized monastery—is strictly organized, and has its work absolutely well regulated and apportioned in all matters of household economy. The instructions with regard to organization are laid down in books which are to be found everywhere. The execution of them depends on the kind and size of the monastery.

At the head is the Abbot, entitled Fang-chang (or

Chu-ch'ih[1]). He is always an elderly monk, but need not necessarily be the oldest, either in age or residence. The obedience of all is due to the Abbot. He holds an independent position. Under him the fully ordained monks range themselves in two divisions, the so-called east and west ranks. The first of these classes, the eastern, deals mostly with the secular and household matters, the western with every kind of ritual and of clerical duty. The so-called Tu-chien possesses the highest position in the eastern division; he is a sort of Prior, and next to the Abbot he is the most influential person. He is the Abbot's representative, and must keep himself informed about every important question, in order to report it to the Abbot. After him come numberless other officials: a book-keeper, a man to look after the guests, a commissioner of stores, a superintendent of field-labour, a superintendent of the water-supply, an overseer of the kitchens, a manager of the clothing department, another for giving out the tea, a superintendent of repairs, etc. At the head of the western division—namely, of the religious side—is a so-called President (Shou-tso); then follow some monks who lead the assembly at certain points of the worship; then, again, others appointed specially to read the sacred books, others to explain the doctrine to laymen, one to act as secretary, one who keeps the ancestor tablets in order, various officers connected with the temple duties, etc.

[1] The term "Chu-ch'ih" means "resident priest." Takakusu (in his translation of I-Tsing, p. 117) thinks that the proper meaning originally was "preserver or maintainer of the Three Jewels." Fang-chang points more to the Abbot's place of residence.

In most monasteries there also live several laymen. Their dwellings often lie outside the monastery wall in an outer circle. They undertake every kind of practical work for the monks, especially agriculture and forestry and handicrafts. It is a free agreement by which they are bound to the monastery. They are generally not badly off—at all events, in comparison with the usual condition of Chinese peasants.

The sustenance of the monks is simple, but not as much one of privation as that of many a poor farmer. They live on a strictly vegetarian diet. That rule is the most scrupulously observed of any, although it is unknown to the original Indian Buddhism. As most of the monks have been accustomed from childhood to the vegetarian diet of the monasteries, it has become second nature to them; meat is repulsive to many. The meals are prepared in the monastery. Chinese Buddhism does not observe the custom of daily begging for food, nor is there any regulation forbidding meals after midday.[1] They usually have three meals a day: in the early morning after first worship a light breakfast; at midday and in the evening are the principal meals. All the common monks assemble for them in the dining-room, where they sit on benches at long tables. A monk superintends from his place on a platform. A general murmured prayer begins and ends the meal. Several serving monks distribute the food out of large tubs, to each man his portion, a bowl of rice and a dish of vegetables. Of rice they are allowed a second helping.

[1] With one exception to be named later (p. 241).

At meal-times there is perfect silence; speech is forbidden. All necessary communications are made by signs. The monks are summoned to meals by the beating of a large wooden fish which hangs from the ceiling of a corridor near the dining-room. The Abbot and the principal monks do not usually have their meals with the ordinary monks, but have a better quality of food served to them in their own cells.

The monks wear the ancient Buddhist dress, with such alteration as to suit climatic requirements. They wear trousers, stockings, and shoes, besides the three garments of Southern Buddhism. The outer garment is of an orange colour or yellowish-brown; the two other articles are generally grey. The Abbot and a few other leading monks are distinguishable during worship by wearing special garments. Their upper garment is red with gold stripes. The Abbot has a peculiar sceptre as a sign of his dignity, which is often adorned with precious stones.

The monks' cells are fitted out according to the varying means of individuals, and they are often quite comfortable. The principal fixture is the bed, which, like the Chinese bed in universal use, consists of a solid bedstead with a wooden frame (from which to hang a mosquito-net), a straw mattress, and woollen coverings. A table and a couple of seats, besides a cupboard in which to keep small things, some strips of paper bearing inscriptions or pictures on the walls, perhaps a flower—that is the usual thing to be seen in the way of furnishing. The monk no longer adheres to the old rules as to couch and to absence of possessions. He receives without a scruple gold, silver, or any kind of presents.

Above all, there can be no question—in the case of average monks—of any intimate conception of the Buddha's teachings. The monastic life is a purely conventional thing. The discrepancy is consequently not unnatural, great strictness of accepted ritual and monastic regulations being combined with great laxity in the observance of moral precepts. A monk who failed to appear in correct dress and attitude at public worship, or made a disturbance during meal-time by speaking, or neglected some wonted ceremony, would without doubt incur a penalty. On the other hand, monks who spend whole nights gambling, who lie, who quarrel, who smoke opium, are free from blame and have no compunction of conscience. The same monks that hold vegetarian doctrines most rigidly may take pleasure in shooting birds or squirrels with European firearms, without seeming to be aware of any wrong-doing. The usual moral standard is not only lower than that of real Buddhist ethics, but also lower than that of the surrounding non-monastic community. Nevertheless, outward decorum is observed to a certain extent.

On the other hand, individual monks are inclined to asceticism, which is very surprising, not only on account of the usual lukewarmness of Chinese Buddhism, but especially because of the intrinsic character of Buddhism, which is not outwardly ascetic. There are monks who, not satisfied with the branding received at their ordination, have it renewed from time to time, either on the head, or the neck, or the chest, or the arms, and that to an amazing extent. They go even farther, and there are monks to be found who have had one or more fingers burnt off.[1] Yet more terrible, here and there a monk has actually given his living body to be burned on a funeral pile, even in the most recent times. At such a drama there are many spectators present, and the authorities take no steps to prevent it. The self-immolating victim is usually seated cross-legged in a wooden frame, closely surrounded by inflammable material, which he himself sets alight with a torch. His ashes are treasured as those of a saint.[2] Another form of asceticism is that of voluntary incarceration. A monk takes a vow that he will not leave a little room, in which he shuts himself up, for a certain number of years or for his lifetime. Through a small opening—generally the only one for the admission of light and air—some food is daily handed to him. He speaks with no one. His hair is never cut nor does he wash his face. His only occupation is the muttering of prayers and sacred formulæ. If the door is not entirely walled up, it is at all events pasted over with strips of paper, containing certain inscriptions, so that it cannot be

[1] J. J. M. de Groot, in his very learned and instructive book, "Le Code du Mahâyâna en Chine" (Amsterdam, 1893), expresses doubt (p. 227) as to the continuance of this practice, and refers to evidence that it was done in past times. But I can speak with the assurance of personal knowledge that the custom is still in vogue. The Abbot of the great monastery Fa yü ssŭ, on the island of Pu t'o, has lost the fourth finger of both hands in this way.

[2] A modern instance is recorded by Macgowan, *Chinese Recorder*, xix., No. 11, pp. 508-521.

opened without observation. Some strict ascetics also shut themselves up in small caves of mountains, devoid of all daylight. When the inhabitant of such a prison dies, his body (which has become greatly emaciated by the scant nourishment it has received) is embalmed and prepared in a special manner, then painted and gilt, and set up in the temple to be worshipped under the name of "flesh body" (*jou shên*).

The ordinary monk is cremated after death. The corpse for that purpose is seated in an iron chair in the meditation attitude, and faggots are heaped around it, which are lighted. The ashes are either placed in a grave under a monument, or let down into a common pit, in a peculiar building. For more distinguished individuals the large monasteries have a special mausoleum, in which are niches for the funeral urns to stand in. It is remarkable that the universal custom of Chinese ancestor worship has made its way even into Buddhist monasteries, despite its fundamental opposition to the leading doctrine of Buddhism. For ancestral tablets are erected in a special room of the monastery to the souls of the cremated members of the community, in exactly the same manner as the usual monuments of the kind. On the appointed days an offering is brought to the dead man, and an extract from the sacred writings is read before the ancestral tablet. Once every year a festive rite, accompanied by an offering, takes place before all the ancestral tablets in the monastery. In many places it is customary also for laymen who were closely connected with the monastery, and whose relatives are willing to pay a sum of money for it, to have an ancestral tablet erected there to their memory after their death. Such tablets, belonging to laymen, are housed in a room apart: to them also offerings are brought by the monks.

Besides the regular monks, there are also many Buddhist hermits living in China. Their abodes are poor huts or holes in the mountains, where they are maintained by alms or by help of a monastery near by with which they are connected. The people style them *mao-p'êng*, from the "mat shed buildings" where they live. The hermits do not shave their heads, but wear their hair long, hanging loose. Their appearance is sometimes very awkward.

### D. The Canon.

The sacred canon is used in the Chinese language. It contains the three ancient divisions: Sûtra Pitaka (Chinese, Ching-ts'ang), Vinaya Pitaka (Lü-ts'ang), and Abidharma Pitaka (Lun-ts'ang). After these comes a fourth section of mixed works, all sorts of additions, translations in different versions, and commentaries. Each of the three principal divisions subdivides again into the Mahâyâna writings, the Hînayâna writings, and the mixed treatises of both collections. From it you see clearly that the Mahâyâna school has not forsaken the original root and origin of the Hînayâna, but has merely far outgrown it. The Chinese text is founded on the original Sanskrit, and in many particulars is only a transcript from it into Chinese sounds. A number of the works included in the canon were, indeed, originally Chinese, such, for instance, as the description of the travels of the famous Indo-Chinese pilgrims, Fa Hsian and Yüan Chuang. The compiling of the Chinese canon was a very long process, for additions were made to it as late as the fourteenth century A.D. Till nearly the end of the tenth century A.D., the canonical writings existed only in manuscripts. The Emperor T'ai Tsu, the first ruler of the northern Sung dynasty, in the year 972 caused the whole of the extant canon to be printed for the first time (from 130,000 woodblocks). Since then many printed copies have appeared. Although noted monasteries possess specially prized books even now, in the shape of beautifully written manuscripts, not infrequently decorated with miniatures, executed in gold and silver and colours, the canonical books in common use to-day are invariably printed.[1] Type and binding are of the usual Chinese kind. A large canonical book consisting of a number of parts is bound between two wooden covers or pasteboards. As Chinese books *lie* instead of *stand* in a library, the parts of the canon lie in single compartments, on which a label is attached, bearing the title. The whole canon usually fills ten large bookcases. The doors are sometimes decorated with ornate paintings of the tutelary deities. In the noted monasteries the library usually is a present from an Emperor. A special building is set apart for it, the so-called *san-ts'ang-lou* (the building of the three treasures—namely, the three sections of the canon). Within this

[1] Here and there you find a manuscript written with human blood, as it is deemed very meritorious to write a sacred book using one's own blood as ink.

building you see images and altars, and the library is as good a place for pious prayer as any other room. Most of the monasteries possess the requisite wood-blocks (and themselves do the printing) for the setting up of special popular treatises from the canon, or short practical writings of importance (for instance, the appeal for gifts to be made to the monastery, which the monks carry round from time to time for the purpose of collecting). Pictures also of the favourite deities, both coloured and black and white, and woodcuts of celebrated localities, are produced for sale by the monks.

### E. Organization.

A hierarchical system has not been developed by Chinese Buddhism. There is no supreme authority over all the monks in China,[1] nor is there an official head over those of each province. The growth of organization, so far as it proceeded from the religion itself, ceased with the Abbot of each individual monastery. Hence many varieties of influence and power arising from local or individual causes, but never cementing into a permanent system. The leading personalities of some large and celebrated monastery became—from the nature of the case—of greater importance than the Abbot of some obscure place. Men who distinguished themselves by some ascetic act, or by

[1] This is the more remarkable because in Taoism this office does exist. The head is the High-priest of the "Dragon and Tiger Mountains," Ch'ang-tao-ling; he lives in the west of the province of Kiangsi, not far from the borders of the province of Fukien, in a place called Shang Ching.

their learning or magic power, or by some other marked quality, won a higher reputation than others; but that was all. Even the renowned heads of schools and the six Chinese patriarchs have not taken the first step towards a hierarchical development.

But the Chinese Government—in which degrees of rank play so important a rôle—has laid hold upon it and introduced a kind of higher organization. It recognized the necessity of keeping a certain control over the monastic communities, and for that purpose it conferred upon certain Abbots the position of Government superintendents, with a corresponding rank. It follows the well-known Chinese order of administration, which recognizes in every province, first a number of *fu* (prefectures), next *chou* (departments), and lastly *hsien* (districts). Three degrees of rank were created for persons of varying importance, the lowest title (for the *hsien*) being *Sêng-huî*, next (for the *chou*) *Sêng-chêng*, lastly (for the *fu*) *Sêng-kang*. The common designation for these clerical officials is *Sêng-lu-ssŭ*. Their concern is, above all things, to act as negotiators between the Government and the monasteries whenever the State comes into contact with the monks, and, furthermore, to exercise control over the doings in the monasteries in their jurisdiction. They are responsible for wrong-doings of the monks, and for cases of flagrant and public excesses. As it has been a long-standing practice to choose men of high reputation and esteem for these posts, they naturally enjoy a certain respect; this is specially the case with those *Sêng-kang* who live in prefectural towns. But it is not in any true sense a hierarchy. Their authority only extends to cases of discipline, if the monks give occasion for it; as a matter of fact, it is only in the most aggravated and notorious cases that any action is taken. For less offences the office has no practical existence.

### F. Famous Monasteries.

The renown for popularity of individual monasteries has been achieved by other means than those of hierarchical supremacy. Age, legends, the fame of certain divinities, beauty of situation, and other such things, have contributed to it. From remote times, the sanctuaries in the neighbourhood of *Hangchow* (in the province of Chekiang, which is perhaps the most Buddhist province in China) have been very celebrated. This former capital of the Chinese Empire is proverbially famous on account of its beautiful situation near the Hangchow Bay, on the so-called "western lake." In early days monks established themselves there in the woods, and on the hills and shores. But the celebrated monasteries of Hangchow suffered very much during the long years of the Taiping Rebellion, and many of the most noted ones of earlier period are now partly or wholly in ruins. At the foot of the wide, picturesque *Lu-shan*—a hill west of Lake Poyang, and south of the noted town of Kiukiang on the Yangtze—there were also formerly famous monasteries, of which the majority, indeed, were also destroyed by the Taipings, and the remainder drag out a miserable existence. The monasteries situated to the north of Kiukiang, in the *Huang-mei Mountains*—where the Chinese patriarchs lived—were not so much exposed to the wrath of the Taipings; nevertheless, they are of no greater consideration than the others at the present time. But the monasteries on the *T'ien-t'ai Mountains*, in the province of Chekiang, being amongst the most ancient in Central China, have a wide renown even to-day. Here is still extant the memory of the founder of the so-called T'ien-t'ai school, Tzŭ-kai, a very celebrated and influential representative of Chinese Buddhism, of whose works no less than twenty-two have been included in the canon. He lived in the sixth century A.D. His begging-bowl and mantle are still shown to visitors at the monastery of Kao-ming-ssŭ, while another monastery guards the ashes of his cremated body under a beautiful unique pagoda in the principal hall. Numberless legends associate his name with curious rocks or waterfalls in the neighbourhood. There are many celebrated and flourishing monasteries still to be found at the mouth of the Yangtze, in and near the towns of Nanking, Chinkiang, and Yangchow.

But all these and many other sacred Buddhist places in China are overshadowed by four which are the most noted places of pilgrimage throughout the Chinese Empire. They are called Pu-t'o-shan, Chiu-hua-shan, Wu-t'ai-shan, and O-mi-shan.[1]

[1] These four famous places of Chinese Buddhism must not be mixed up with the five sacred peaks (*wu yo*) of the Chinese State religion, which are the T'ai-shan (Shantung), the Hua-shan (Shensi), the Hêng-shan (Shansi), another Hêng-shan (Hunan), and the Sung-shan (Honan).

*Pu-t'o-shan* is a sacred island in the Chusan archipelago, east of the well-known port of Ningpo. The island is covered with monasteries and chapels, and is almost entirely inhabited by monks. It is specially dedicated to the female Bodhisattva Kwanyin, whose image is always in the centre of the principal hall. The small island, round which roars the thunder of the waves of the Pacific, whose wooded heights are crowned with trees, whilst green meadows and cultured fields cover the slopes, is a most charming spot. It is easy to understand the reason of the monks appropriating it and attracting yearly many thousands of pilgrims. The goddess Kwanyin of Pu-t'o-shan is specially the patroness of mariners and fisher-folk.

*Chiu-hua-shan* is a mountain crater, two days journey east of the city of Nganking, on the middle Yangtze. Here the Bodhisattva Ti-ts'ang, the overlord of hell, has the first position. In the very centre of all the temples which crown the hill-tops here stands a pagoda sacred to Ti-ts'ang, ornamented with stone carvings representing this god. The monastic communities of Chiu-hua-shan suffered greatly at the time of the Taiping Rebellion, and in consequence many of the monasteries are new and unimportant. But the enchanting panorama of mountains lends the place a great charm.

The third of the great places of pilgrimage is *Wu-t'ai-shan*, a five-peaked mountain in the province of Shansi, not far from the town of Tai-chou. Here the highly venerated divinity is the Bodhisattva Wen-shu (Manjuśrî). This place of pilgrimage, adjacent to Mongolian territory, may almost be said to have lamaistic features. Mongo llamas share both the temples and the images of the gods with the Chinese *ho-shang*. Tibetan sacred pictures, prayer-wheels, and inscriptions, are common, and amongst the pilgrims may be reckoned more Mongols than Chinese. They have also the lama mask dances.

In the far west of China, in the province of Ssŭchuan, is the most beautiful (as to situation) of the four holy places, *Mount Omi*. The temples on this mountain are dedicated to the Bodhisattva P'u-hsien (Samantabhadra), of whom there is a wonderfully fine and powerful bronze figure in one of the largest monasteries seated upon the sacred elephant. Mount Omi is in itself a most remarkable formation, for it rises almost without interruption from the plain to a height of some 11,000 feet. The view towards the east over the fruitful Chinese plains, and towards the west to the snow mountains of Tibet, is of unrivalled grandeur. But most of the temples of Omi are poor and in decay; nevertheless, it is easy to see that formerly they were not devoid of splendour.

### G. Schools of Chinese Buddhism.

Various schools or sects have arisen in Chinese Buddhism, but at the present time many of the differences have been practically obliterated, and on the other hand much has been freely interchanged between them, so that the mass of ordinary monks would be equally unable to give information to an inquirer as to their own sect or as to the subject in general.[1]

[1] It is not easy, indeed, to make one's way amongst the various sects, as even Chinese writers and informants often take

Nevertheless, there exist many finely-drawn distinctions, and occasionally these stand out clearly.

According to Chinese reckoning, there are ten principal schools of thought. These main divisions are called *tsung;* subdivisions are known as *p'ai.* The ten *tsung* are as follows:

| | |
|---|---|
| 1. Lü tsung. | 6. Hsien shou tsung. |
| 2. (Chü shê tsung.) | 7. Tz'ŭ ên tsung. |
| 3. (Chêng shih tsung.) | 8. Ch'an tsung. |
| 4. (San lun tsung.) | 9. (Mi tsung.) |
| 5. T'ien t'ai tsung. | 10. Ching t'u tsung. |

From these may be excluded those in parentheses—2, 3, 4, and 9—as they no longer play any part in Chinese Buddhism. We shall meet them again in Japan, where their offshoots still exist to a certain extent. The six remaining schools fall naturally into two essentially different groups. The first group consists in the adherents of Ch'an tsung (No. 8 in the list); all the rest may be included in the second group.

The difference between these two groups is a profound and radical one; it is indicated in the name Ch'an tsung. *Ch'an* is the Chinese expression for Buddhistic meditation (Sanskrit *dhyâna*). This school accomplished that change which made in-

---

a very partial and one-sided view of things. De Groot's remarks on the sects at the beginning of the before-mentioned book, "Le Code du Mahâyâna en Chine," I cannot accept as either accurate or complete, judging by the information and authorities I possess. In chapter vii. of "Chinese Buddhism," by Edkins, the information is accurate, but not clearly stated.

wardness the one quality needful, and thereby meditation became naturally the most important fulfilment of the Buddhist injunctions. Bodhidharma, the first Chinese patriarch, was the founder of the Ch'an school (see p. 80). He opposed study of the writings and outward ritual. He laid stress upon the inner being of Buddha (his heart, his nature), and urged the true disciples to become like him in that respect. In order to avoid the fruitless use of books, the disciples were only to be instructed by word of mouth. The "inward look" was to be practised. The characteristic of Bodhidharma's teaching was a vivid abstraction, as is the principle of the old Buddhist meditation. The philosophy based upon this was the "emptying of consciousness"—that is to say, the complete subjectivity of our human conceptions and impressions. In the popular legend he was called the "Wallgazer," because, according to tradition, he had sat in front of a wall for nine years, wrapped in meditation; for which reason he is still frequently portrayed in that position, his back being turned to the observer. Every outward manifestation was indeed superfluous as far as Bodhidharma's contemplative aim was concerned—whether worship, image, or recitation; and it may be that in those early times his school had really discarded these things, although, naturally, such is no longer the case. Indeed, in the older writings of the school (for, although the teaching was to be handed down verbally from generation to generation, it was of necessity soon transmitted to books), the generally accepted difference between good and evil is held to be the imperfection of a lower standpoint, above which the person who meditates raises himself. Having been absolutely emptied of content (for all apparent living beings are subjective illusions), the disciple is utterly indifferent to everything, when once Buddha has taken possession of his heart.

This school — whose founder has strongly and rightly guided back into the original channel of the Buddha Gautama—became split up after a time into five subdivisions, of which each assumed such importance that it also received the title of school (*tsung*). They are also sometimes called the *wu chia*, or five families (houses). These still existing divisions of the Ch'an school are: (1) Lin chi tsung, (2) Ts'ao tung tsung, (3) Hui (Wei) yang tsung, (4) Fa yen tsung, (5) Yün mên tsung. They derive their names from the places where their founders lived. None of them has deviated far from the others in doctrine; but the Lin chi school had the greatest practical result, and in more recent times the other four schools have quite retired into the background.

In contradistinction to this whole doctrine, originating from the Ch'an school, we have the group of the five others aforementioned. Each of them has its distinguishing characteristic, which it emphasizes, but they share in common opposition to the absolute subjectivism of the Ch'an school by their teaching of objectivism and of the importance of externals.

The Lü tsung is the school of discipline. Lü is the translation of the Indian Vinaya, the rule of discipline which constitutes one part of the Buddhist canon. This school, founded by Tao hsüan (died A.D. 667), sets the greatest value on the strict observance of the old monastic regulations. Even to-day one notices something particularly severe in the external conduct of their life at the chief monastery, Pao-hua-shan, a day's journey to the east of Nanking, on the Yangtze. Here the monks are only allowed two meals a day—morning and midday; the evening meal is forbidden in accordance with the ancient Indian regulation. They are only allowed tea to drink. They are also stricter in keeping their devotional assemblies, and in learning and reciting the sacred texts.

The T'ien t'ai tsung, founded by the before-mentioned Tzŭ-kai (died A.D. 597; his monastic name was Tzŭ-i; he is also frequently called "the sage of T'ien-t'ai"), tried to combine the method of Bodhidharma—putting meditation in the first place—with the use of books, in due proportion and with external ceremonial. From amongst all the writings of the sacred canon, the founder selected one in particular, which contains the quintessence of real Buddhism, the Miao fa lien hua ching (Sanskrit, Saddharma pundarîka sutra).[1] He has written several commentaries on it.

The Hsien shou tsung, so called after one of their most illustrious teachers (not the founder, who was Tu fa shun, died A.D. 640), chose as their principal text-book the Hua yen ching, which was said to have been composed by Nagarjuna, the great exponent of the Mahâyâna. It is a book full of legendary em-

[1] Translated by Burnouf, "Le Lotus de la bonne Loi," and by Kern, "The Lotus of the True Law" ("Sacred Books of the East," vol. xxi.).

bellishments and fantastic glorifications of the Buddha, and in it he relates the Buddha's supernatural appearances in various heavens, as well as on earth, before numberless supernatural beings, accompanied by all sorts of brilliant miracles. This book and the above-mentioned one (Miao fa lien hua ching) are perhaps the most highly esteemed by all Chinese Buddhists. By means of a very arbitrary symbolical interpretation of the text, the whole Mahâyâna philosophy is derived from it, while the legend has found in it ample nourishment for a lively play of the imagination about the supernatural beings. The school is, after its favourite book, also called Hua yen tsung. Still another name it bears is Fa hsing tsung (school of the Dharma-nature).

The Tz'ŭ ên tsung, in like manner, has taken a particular canonical book as the foundation of its teaching, the so-called Wei shih lun,[1] a work which originated from the Mahâyâna teacher Vasubandhu, and was translated by the celebrated pilgrim Yüan Chuang. A remarkable psychology attached itself to this work, of a thoroughly Mahâyânish character: things are unreal; they proceed from man's mind, and, indeed, spring from different kinds of perception. The illustrations of this fundamental idea are often extraordinary and incomprehensible; they cannot be further dealt with here. A special doctrine of meditation was built upon this psychology. Nevertheless, they gave weight also to the value of kindness and

[1] Apparently after this favourite book, Edkins ("Chinese Buddhism," p. 169) gives the name of this school as "Wei shi siang Kiau."

friendliness towards all beings, and esteemed as the highest of all outward religious signs the exercise of love and sympathy. Hence the name of the school, for Tzŭ ên means "kindness and compassion."[1] The founder was Chieh hsien.

The Ching t'u tsung obtained its special characteristic by developing and popularizing the doctrine of a western Paradise (the pure land, Ching t'u—hence its name). This idea (see p. 190) appears to have arisen at the same time as the belief in the Buddha Amitâbha and the Bodhisattva Kwanyin, and the explicit removal of the Paradise to the west thoroughly confirms the opinion of some investigators, that the features of Amitâbha and Kwanyin (originally Avalokita) have penetrated from the west, perhaps from Persia to Northern India, Tibet, and China. The western Paradise is ruled by Amitâbha. The Bodhisattvas Kwanyin and Ta-shih-chi rule beside him. All three—the "three holy ones of the western land"—are invoked and worshipped by the faithful, in order that they may reach Paradise, and it is, doubtless, their connection with this popular doctrine about Paradise which has brought about the notoriety of the three holy ones, especially of the two first named.

The special writings of the Ching t'u school are two works in praise of Amitâbha, O mi to ching and Wu liang shou ching. The school was founded by Hui yüan or Yüan kung (fourth century A.D.). It is also often styled the Lotos school (Lien tsung).

[1] Another explanation is that the name has been derived from a monastery known as the Tzŭ ên ssŭ.

Each of the above schools has its special chain of traditions, tracing their way backwards by the various noted teachers to the founder, and from him still farther back to some celebrated personality among those surrounding the Buddha, or to himself, or to one of the imaginary Buddhas and Bodhisattvas. Naturally, this last slender thread in the line of tradition is only a means conceived for the purpose of giving the highest possible authority to the doctrine. All sorts of fancies attach themselves also to the favourite writings of each school. So it is held that the famous book Hua yen ching, the authority of the Hsien shou school, originated in six forms. The two first were never written down, but only live in the memory of certain Bodhisattvas; the two following, as soon as they were written, were transmitted for safe guardianship to the Dragon Palace under the sea. The fifth edition was written out by Nagarjuna. The sixth is the Chinese version of the fifth.

It has been already remarked that the individual characteristics of each sect have at the present day very much disappeared. Nevertheless, the majority of the monasteries still adhere to the names of their doctrinal authorities, and are attached to their special books. A close inspection shows that there are all sorts of differences in their inner working, in the method of their meditation, in the passages which they recite, and in the details of worship. From the outside one notices but little of this. The energy of spiritual independence is almost everywhere extinct.

There are not a few nunneries in China. The southern part of the empire contains more than the north; in Canton alone there are over eighty. But most of the convents are small. They are established and organized in the same way as the monasteries, and are under their control. The nuns have their heads completely shaven, like the monks, but always wear a cap to cover the whole skull. Their habit on the whole resembles the dress of the monks.[1]

### H. The Character of Monasticism.

The Chinese Buddhist monks receive but little sympathy from the bulk of the population. Their whole manner of life is essentially opposed to Chinese ideas, and that fact is continuously kept before them. It tends to loosen the social bonds, and is an unproductive life as well. So the monks are proverbially spoken of as "the drones in the beehive," or as "not being so useful as the silkworm." In addition to this, it comes about that almost all the monks are drawn from the lowest ranks of the population. It is very rarely the case that a wealthy man, or a member of a high-class family, assumes the yellow robe; and when it does occur, the individual quickly attains the rank of an Abbot. It may be taken for granted that the majority of monks are peasants and people of no importance. They even fail to attain that which is so highly prized by the Chinese—literary culture. It is true that many monks receive a literary training during long years, but this training follows entirely the Buddhist line, so that the monks are unable to devote themselves to the study of the

[1] Details on nuns and nunneries are to be found in W. C. Milne's "Life in China," pp. 134-145 (London, 1858).

classics, which alone entitles a man to respect in the eyes of the Chinese. Here yawns the great gulf, fixed from the very beginning, which prevents this foreign religion from getting hold of the Chinese national character. All the spiritual receptivity and strenuousness of the Chinese nation, all its ideals, all its opinions, are rooted in its antiquity, and in the writings which are so intimately bound up with it. The study of these writings is therefore the nerve centre of its life. But the Buddhist monk takes up an altogether different and opposite position. He has his own literature, an all-absorbing one; and it is, moreover, of Indian origin, and not infrequently Indian in expression. Here, also, the uniqueness of Chinese written characters plays a momentous part in the history of Chinese Buddhism. As the Chinese language possesses no alphabet, only characters, each conception has therefore to be written by a symbol of its own (in the same way as we use numerical figures); consequently the characters are innumerable, just in proportion as the conceptions are innumerable. From this it follows that all people cannot equally well read any book. Different intellectual departments require different characters to express their meaning, apart from all peculiarities of style. Thus, a person who is tolerably well acquainted with Buddhist literature may not unnaturally find the classics a sealed book.

As regards all the facts above-mentioned—which rob the monk of the sympathy and esteem of the people—he is personally free from blame. But, unfortunately, there is much besides, contributing to this state of affairs, for which he is responsible.

The moral level of the monks is a very low one. They have not sufficient strength of character to withstand the temptations closely attending their trying position. Their religious duties are purely mechanical, carried out within their own restricted circle, and their life, instead of being an example of self-conquest, becomes a life of utter idleness. Not only so, but the very fact that they are encouraged to rely wholly upon the assistance of the laity, and to expect everything to be provided for them in the shape of offerings, alms, and gifts, produces in them the most aggressive and offensive cupidity. All their intercourse with laymen is in connection with business. The money obtained is sometimes handed to the monastery, sometimes to the individual, for the old fundamental rule forbidding monks to possess personal property has been long ago forgotten. Another of the injurious results of the monastic system is the inability of keeping the enforced celibacy. Immorality of various kinds is but too common. Where the monks are under the rule of a strict Abbot who cares for the reputation of his monastery, these things are kept in the dark. Elsewhere they are done openly, and frequently to such an extent that public indignation is aroused. Thus, all the convents in Foochow were suppressed by the authorities in the thirties of the nineteenth century because they had become too notoriously the haunts of vice. Also in Suchow in 1840 all nunneries were broken up from the same reason.

The use of opium is indeed becoming increasingly widespread. Whoever is familiar with the outward signs of opium-smoking can recognize smokers among the monks frequently enough, especially in the larger town monasteries. And if you spend some time living with the monks, and are trusted within all their precincts, in one or another of their cells you are reminded of the dreadful fiend by the fatal, sickly exhalation which it is impossible to mistake. In town monasteries the pleasures of the opium habit are frequently indulged in without any disguise. Acquaintances of the monks visit them in order to enjoy smoking undisturbed in the quiet of their cells.

Another injurious effect of the monastic life is that many of the monks drift by its means into a sort of religious vagabondage and become quite lawless. Every monk who is fully ordained has the right to leave the monastery originally selected in order to go to another monastery which he wishes to enter, or merely to assume an itinerant life. He is received into any monastery on showing a pass from his Abbot, and receives accommodation and the usual food for a few days. This should be a help for those who go about begging for their temple, but is frequently misused by those whom a spirit of unrest has taken possession of, and who after a time give themselves up entirely to a life of vagabondage. This type of monk is well known to the people, who call them "wild monks."

### I. Buddhism and the People.

Although the followers of Buddhism, for the above-mentioned reasons, are not much esteemed in China, yet their services are widely and eagerly sought. It is difficult to imagine the life of an ordinary man deprived of Buddhist monks and monasteries. The very outward aspect of the country bears unmistakable signs of Buddhism. The pagodas, for instance, have spread outside the narrow borders of Buddhist sanctuaries in China. Although many pagodas still belong to monasteries, thousands are built without any such connection. Here they have assumed a totally different significance from their original one—that of monuments to the memory of a saint or in honour of the Buddha. They have been incorporated into the so-called doctrine of Fêng-shui. This doctrine, literally translated the "Wind-water Doctrine," is a theory about the connection of human fate with the influences of nature. It deals with very strange manifestations, and these have in time become associated with the pagodas. Pagodas have the power to change the influence otherwise possessed by mountain and valley, by stream and hollow, on human circumstance; they can—if their situation is rightly selected—secure to any place a favourable lot. This is the reason why you so frequently see a town with a pagoda crowning the summit of a neighbouring hill, although the pagoda is quite unconnected with Buddhism, and is only one of the signs of a Chinese landscape and of Chinese imagination.

The Chinese pagoda (the word "pagoda" has been derived, in very different ways, from the Portuguese *pagão* or from the Indian "dagaba" in Portuguese pronunciation, or from Hindustani *ponthkoda*) is called *t'a*, an abbreviation of *t'a-p'o*, transcribing the Sanskrit *stûpa*, Pâli *thûpa*. It has generally seven or nine stories, sometimes eleven and even thirteen; the number must be an odd one. Buildings with less than seven stories should not properly be called *t'a*, but bear other names, as K'anghsi's dictionary, the great Chinese authority, states.

Other visible tokens of Buddhist life are the shrines and chapels by the roadside. They are specially common in Western China. Inside these little buildings (which are of stone or wood) there is an image of the gods or an inscribed tablet. The pious passer-by lights a couple of incense sticks before it. In other places — especially in the neighbourhood of water or before bridges—are remarkable quadrilateral or hexagonal pillars, which not infrequently end above in a roughly carved, projecting head. On the pillars are inscribed the names of gods, prefaced by the Buddhist (Indian) *namu* (adoration to . . .). Such pillars are for the purpose of counteracting the influence of evil water-spirits, who strive to draw people down into their element.

These are some of the Buddhist features of the landscape besides the monasteries themselves. Countless are the evidences of the influence of Buddhism on the life of the individual man.

Without entering fully into Buddhist doctrine and theories, the Chinese concentrates his attention upon the divinities in the temples, just as upon any other gods, as his ultimate helpers in the emergencies of life. He deals with them according to the advice of the monks, who may be supposed to know what is fitting. Thus, he brings offerings in the shape of rice, fruits, cakes, money, which naturally all belong to the monastery. He brings candles for the altar, incense to be burnt. He kneels before the images and recites sacred formulæ. He provides for a procession of the monks (at a high price), with the Abbot at the head—behind whom he himself walks—while the monks recite prayers. He presents an image of Buddha, or shares in some greater gifts, either a huge bronze bell or the restoration of a temple which had fallen into decay, or the building of a new one. He invites the monks to his own house, where they perform prescribed ceremonies and recitations. These customary means taken by the Chinese to obtain the help of the Buddhist deities are forced on him by the practical needs of life. If there is illness in a house, or a childless woman desires a son, or a man has some perilous business on hand or has come into conflict with the authorities, it then depends upon his means which temple he must visit or what god is to be invoked, and at what cost. If the prayer prove successful, thanks are expressed not seldom by hanging some votive offering in the temple, a heart or an eye or a hand or a foot made of wood or of cloth. One may see heaps of such ex-voto presents depending from some altars of famous sanctuaries. The way in which certain oracles are obtained from the divinity is most strange. On almost every temple altar lie two worn, semicircular pieces of wood, shaped like a crescent, with one surface convex, the other flat. The man who undertakes a doubtful and important enterprise goes to the temple with his offering, which he presents to the god, burns incense, and then swings the two pieces of wood (with their flat sides together) in the incense, and throws them down on the left-hand side. The way in which they fall shows him whether he will succeed or not. The favourable omen is when one of the pieces falls with the flat, and the other with the convex, side uppermost. If they both fall with the flat side undermost, that is a bad outlook. If both the convex sides are undermost, the result is uncertain. Another method is by drawing lots. Every temple possesses a wooden box, containing a large number of little wooden sticks. This box is shaken in front of an image with certain appropriate ceremonies till one of the sticks falls out. The number marked on the stick corresponds with a passage in a collection of oracular sayings, which are usually of so universal or ambiguous a nature that they might equally apply to any kind of result.

A common way of obtaining the favour of the gods or of relieving a burdened conscience is by pilgrimage. Frequently there are celebrated places within easy reach; but long journeys are not shunned. Every year thousands of pilgrims from every part of the empire pour into the four great sacred places, where the four most renowned Bodhisattvas are worshipped. At Mount Omi, in the far west of China, may be met pilgrims coming from Peking, or the east coast, a journey of several months. Here and there you meet special ascetics bent on this pilgrimage. There are people who do penance on the journey by prostrating themselves every tenth step, and praying with their forehead touching the ground. Pilgrims often travel in parties who adopt a common name and a common banner. Their most important duty when they reach their destination is to burn several sticks of incense before each god, kneeling down and repeating certain formulæ. At celebrated shrines you see an innumerable crowd like a swarm of ants engaged in this business, hastening from altar to altar and from room to room. Much else is going on at the same time. The monks erect booths, where all sorts of talismanic pictures, verses, and symbols, may be obtained; they are eagerly bought by the faithful. Sick people rub the diseased limb upon the wonder-working image. Money pours into the large chests, which are set ready to receive offerings in every hall.

Another meritorious custom inculcated on the people by Buddhism is the temporary abstention from eating meat. Sometimes the people who are observing this custom reside for the appointed time as guests in the monastery, living for a few weeks on the same diet as the monks, and taking part in all their religious observances. The high estimation of an entirely vegetarian diet has even brought a peculiar sect into existence, called the "vegetarian sect," which cannot be reckoned among the ordinary schools of Buddhism, although this was doubtless its origin. It is a lay community. They repudiate all image worship, and have given up all the religious ceremonies of Buddhism. They only venerate heaven and earth, the ruler of the empire, parents and teachers, and this they do in the simplest manner, by placing offerings of tea and rice before the memorial tablets of their great ones in the halls for devotion. They possess books and deep-reaching conceptions, but it is all kept very secret, chiefly because the State often persecutes this society. But what is outwardly very noticeable is the strict fasting from meat; this is their most important religious duty. Their origin is derived from the already frequently mentioned Bodhidharma. Contemplation plays also an important rôle with them.—For fasting from meat, which Buddhism counsels, the common people generally account by the idea of metempsychosis: you do not know whom you are wronging when you kill an animal and consume its flesh, for a friend or relative may be doomed to this existence. The positive side of abstinence from meat is the "saving of life"—namely, the housing of animals in a monastery where they are cared for till they die a natural death: the cost of this is met by laymen. While such a practice has been assiduously cultivated by many people, yet Buddhism has never been able to establish a kind and considerate treatment of animals by the people in general. Extreme cruelty to animals is quite common, and is the result of lack of thought. That the people have no sensibility for the torture of animals can be only too easily understood in a country where the most terrible tortures are daily inflicted upon men by the authority of the magistrates, without exciting any general feeling of horror.

The laity in China have only assimilated Buddhist ideas in so far as they were easy to bring into line with the existing Chinese religious ideas. Such are those of recompense, of reward and punishment for every deed, and of reincarnation, always under the form of metempsychosis. The ancient State religion recognizes also the moral surveillance exercised by the higher powers, divine rewards and divine punishments. They also believe in the continuance of the soul after death in happy or unhappy surroundings, and their most salient characteristic—the veneration of ancestors—is most closely attached to it. All this has taken on a brighter and more vivid colouring through the influence of Mahâyâna Buddhism—in fact, a thoroughly Chinese complexion. The other world exists in their imagination as heaven or hells, and between these two lie the six kinds of reincarnation—as high-born people (mandarins), poor people, quadrupeds, birds, fishes, and insects. The most vivid impression is made by the hells. The fate of the soul which goes down there is portrayed in an incredibly dramatic way, both in words and pictures. Buddhism has been compelled to assume the rôle of deliverer from the torments of hell. However incompatible this may be with its fundamental tenor, it has become a universal belief that the lot of those who have died can be influenced from this world. At the death of a monk and after the death of a monk, therefore, special extracts from the canon are recited, with a musical accompaniment (especially extracts from the Amitâbha-Sutra): this is done because the sacred word has power to improve the position of the soul. When, also, the customary offerings to the ancestors are brought by the wealthy layman, he gladly consults the Buddhist monks, and by paying ascertains what passages of the sacred writings should be recited to bring a blessing to the deceased.

It is often maintained that the faithful adherence

to Buddhism, as regards the laity, is confined to the lower classes. It may well be that the cultured Chinese, the official, contemptuously smiles and scoffs at the superstitions of Buddhism. But this apparent contempt is not always genuine. Even high-placed officials, especially of mature age, not infrequently submit to Buddhism, when the thought of death and the uncertainty of their future fate begins to weigh upon them.[1] They generally arrange matters so as to court observation as little as possible. A private chapel near their house or place of business is the scene of their devotions, and the help they afford to monks and monasteries is rendered with all privacy.

It is perhaps worthy of notice that Buddhism has given a certain tinge to Chinese literature. The popular novelistic literature contains a number of stories about the legendary figures of Buddhism. The unbridled fancy of these fabulous stories is so attractive to the ordinary individual that some of these books may be counted as the most read in Chinese literature. Pictorial art as well shows marked traces of Buddhist influence. Many famous painters have been monks, and a great deal of the subject-matter of Chinese paintings is Buddhist material.

Despite all the influence brought to bear on the Chinese laity by Buddhism, it must always be remembered—as was explained at the beginning of this

[1] It is said even of the late Empress-Dowager, that she was "addicted to the pietism of the Northern Buddhism" (Wen Ching, "The Chinese Crisis from Within," London, 1901, p. 136).

chapter—that the laity cannot rightly be considered a Buddhist people. In the statistics of Chinese religions, only the monks should be reckoned as Buddhists. The laity merely have to do with Buddhism as regards its externals, and share very little of its genuine ideas. The Chinese layman essentially belongs to his indigenous religion, which most clearly asserts its supremacy over the Indian import by the introduction of the ancestral tablets into Buddhist monasteries.

## Chapter VII.—BUDDHISM IN KOREA.

The picture of Buddhism which confronts the student in Korea is on the whole a very dull and faded one. The lethargy which for so long a time has mastered Korean culture and intellectual life is also characteristic of the Buddhism of this country. But its principal features show unmistakably its Chinese origin. The architecture of the sacred buildings, the dress and mode of life of the monks, the organization still extant, the images of the gods, the ritual of worship—all these things at the first glance are seen to be of a Chinese type. Here and there, it is true, a trait appears which is not Chinese, and is either Tibeto-Mongolian or Japanese in origin. Korean Buddhism only appears to have had the most limited capacity for originating new features, peculiar to itself.

### A. Monasteries and Monks.

Korean monasteries include partly dwellings, partly temples. Both are frequently combined in such a way that the front part of a house is a temple, while the back is a dwelling. But the larger monasteries have always at least two or three buildings entirely consecrated to the divinities. Among them the most important is the one known to us in Chinese Buddhism as the *ta hsiung pao tien*, the Precious Hall of the Great Hero. Besides this hall you also frequently find a special hall of Ti-tsang, the god of hell. Both these much-esteemed temples stand in the square courtyard which is enclosed by the dwelling-houses. The more important establishments possess besides a wooden tower for the big drum, an entrance-hall with images of the four great Deva Kings, a small pagoda, and a wooden portal, through which you enter the temple precincts. Sometimes there is also a hall, roofed, but open at the four sides, which serves to shelter the votive offerings brought to the monastery by visitors. The inhabited buildings are simple wooden constructions, generally mean and neglected. One particular feature in this country is that the entire outside walls of the temple halls are covered with paintings of gods, or scenes from the life of the Buddha or of a Bodhisattva. These paintings are executed in strong colours —red, blue, and green—and occupy the whole expanse of boarding; while the pillars and beams and scaffolding under the roof are also painted with every kind of device, producing a bright and pretty effect so long as the building is new and the colours fresh. This tendency to picturesque adornments of the exterior corresponds with a special feature of the interior—namely, with the custom in Korean monasteries of having the walls hung with pictures, both small and large, on religious subjects. Such a thing is unknown in Chinese or Japanese Buddhism, although one may occasionally see a single picture hanging in one of their temples ; Korean Buddhism, on the contrary, is in the habit of covering all the inner walls completely with pictures. The subject as well as the execution of these pictures is stereotyped. They represent the Buddha Gautama in the midst of his disciples and Bodhisattvas, also other higher beings, as well as scenes from the Buddhist legends. A continually recurring subject is a representation of the course of earthly life, with all its characteristic troubles and features, and then man's exit from this life, either to heaven or hell. In the hall of Ti-tsang may usually be found, together with a representation of the Bodhisattva himself, the pictures of ten of the nether Princes, his underlings, acting as judges. These pictures are highly coloured—green, red, blue, like those on the outside of the building—and frequently they are executed not without skill, especially in the drawing of the faces. They are painted on strong paper, covered with fine gauze, and mounted on silk. Many of them are several square yards in size, and cover walls of considerable dimensions. These pictures give the interior of the Korean Buddhist temples their unique character. In comparison with them, the statues of the gods at the present time have become very limited in number. Generally there is only one figure, or at most a few, on the principal altar, small in size, made of wood or clay, and gilded.

The pictures which adorn the walls of the sacred buildings in Korea remind anyone who is familiar with Tibetan temples of the art shown there in the decoration of the interiors. Judging by the evidences of Mongolian influence which run through Korean history, it seems not improbable that Korea has adopted that style of temple decoration from Tibet.

The celestial beings usually worshipped in Korea are the same as those in China—Śâkyamuni; the seven or the five great Buddhas (see p. 158); the Buddha Amitâbha; the Bodhisattvas Kwanyin, P'u-hsien, Wen-shu, Ti-tsang, Ta-shih-chi; the four heavenly Kings; the larger and smaller groups of the disciples of Gautama (the five hundred and the sixteen, not in this case eighteen, Lo-han). Also others—not originally Buddhist divinities—are mixed up with the crowd: most frequently the mountain-god, accompanied by the tiger for his escutcheon, as in China; also the kitchen-god. It should be particularly noted that in many monasteries there is a special chapel for the worship of the constellation of stars known to us as the Great Bear, and also that the sun and moon still retain a dim religious significance.

The sacred language is Chinese, as is the language of all culture in Korea. The names, inscriptions, notices, to be met with in a Korean monastery, are in Chinese characters. The sacred canon is also entirely Chinese. The Chinese written characters (denoting ideas) are pronounced differently by the Koreans, but have the same meaning, so that a Korean and a Chinese would understand one another in writing, when they would be unable to do so in speech. Besides the Chinese characters, there is also an alphabetic form of writing common in Korea, but it is not much esteemed (see p. 87). In order to facilitate the reading of Buddhist books by students, there are copies of the most important ones with a double text—one in Chinese characters, the other translated, or only transcribed, into Korean lettering.

The monks wear practically the same dress as those in China. But the long cloak with sleeves, over which the mantle covering the left shoulder hangs, is usually white, in accordance with the Korean partiality for this colour in dress. They wear wider trousers. The head is, of course, completely shaved, except as regards the beard. On the shaved crown there are no marks of branding which Chinese monks receive at ordination, but in Korea these marks are most frequently to be seen on the arms, and occasionally on the breast. The monastic communities are small; monasteries containing thirty or more monks are rare. Worship is much neglected. Of the daily services only a slight trace is to be found in the early morning, and at midday between eleven and twelve o'clock. Generally it is only single monks who, at the sound of the bell and the wooden fish, light a couple of little incense sticks before the pictures of the gods and recite a long string of ceaselessly repeated names or some sacred formula, like "Namu omitobul" or "Om mani padme hûm." A larger general ceremony takes place on special occasions (as, for instance, at the New Year), and at the instigation of a layman who is able to bear the expense. The organization of the monasteries has dwindled to a mere shadow. The Abbot's office still retains a certain prestige. There is no trace of any wider organization. Though some monasteries still enjoy a certain reputation, they have no jurisdiction over others.

The monks (named *puchung*, or simply *chung* in Korean) keep up their numbers by admitting children, who are either dedicated to this life by their parents, or are received by the monastery for a monetary compensation. It is but seldom that full-grown men enter them. The rules and customs for admission are similar to those in China. The inmates of monasteries are almost exclusively drawn from the poorest classes. The monasteries possess a little landed property—gardens and fields—which are cultivated by means of lay help. For the rest they are dependent on the charity of the laity, which does not flow in liberally. In consequence, their way of life is very simple: a meat dish is categorically forbidden, as in Chinese Buddhism. Personally, the Korean monks do not make a bad impression on the visitor. They receive him with friendliness, even if he is a European; they give information willingly, as far as they are able to do so; they exhibit that gentle, good-natured indolence which is characteristic of the bulk of the Korean people.

The number as well as the standing of the monasteries has steadily declined for a long time past. The monastic colonies in the so-called Diamond Mountains (Kim-gang-san, to the south-west of Cape Duroch) still enjoy a certain celebrity. There are more than forty-five of them. Amongst them the most noted is the monastery of Chang-an-sa. Another well-known name is that of the monastery of San-wang-sa, a day's journey to the west of Wensan (Gensan), which has a community of more than fifty monks. Small Buddhist monasteries lie thickly sown in the immediate neighbourhood of Seoul, the capital. Whereas not a single Buddhist shrine is allowed within the walls—a law prohibits the entrance of monks because of their share in a certain conspiracy[1]—there exist no less than forty Buddhist monasteries in the neighbourhood. Most of them, however, are very insignificant, some only containing six or less monks. A few of these monasteries serve also another purpose, being designed as fortresses, and picturesque summits are crowned by them. At a distance of several hours' journey to the south of Seoul are to be seen the ruins of a large and once famous monastery fortress on Mount Nam-han-sa. A mighty wall still protects the extensive building on the loftiest height, within which at a former date were houses for the entertainment of royalty, together with a number of shrines and monastic dwellings. To-day a village occupies the site. In the north of Seoul lies a similar temple fortress (Puk-han-sa). Such monastery fortresses as these were formerly of great importance for the Sovereign. The inhabitants formed a warlike band, among whom he could take refuge in the time of danger, and it was by the help of these warrior monks that many a conflict was won.

I will put down here the names of some other well-known monasteries which a traveller may take interest in to visit: Ryeng-an-sa, on the border of the Han

[1] Formerly the monks were not even allowed to pass through the streets of the capital. This prohibition has been abolished since 1895.

River, above Han Kang; Pyök-chol, also on the Han River, above Yö-ju, about four days' journey from Seoul; Chun-deung, on the island of Kang-hwa; Ha-in-sa, in the town Hyup-ch'un. A very large monastery of more modern character and tendency is situated at the foot of the Chi-ri Mountain. Of nunneries there exist only few, mostly near Seoul.

### B. The People and Buddhism.

Superficial travellers have been misled into thinking that the Koreans were a people without any religion, and have so delineated them. Such an estimate is far from correct; but it is true that Buddhism has lost its hold on the people here more than elsewhere. Nevertheless, it has not been entirely uprooted; nor may one assert that, because of the decline and withdrawal of Buddhism, the country is without religion. One notices here again, as in the case of other Buddhist countries, that Buddhism tolerates the existence alongside of it of undercurrents of another sort of religious life, which have a greater ascendancy over the people than the religion of Gautama. At the present time, when the power of Buddhism has nearly faded away, these undercurrents have become much more noticeable.

Buddhism is by no means uprooted in Korea. Although the monasteries are in decay and the monks are despised, the laity are not lacking within the temple precincts, and they come to seek assistance at the Buddhist shrines in every kind of need. They bring offerings; they fill the brass dishes on the altar with rice, cake, nuts, apples, and pears; they light candles before the images and burn incense; they hire the monks to recite sacred passages to the sounds of drums, bells, and cymbals; they fling themselves meanwhile repeatedly before the altar in prayer, with their foreheads in the dust, murmuring softly the words of supplication, of prayer, of sorrow. Such scenes are of daily occurrence, and anyone who spends sufficient time in a larger temple will witness them. Even to-day the Buddhist teaching suits many people by its accounts of the recompense awarded either in heaven or hell; and the great Ti-tsang—the Bodhisattva of the nether world—together with his ten underlings and their three constables, whose duty it is to drive the souls of the dead before the tribunal, are not played out. Of those who are still in touch with Buddhism, certainly the lower classes preponderate, and there is nothing to be found amongst the people of the deeper ideas of this religion; they make a blunt external use of those gods who are supposed to be serviceable. At the same time, we must not overlook the fact that from time to time, and even quite recently, Buddhism has been supported by the ruling classes. Not only did the Emperor sometimes spend large sums of money on the embellishment and restoration of a monastery, as in a remarkable case in the sixties of last century, but also you may read the following notice in the *Korean Review*, a good English monthly periodical, under date of January, 1902: "The Government is building an enormous Buddhist monastery about a mile outside the East Gate [of Seoul]. It is intended that this will be the head monastery in Korea, and will hold the same relation to Buddhism in Korea that the Vatican does to Roman Catholicism throughout the world (!). It will contain between three and four hundred *kan* of buildings, and the plan is the same as that of the great Ch'un-ch'uk monastery in Tibet. The ceremonies connected with the commencement of this work took place on the 4th instant. Monks from all over the country, to the number of eight hundred or more, congregated at this spot, together with Japanese monks from the Japanese quarter of Seoul. An immense crowd of Koreans surrounded the place to view the scene" (p. 26). Later on it is remarked (p. 29): "At the new monastery there will be placed one director, one assistant director, one secretary, one assistant secretary, nine clerks, two accountants, four messengers, fifteen *kisus* (runners), five policemen, and fifty 'soldier monks.'"

It would not be impossible for Korean Buddhism, precisely owing to the last change in the history of the country, to take a new lease of life, by means of the help given to it by Japanese Buddhism. For some time past the Japanese have made efforts in this direction. Japanese Buddhist monasteries have been founded in Korea; Japanese monks have been sent over to instruct and stimulate their Korean brethren in the faith. Likewise they have transferred Korean monks to Japan for them to be brought up there. The above-mentioned *Review* has the following remarks in one of its numbers (1905, p. 278): "It is reported that the number of Japanese Buddhists in Korea have very greatly increased, and a circular has been sent throughout the country to the effect that this religion will be taught in all parts of the interior, and schools will be established to properly educate the young men." One may say in advance that these efforts will be expended on a very hard field of labour; for although it cannot be maintained that Buddhism is entirely spent there, yet it has certainly wasted away to a great extent.

What has come into prominence whilst Buddhism is driven into the background is the Chinese type of ancestor worship, and with it an ancient form of nature and demon worship, which from early times is ingrained in the Mongolian race, and was only slightly veiled by Buddhism. Demon worship is specially noticeable amongst the bulk of the population. The stars, mountains, rivers, caves, have their demons, besides numberless remarkable or peculiar places and objects. Amongst animals, snakes are particularly feared and worshipped as spirits. They are often kept and fed near the houses as guardians of the dwellings. The tiger is frequently looked on as the manifestation of a spirit. The discovery of the influence of an evil spirit and its exorcism are important, and practically daily occurrences. The people who rely on their skill in dealing with these matters for their livelihood, and to whom everyone applies in such a case, are always, strange to say, women—the so-called *mudang*. There are, indeed, men of a similar occupation—the so-called *pansu*. These, however, are nothing more than soothsayers, transplanted from China and Korea—usually blind men, whose means and methods are similar to those employed in China. Their business is principally to foretell the future or to discover hidden things; it is only incidentally that they are employed for exorcising demons.[1] This is far more the prerogative of the *mudang*. Her assistance is called in for all sorts of illness; for the appeasing of the spirit of a dead person; for the wished-for intercourse with the dead; for the warding off of epidemics (smallpox); for the ceremonies to propitiate the spirits of water, of rivers, and of fishcraft; for long journeys and other important undertakings. The exorcism of a *mudang* is called *kut*. Such a *kut* is performed in various ways, according to its object and surroundings, but usually to the accompaniment of an ecstatic dance led by noisy music. During this dance the woman herself is supposed to be possessed by the spirit, and through her mouth the cause of the evil is indicated, as well as the means of healing. Offerings always play a large part on these occasions. Sometimes (as at a séance with the dead) she sits quietly sunk in thought, and experiences inward communion with the spirits. The *mudang* is accounted a friend of the ghostly powers. She does not compel them by force, but makes use of the favour in which she stands with them to obtain the necessary information. There are special little chapels in which the *mudang* exercises her art if the house of those concerned or of the witch herself does not seem suitable. These chapels, called by different appellations, are very common on the roads or on the hill-tops. These exorcisms take place also on those stone heaps which every traveller in Korea must have had frequent opportunity to observe, and which are usually

[1] If they practise as exorcists, they put on female clothing for such purpose!

augmented by one stone from every passing Korean. They are crude memorials to an indwelling spirit, close to a bush or a tree, on which hang rags and little streamers as votive offerings. Although the *mudang* is despised, and although she is surrounded by most sinister reports, yet her services are always in requisition ; and there are many men who marry a *mudang* simply on account of the income for her services, which will enable them to live free from care. It is very remarkable that the *mudang* has entirely ousted the Buddhist monk, who formerly used to be employed for the overcoming of supernatural agencies. For instance, the rites required at the death of a person, in order to facilitate his passage into the other world, were originally performed by Buddhist monks ; now the *mudang* only is employed. The more the hand of Buddhism is palsied in Korea, the more strongly is the hold of early superstitious customs and habits shown, which were glossed over, but never completely lost. How these dominate the people can be seen by a glance at the rich literature of popular anecdotes, fairy-tales, legends, and novels ; they are all full to overflowing of references to spirits.

## Chapter VIII.—JAPANESE BUDDHISM.

Amongst the Buddhist countries of the East, Japan is unquestionably the most important. From early times it was the aim of this people to work out independently the leading conceptions of Gautama's religion. More recently, also, there has not been lacking the endeavour to combine the Buddhist gospel with Western knowledge, and to show its permanent value in theological terms. Such endeavours are undertaken by clever and even learned laymen, or members of the aristocracy and high officials, as well as by prominent monks.

In the historical survey (see p. 92) it was pointed out that, at the time when a change was made in Japan to a new era (1868), the Government officially dropped Buddhism. From that date till 1888 the turn to Western culture and the influence of Western science was so strong that Buddhism was completely driven to the wall. It was genuinely supposed for a time that Christianity would become the State religion. But in the years 1888 and 1889 this tendency suffered a powerful recoil. A more critical and sober estimate was taken of Europeanism. Warning voices were raised to the effect that the special features of Japanese individuality should not be blindly sacrificed for the sake of foreign ways, in whose wake would follow danger and difficulty. After this revulsion of feeling Buddhism advanced with new energy, and made noticeable efforts to deepen its fundamental ideas and to infuse them with new life.

The Buddhist current is, indeed, only one among many passing through modern Japan. All sorts of attempts to establish a common religious basis cross one another here, since the old world of this remarkable people has fallen out of joint and a new one is beginning to be fashioned. Alongside of Buddhism there are Shintoism, the moral philosophy of Confucius, Christian dogma of all shades, besides a multitude of newly-devised systems, sometimes transformations of Western philosophies, sometimes a blend of all sorts of different elements drawn from European and Asiatic sources, which some speculative mind has worked out for itself and then thrown into the common chaos.

Though Buddhism plays a certain part amongst all these heterogeneous elements which surround the soul of the people, and emerges with its highest conceptions, nevertheless one must not argue from such fact that this spiritual and inward character is at all universal. It is peculiar to certain groups only of the higher circle. As regards the broad masses of the population, and also the majority of the monks, Buddhism is more or less a traditional and external cult, and in this form it is superciliously ignored by the educated, or treated with a smile of contempt.

## A. The Externals.

In its outward manifestations, Japanese Buddhism is very similar to Chinese, as is natural from its historical development. The usual arrangement of the buildings within a temple enclosure evidently follows the Chinese plan, where the gateway leads into a right-angled court, whose centre is occupied by the buildings for worship, while in the background and at the sides are dwelling-rooms and places for entertaining guests, small sanctuaries, and the like. This original design, indeed, is frequently set aside. The rooms for worship often stand alone; Abbot and monks live near. The most important places of worship are a main hall, called *hondô*, and a hall dedicated to the founder of the sect to which the temple belongs, or to some other noted saint; this hall is called *soshidô*. Besides, some special halls may be found in large temples for the worship of a renowned divinity—for instance, of Amida (Amitâbha) or Kwannon (the Chinese Kwanyin). The architecture of the buildings shows fundamental traces of Chinese style, but with that slight alteration of the Chinese model which the artistic Japanese instinct has stamped upon most of the departments of its culture. The curved roofs, often rising one above the other, the wooden walls, the elaborately twisted wooden pillars, the verandas with wooden balustrades, the lattice windows, paper-covered—all this is a sight familiar to the visitors of Chinese temples. But here everything is generally finer in execution and kept in better repair; also, the colour-loving Japanese decorate the woodwork more tastefully in subdued colours. The more prominent buildings are erected on a wooden or stone platform, leading up to which is a flight of steps. The roof is generally tiled in the Chinese manner, or covered with sheet copper; but here and there one comes across roofs thatched with fine shingles or bark on the model of the Shinto temples, and these were executed when Shintoism and Buddhism became associated with one another. In the same way, you not infrequently see Buddhist temples showing that peculiar upward curve of the overhanging part of the roof above the entrance-gate, with a corresponding curved little sheltering roof above it again, which originally belongs to Shinto architecture.

The halls set apart for worship are so arranged internally, as a rule, that the part containing the images of the gods is separated from the other part by a partition. Behind it are one or two altars, and on them—mostly in richly decorated little shrines—are the images of the gods. Silken embroideries, bronze lotos-blossoms, incense bowls, candles, lanterns, and costly paintings, etc., form the remainder of the furniture of the shrine. The part of the temple reserved for the laity, generally divided into naves by rows of pillars, not infrequently shows in the more noted temples a great wealth of votive offerings, pictures, carvings, lanterns, etc., which are attached to the walls, pillars, or ceiling. The ground is covered with mats, as is customary in every private house, and is therefore not to be trodden on with shoes or sandals.

In many temples there is also a special hall for offerings (called *emadô*[1]), as well as a wooden tower in which the great principal bell is hung (*shôrô*). You find also frequently a tower for a large drum (*kôro*). A tank is close at hand, wherever this is possible, in which lotos grows, and populated with highly-fed fishes or tortoises, spanned by an elegant bridge. A sacred tree—not, indeed, the celebrated Indian Bo-tree, but generally an aniseed (*Illicium religiosum*) or a Chinese juniper—is planted in the courtyard. A

[1] This name has been derived from Shintoism. It means "horse hall," and refers to the presents of horses made to Shinto shrines. *Cf.* W. G. Aston, "Shintoism," p. 221 *et seq.* (London, 1905).

pagoda in Chinese style, five or seven stories in height, rises within the circumference of the temple precincts.

As things of a specially Japanese character, one cannot but notice in the neighbourhood of most temples rotatory book-shrines, the so-called *rinzô*. They are little wooden houses which turn on a perpendicular axle. Within them lie the sacred Buddhist scriptures—not always the complete canon—and it constitutes an act of merit to turn the repository, with its whole bulk of sacred writings, round two or three times. In the eyes of the people, the turning of the shrine, if it is done with the earnest wish to be able to read the scriptures, is of equal value with having read the text, and wins much favour and blessing. The invention of the turning library is attributed to a Chinese Buddhist of the sixth century A.D., on account of which he and his two sons are usually represented at the entrance of the shrine.

The so-called "prayer-wheels," so common in Tibet, are also to be found in the Japanese temples (*goshô-guruma*), but their use is confined to the adherents of certain sects (Tendai and Shingon). The Japanese instrument also may be distinguished from the Tibetan by the fact that it contains no written prayers, but is a simple wheel set in motion with the pious wish that a deity will procure a favourable reincarnation of the man who prays.

In the environs of the temple the visitor's eye will often be arrested by the great number of stone or bronze lanterns (*tôrô*). These are votive offerings erected in the shape of a monument, in the upper part of which, with open lattice-work sides, burn lights on special occasions. These lanterns often reach a height of 6 to 9 feet, and have a very picturesque appearance.[1] At celebrated temples you may count them by the hundred. Another characteristic adornment of the temple environs is the *torii*. This is a portico of wood or stone. Although the Japanese attribute it to a Shinto origin, it is undoubtedly derived from the Chinese and Korean portals which characterize their temple entrances, and lastly points back to the Indian *torâna*. The *torii*, in red lacquered wood or grey moss-covered stone, rising from the midst of the green trees, is highly decorative in effect; and the simple beauty of the Japanese *torii*, compared with the Chinese or Korean original, accentuates well the superior artistic capacity of the islanders.

The elegant taste of the Japanese has found a specially wide field for its exercise in shaping all the manifold implements of the Buddhist temples. Especially the wood-carving, painting, and the bronzes, are to be mentioned. The carver's art finds scope in the altars, the partitions, the shrines for the pictures or images of the gods, the wall decorations, window lattices, and pillars. Of fine old paintings, every noted temple possesses at least a few examples, sometimes of great antiquity, generally in the shape of so-called

[1] The famous one in front of the Tôdaiji temple at Nara is the finest and the earliest specimen of the kind.

*kakemonos*, unframed, mounted on silk, and fastened to two sticks. Decorative art is prominent in the paintings of walls and ceilings, with brilliant effect. Bronze-casting and ironwork find their place in incense-burners, lanterns, the metal lotos-blossoms which often adorn the altars, also in gongs, storks used as candlesticks standing on the back of a tortoise, great candelabra vases, but above all in the huge bells and bronze figures of the gods. Japan's three greatest bells are—(1) The one in connection with the great Buddha (Daibutsu) at Kyôto, the height of which is about 14 feet, the thickness 9 inches, the diameter about 9 feet, the weight about 63 tons. (2) That of the temple of Chionin at Kyôto; the height 10·8 feet, the thickness 9½ inches, the diameter 9 feet, weight nearly 74 tons. (3) That of the temple of Tôdaiji at Nara; the height 13 feet 6 inches, the thickness 8 inches, the diameter 9 feet. Amongst the gigantic bronze figures, the most celebrated is the so-called Daibutsu of Kamakura, a representation of Amitâbha, of the height of upwards of 49 feet, and unique in beauty. Yet larger than this image, but of nothing like the same artistic merit, is the great Buddha of the temple of Tôdaiji at Nara (a representation of the "celestial Buddha" Vairochana), about 53 feet high.

Mention may also be made of the representation of the "footprint of the Buddha," which is so common in Southern Buddhism, and is also sometimes to be found in Japanese temples (*bussoku seki*). Here it is not subdivided into 108 squares, as in Ceylon, but merely exhibits several symbolic figures, such as a wheel, a sceptre, the *svastika*, the conch-shell, fishes, and lotos-blossoms. Meditative contemplation of the footprint is considered meritorious.[1]

### B. The Divinities.

Japanese Buddhism recognizes—as does the Mahâyâna doctrine everywhere—a very large number of celestial, or at all events of worshipful, beings. In their origin some are thoroughly Buddhist, some Hindu (Brahman), some Shinto, and a few also Chinese.

The Buddhist speculations about higher Buddhas (Japanese Butsu) and a highest Buddha-god, which we noticed already in connection with Lamaism (*cf.* p. 159), are the foundation of the system in Japan also. The historic figure of a Buddha is associated with a supernatural celestial Buddha and with a sort of intermediate being—a Bodhisattva. This combination of a historic Buddha, a celestial Buddha, and a Bodhisattva, is five times repeated, as there are five "historic" Buddhas of the present epoch especially well known and revered. Thus we have five triads. The edifice culminates in a supreme Buddha, who dominates the whole. Now, this plan unfolds itself with various peculiar features amongst the different sects, and even the names of the individual representations are not always the same. The

[1] K. Florenz, in his "Geschichte der Japanischen Literatur" (Leipzig, 1906), mentions (on p. 18) two poems in honour of the Buddha's footprint, written in a peculiar form, called "the Buddha footprints form" (*bussoku sekitai*).

doctrine, also, of the supreme Buddha often sinks into the background.

Amongst the celestial Buddhas (Dhyâni Buddhas), the most prominent are Vairochana and Amitâbha. Each of them is conceived in certain sects as the highest and most surpassing of all Buddhas, with such attributes as the Christian conception of God is wont to embrace—eternal, almighty, compassionate, the spring of all being. Vairochana (*cf.* p. 209) is called in Japanese Dainichi; Amitâbha is known by the abbreviated form of his name, Amida (also Mida). The popular conception—as many of the representations of them in the temples show—confuses the historic Buddha Śâkyamuni (usually called Shaka in Japan) with the celestial Buddhas, and ranks him among their number, which is not in harmony with the system; for Śâkyamuni was one of the human (*manushi*) Buddhas—a temporary apparition, and an emanation from one of the celestial Buddhas. The correct numbering of the five celestial Buddhas is: Dainichi, Ashuku (Indian Akśobya), Hôshô (Indian Ratna Sambhava), Amida, Fukujoju (Indian Amoghasiddhi); but the last is frequently confounded with Shaka. To each of these names may be added the title Nyorai (corresponding to the Indian Tathâgata, one of the designations of the Buddha).

Equally worthy of notice amongst the Buddhas is the so-called "healing" Buddha, Yakushi Nyorai, included by many people amongst the five Dhyâni Buddhas.

As Dainichi and Amida, together with Shaka, are the most popular Buddhas, amongst Bodhisattvas

(Japanese Bosatsu) Kwannon is the first. She is the Chinese Kwanyin (see p. 210). Both conception and representation of her correspond entirely with the Chinese, so that we need do no more than refer to what has already been stated on the subject. Other Bodhisattvas, also familiar to us from the Chinese, are Fugen (Chinese P'u-hsien) and Monju (Chinese Wen-shu), frequently standing at the sides of Kwannon or Shaka; also Daiseishi or Seishi (Chinese Ta-shih-chi), who, together with Kwannon and Amida, shares the authority over the western Paradise. Sun and moon are also conceived as Bodhisattvas, and, under the name of Nikkô Bosatsu and Gwakkô Bosatsu, are the customary companions of Yakushi Niorai.

In Japan, the place of Ti-tsang, the Chinese King of Hell, is taken by Emma-Ô. This name is the corruption of the Indian Yâma-râja. The Indian nether god Yâma belongs in China to the ten rulers of hell, who are subordinate to Ti-tsang; in Japan, on the other hand, Yâma as Emma-Ô is the supreme ruler; while the figure of Ti-tsang corresponds to the well-known and highly revered figure of Jisô. This is (like Ti-tsang) a mild, compassionate deity who specially comes to the assistance of children in the under world, when they—as folklore asserts—are terrified by a certain witch (Shôzuka no baba) who lies in wait for them on the banks of the Buddhist Styx.

The Bodhisattva Maitrêya (Japanese Miroku), who is said to come next in order to Gautama when his time of appearance has expired, is in nearest connection with Kwannon, Fugen, and Monju. Gigantic figures of him have been carved in rocks.

Amongst the disciples of Gautama, the most celebrated are Ânanda and Kâśyapa (Anan and Kashô), and, as in China, they are frequently placed beside Shaka. Equally well-known and much-represented figures are the smaller and the greater circle of the Arhat (Japanese Rakan). The smaller group includes sixteen, as in Korea. Of these the most popular is Binzuru (Indian Pindola), who is usually removed from the group into a place of his own, because Buddha once was obliged to punish him for a sin; nevertheless, he is specially honoured by the people as a guardian from disease, and people rub the particular part of the body of the statue where the suppliant is afflicted, with full confidence that the disease will disappear. The larger group of 500 Rakan has also sometimes its special hall in the temple, as in China.

Another familiar figure in the temples is (as in China) that of the patriarch Bodhidharma (see p. 239); in Japan he is called Daruma.

The four heavenly Kings who stand at the entrance of Chinese temples are not unknown in Japan, called the Shitennô; their single names are Bishamon, Zocho, Kômoku, Jikoku. But they do not usually stand in the entrance-hall, where instead are to be found the so-called Ni-Ô, the two Deva Kings, namely, Indra (Taishaku) and Brahma (Bonten), who stand menacingly on the right-hand and the left-hand side. The figure of the tutelary deity, Weito (Veda, see p. 213), here meets us also, but it is mixed up with one of the heavenly Kings, and therefore often called Bishamon. Under this name it has become even one of the gods of happiness—namely, the god of wealth. But Weito keeps its proper place alongside under another guise, as Idaten (the Japanese Ten corresponding with the Indian Deva).

Fudo must not be overlooked as an originally Hindu deity who has been adopted into Japanese Buddhism, and is much and zealously worshipped. He seems to correspond to the Indian god Siva. His appearance is fierce and angry, the face often coloured black; in his right hand he holds a sword, and in his left a rope; tongues of flame form the background. The popular superstition places him amongst the celestial Buddhas, identifies him, indeed, with Dainichi (Vairochana).—The Hindu deities Ganesa, Hâritî, Kumbhîra, and Marîchî, appear on Buddhist altars in the Japanese form of Shôden (also Kwangiten), Kishibojin, Kompira, and Marishiten. The first-named is specially attractive with his elephant head, which denotes his sagacity.

From Shintoism, Japanese Buddhism has incorporated the god of war, Hachiman, an ancient Emperor (Ôjin) raised to the rank of a god. But with him may sometimes be seen also the Chinese war-god, Kwanti'as Kwanwu.

A special class of celestial beings is that of the Tennin and Tengu, of Indian origin. The former (the Indian Apsara) corresponds somewhat to our angels—womanly and youthful, with bright, flowing, outstretched garments; their figures often occur in wall-paintings. The Tengu, on the other hand, are a kind of demons (the Indian Garuda), half man, half bird, with wings, claws, and long sharp beaks. They play a great rôle in popular tales as beings of high supernatural powers (for instance, infinite vision) and much interfering with human affairs. Other classes of demons are the Shôjô and the Sennin. These come from Chinese conceptions.

It is in the nature of things that the most celebrated teachers of Japanese Buddhism should be honoured as saints. They enjoy the title of Daishi (" the great sage," from the Chinese *ta shih*). The most important ones of them will be mentioned in connection with the sects which they have founded. In this place it may suffice to name Shotoku Daishi, that Prince of the seventh century A.D. to whom is mainly due the introduction of Buddhism into Japan (see p. 89).

### C. Principal Sanctuaries.

The Japanese city where most of the renowned temples are to be found, and the religious life of Buddhism can best be studied, is *Kyôto*, the ancient capital of the country (from 793 to 1868 A.D.). The enumeration of all its more eminent temples would lead too far, but the following must at all events be mentioned: the Sanjusangendô, the two Hongwanji temples, the Kyomizu, and the Chionin. The first-mentioned takes its name from the 33,333 images of Kwannon which it contains. The Hongwanji temples and that of Kyomizu are specially worthy of notice for their elegance of design, and the latter for the beauty of the situation. The Chionin temple is rich in unique works of art. To the north-east of Kyôto lies the mountain of Hieizan, celebrated above all others in the history of Japanese Buddhism, said to have been studded with thousands of temples and shrines in the Middle Ages. The monks of this locality have often played a warlike part; but to-day there is little remaining of the brilliant past. In *Ôsaka*, the neighbour town of Kyôto, may be mentioned the famous Tennōji temple. South of Kyôto, two hours by rail bring us to *Nara*, another of the Buddhist places most worthy of a visit. Here is to be found the large temple of Tôdaiji, with the greatest image of the Buddha in the whole country. South-west of Nara, the little place called *Hôriûji* contains the oldest Buddhist temple in Japan; it dates from the beginning of the seventh century A.D. The contents of this temple are of the highest importance as regards the history of ancient Japanese art. On the south-west border of the province of Yamato, in which are Nara and Hôriûji, rises one of the most noted hills for pilgrimage in Japan, *Kôyasan*, which has been held in high esteem since the beginning of the ninth century A.D. There are always thousands of pilgrims praying here, and thousands of the dead lie in the huge cemetery under the shade of the cryptomerias, within the sacred earth of the mountain. The name of Kobo Daishi (see pp. 91 and 291) is closely associated with that of Kôyasan.

*Tôkyô*, the modern capital, naturally also possesses important temples. The most popular one is that of Kwannon, in the Asakusa quarter of the town. To the south of Tôkyô lies the hamlet *Ikegami*, which possesses a very noted temple (Hommonji), the burial-place of the saint Nichiren. Two hours by rail to the east of Tôkyô we find at *Narita* a flourishing and far-famed temple of Fudo. *Kamakura,* a village to the south of Yokohama, possesses an almost world-wide renown on account of its colossal statue of Amida. The temples of *Nikko* have a similar reputation; they are five hours by rail to the north of Tôkyô. These sanctuaries, of whose beauty the Japanese proverb says, "Call nothing beautiful till you have seen Nikko," are more of Shinto than Buddhist origin, although Buddhism and its saints have given the place its celebrity. In Central Japan the town of *Nagano* must be mentioned, with its much-renowned shrine of Zenkôji. This temple belongs to the earliest Japanese period, for it is said to have been founded as early as 642 A.D. They pretend to guard there a picture of the three divinities, Amida, Kwannon, and Daiseishi, which was presented to the Mikado by the King of Korea when Buddhism was first introduced into the country. But the picture is concealed within seven cases, and is not to be seen by visitors.

### D. The Monks.

The name of "monk" cannot be accurately applied to the members of all Buddhist Orders in Japan, for one of the most numerous sects allows its adherents to marry, as we shall see later on. But in speaking of these communities we retain the name of "monk" for convenience' sake.

The great majority of the monks issue from the lower ranks of society. Some are dedicated to the monastic life from childhood, and in that case they grow up in the temples under the priestly care and teaching. The larger establishments generally have an institute of their own (the seminary of the priests) for the education of their monks. The State supervision which (through a department of the Home Office) is exercised on Buddhism does not concern itself with religious questions, and therefore not with the methods of education, but merely keeps an eye on the public doings of the Orders. The scope of their culture is consequently very various, depending on the differing sects and personalities. The knowledge of the average monk is confined to practical necessities. Many of them are not even sufficiently versed in the Chinese characters to be able to read the sacred canon, which is in Chinese. There are, however, also very learned men amongst them.

In their organization, dress, shaven heads, and vegetarian diet, they resemble the Chinese monks, but they differ in a number of minor points, which we may afford to ignore. It must be observed, however, that the branding which the Chinese monk endures upon the head, at the completion of his ordination, the Japanese monk usually has upon his arm instead. The religious duties of the monks consist partly in ritual observances in the temple, partly in recitation of the sacred text, partly in meditation. They are in constant communication with the people. Their help is especially sought in connection with funerals and the offerings to ancestors. They also read the sacred books on certain occasions in private houses. They may even feel an obligation to preach to the people.

In some temples the rule is that a daily sermon should be delivered, in others every ten days, in others twice or once a month.[1] Generally, however, this is limited to a certain time of the year which is set apart for the purpose. At birth and at marriage the Buddhist monk has no official part to play.

The monks do not hold a high place in the common estimation. Their ignorance, and especially their greed and immorality, make them the butt of much remark by cultured men. In the summer of 1902 the newspapers were full of accounts of the deplorable private life of the principal of the chief sect in Japan, and also of great embezzlements which had been going on in the same community. Anyone happening to be in Japan at the time would constantly hear remarks to the effect that such things were not at all surprising, but quite in keeping with the common expectation.

The monks rely for their means of subsistence upon the gifts and fees of adherents. Special temple property, which was formerly of considerable value, in the new era no longer exists; the Government has confiscated it in return for exemption from taxes.

### E. The Sects.

Japanese Buddhism has split up into a great number of different forms. These divisions are of great antiquity. None of the principal schools is of later date than the thirteenth century of our era; only some insignificant groups have been formed in more modern times. The cause of the divisions is the same as that

[1] Lloyd, "Developments of Japanese Buddhism" ("Transactions of the Asiatic Society of Japan," vol. xii., p. 402).

which we have already noticed in China; for by far the greater number of the Japanese sects are only offshoots from the Chinese sectarian developments. From the large number of sacred books, one or another was selected for special study. A highly gifted teacher would develop an original view of Buddhist doctrine from his own individual standpoint out of his favourite book. The philosophical and psychological observations which had focussed themselves on the Mahâyâna doctrine (for this was the only one to penetrate into Japan) were modified, and this was very easily accomplished owing to the vagueness and arbitrariness of this kind of philosophy. Thus there arose a new school, which in course of time acquired special features in many external ways, such as the colour of the clothing, the ritual observances, the internal arrangements of the temples, and in more intimate ways in connection with their habits of life. To enlarge upon the differences between the sects is impossible in our limited survey of Buddhism; it is also of little moment. The differences lead to abstruse distinctions, and the points of divergence are, to our thinking, frequently far from clear. But in some sects there is a religious originality which marks them out, and will be dealt with later on.

The enumeration of the sects varies somewhat. Sometimes are included those from an earlier period which have ceased to exist. According to this historic reckoning there are the following twelve:

| | | |
|---|---|---|
| 1. Kusha. | 5. Sanron. | 9. Jôdo. |
| 2. Jojitsu. | 6. Kegon. | 10. Zen. |
| 3. Ritsu. | 7. Tendai. | 11. Shin. |
| 4. Hossô. | 8. Shingon. | 12. Nichiren. |

Numbers 1, 2, 3, and 5, are no longer in existence. If these are excluded from the list, usually two other small sects are added which were omitted in the foregoing; besides which, under number 10, are mentioned its three large offshoots, so that the number 12 is again complete, as follows:

| | | |
|---|---|---|
| 1. Hossô. | 5. Yûzû nembutsu. | 9. Ôbaku. |
| 2. Kegon. | 6. Jôdo. | 10. Shin. |
| 3. Tendai. | 7. Rinzai. | 11. Nichiren. |
| 4. Shingon. | 8. Sôtô. | 12. Ji. |

Here those mentioned as 7, 8, and 9, are only subdivisions of number 10 in the first list, called the Zen sect; 5 and 12 are two small schools which were omitted in the former list.

So much by way of general survey.

It must further be noted that the majority of these principal divisions contain quite a number of smaller varieties, so that the total of religious parties may well be reckoned as thirty.

Amongst the schools mentioned in the first list, eight of the most noted have been imported from China. Their names belong originally to Chinese sects, but they are differently pronounced in Japan. Thus, Kusha is the Chinese school of Chü shê, Jojitsu is Chêng shih, Ritsu is Lü, Hossô is Tz'ŭ ên, Sanron is San lun, Kegon is Hwa yen (Hsien shou). Tendai corresponds with T'ien t'ai, and Shingon with the Chinese Mi (*cf.* p. 238). The Japanese tradition records with regard to each of these sects the name of the Chinese teacher from whom they have received the special form of doctrine. The four last divisions of the list—Jôdo, Zen, Shin, and Nichiren—are held by the Japanese to be of Japanese origin. This is only literally true as regards the last two. However, Jôdo and Zen have additionally Japanese founders, though, as far as doctrine is concerned, these two schools are only Japanese parallels of the Chinese schools of "the Pure Land" (Ching t'u) and of "Contemplation" (Ch'an).

The most influential sects at the present day are the Zen, Shin, Shingon, Jôdo, and Nichiren.

As regards the number of temples, the *Zen* is foremost, if all its ramifications are included. This sect, whose Japanese founder is Eisai (A.D. 1191), lays the greatest stress on contemplation and meditation for the maintenance of the religious life, and is indubitably most in harmony with the fundamental teaching of Gautama. They carried this at first to such a pitch of opposition to the use of books that books were entirely discredited. But later on they abandoned this position. None the less, they held fast to the value of those special spiritual exercises in which the founder of Buddhism saw the true means of deliverance from earthly bondage (see p. 24). In connection with such endeavour, the Zen school always laid special stress on the training of the will, for the regulation of all passion and for the conquest of physical desires. Because such exercises proved useful for the development of knightly and warlike valour, many of the nobles (*samurai*) in early times, as well as military officers until quite recently, took part in these self-denying and hardening practices. While it is not possible to assert that the warlike valour and self-sacrifice of the Japanese actually sprang from this root, yet it may at least be said that Buddhism, through the teaching of the Zen school, has greatly strengthened a natural tendency of the race.

The *Shin* sect (its original name was Jôdo-shin sect) is also very worthy of notice. As regards influence, it perhaps ranks higher than the Zen. It has from the very beginning carried to its legitimate conclusion the Mahâyâna ruling principle as to the meaning of the faith. This faith is an inward firm conviction of the good-will and help of the deity, more especially of Amida, who almost entirely holds the position of a highest god in the Western sense. Faith is the foundation of the whole religious life. Compared with the power of faith, all other religious devices—prayer, good works, asceticism, a monastic life — are of secondary value. As a result of such a conception, Buddhism has become more transformed in this sect than in any other. Most remarkable of all, monasticism, the celibate organization of disciples, has ceased to exist. It is true that the Shin sect has priests; but they are allowed to marry, and no peculiar way of life is prescribed. They only differ from laymen in dress when they are actually performing their functions in the temple. Judging by these outward signs, it is plainly evident that the Buddhism of this sect has wholly renounced its aloofness from the world, and that it tends more directly to strengthen the general human life by a simple religious faith. In accordance with this, much is done for the education and instruction of the people, both by preaching and popular literature. The Shin priests show themselves inclined to the adoption of Western methods, yet at the same time they strongly emphasize the permanent value and missionary power of Buddhism. The founder of the Shin sect was Shinran Shonin; A.D. 1224 was the date of its foundation. This school is often designated by other names, as, for instance, the Monto or Hongwanji sect.

The *Shingon* sect, founded A.D. 806 by Kôbô Daishi, is the *mantra* school of Japan—that is to say, the school where the magic word, the magic spell, and the magic posture (especially the *mudrâ*, see p. 195), have obtained a predominant influence. A mystic philosophy, in which all conceivable ideas — even those of Confucianism—are mixed up with Buddhism, lends a somewhat deeper (esoteric) significance to the otherwise grossly superstitious system.

The *Jôdo* sect (deriving from Honen Shonin, also known as Enko Daishi, and founded in A.D. 1175) promulgated mainly the doctrine of the western Paradise, behind which the goal of Nirvâṇa completely disappears. The ruler of the western Paradise is Amida, and beside him are enthroned Kwannon and Daiseishi. These "three holy ones of the western land" receive the highest veneration. Faith in Amida, but at the same time a constant reiteration of his name, procures entrance into Paradise.

Lastly, the *Nichiren* sect deserves a short description. It is known by the name of its founder, Nichiren, who founded it in A.D. 1253. This remarkable man wished to reinstate in his rightful position the historic Buddha Gautama, together with his real teaching, which he found more especially in the "lotos of the good law" (Saddharma pundarîka, see p. 241), in contra-distinction to the worship of Amida and other erroneous doctrines. But the historic Buddha is everywhere taken mystically; the historic advent in itself is nothing. The true Buddha is a greatness permeating all being, the great illumination which we must find in ourselves. Prayer, recitation of the sacred writings (or even of the sacred formula, "Namu myô hô renge kyô," which means "Praised be the book of the lotos of the good law!"), and a number of pious deeds, lead to the right communion with the Buddha of the true illumination. The invocation of Amida on the other hand ("Namu Amida Butsu," or, shorter, "Nembutsu," the usual prayer formula of most other sects), therefore, is a sin, and the doctrine of the efficacy of faith in Amida is a wicked heresy. As the mentioned Saddharma pundarîka sûtra, which is called in Japanese Hokke Kyô, is most highly prized in the Nichiren sect, the sect is often called after it—the Hokke sect.

The Nichiren sect, owing to its origin (which was an opposition to the Shingon and Jôdo sects) and to the character of its founder, is of an aggressive and fanatical type. The other organizations are not much opposed to one another, although a certain spirit of rivalry is not lacking amongst them. When in the summer of 1902, at Yôrô, a small place in Central Japan, a congress was held in which all the schools of Japanese Buddhism took part, it was only the Nichiren sect which declined to send representatives and to come in touch with the others. This fact shows their feeling.

### F. Buddhism and the Life of the People.

The common people do not concern themselves about the philosophical and religious distinctions of Buddhist learning. They are much more concerned about what is called *hôben*. This word comprehends all sorts of outward performances, deeds of virtue, of piety, of asceticism. To this class of action belong prayers in temples, the repetition of sacred formulæ, donations which are cast into the huge chests usually standing before the altars, the maintenance of monks, listening to sermons, abstinence from meat or complete fasting, gifts, legacies, pilgrimages to noted places, and the like. Among the ascetic practices which laymen undertake for the sake of merit are many very peculiar ones. In the temple of the great Buddha at Nara, one of the gigantic wooden pillars supporting the roof has been bored through, so as to make a hole of little more than a foot in diameter. It is held to be meritorious to pass the whole body through this hole in the pillar, and the worn-away edges show how frequently this has been done. In one of the Hongwanji temples of Kyôto, visitors are shown long, thick ropes which were used at the building of the temple. The ropes are composed of human hair, which the zealous adherents have parted with for the service of the sanctuary. Under the principal altar of the greatest temple in Nagano an underground passage extends all round the altars. It is considered meritorious to make a complete tour of this three times in utter darkness. Many similar things might be mentioned.

Of course, it is only the uneducated who practise them. Their object is to avert by it some impending misfortune, or to obtain a more favourable incarnation; for the idea of recompense in the new birth has been deeply impressed on the popular imagination. Many proverbs and proverbial sayings testify to this fact. Thus, it is said of a crippled or sick child, "Ingwa na ko," namely, "It is an *ingwa* child." *Ingwa* (corresponding to the Indian *karma*) is the reward which, in a new span of life, reproduces the effect of the past. Other proverbs of similar meaning are, "The echo answers the voice" (that is to say, The lot of life corresponds with the merit); or, "The flower goes back to its root"; or, "Even a shadow or a water-wave springs from the result of a former life." A number of stories current amongst the people have the idea of retribution as their basis. Another idea which has taken hold of the popular mind owing to Buddhism is the idea of universal transitoriness, of the uncertainty, of the nothingness and illusion, of all events. About this, also, there are many proverbs, such as, "Life is like a light in the wind"; "The world is only a halting-place"; "What increases must decrease"; "In the three forms of existence there is nowhere rest"; "Not to know is to be a Buddha, not to see is Paradise."

The educated and cultured Japanese, so far as he yet adheres to Buddhism, constructs his own system of thought from the Buddhist dogma. He looks down not only on the ignorant people, but also on monasticism and on worship. But the essence of the dogmatic system appears to him in harmony with a tenable scientific aspect of the world, especially with modern scientific research. This view trained Buddhists have promulgated in numerous pamphlets, periodicals, and larger works. The tendency may be associated with the name of Reformed Buddhism, but the individual exponents vary much from one another. Buddhist reform works strenuously for the diffusion of its teachings, of which, naturally, Christendom is the main opponent. The International Buddhist Young Men's Association of Japan (founded in 1902 at Tôkyô), and the Japanese Buddhist Mission in America (at San Francisco), represent such a Buddhist Reform Mission. They carry on their work by means of periodicals, personal influence, translations, and schools.

## CONCLUSION

THE actual course of history is always a powerful corrective to one-sided, theoretical views. In the course of history both the strength and the weakness of the original starting-point become evident. We have reviewed the historic development of Buddhism and the present result of its growth as seen in widely differing countries. What does history tell us of its value as a religion?

Wherever Buddhism has become the ruling factor, there is a striking uniformity in some results of both social and religious life. They are as follows:

1. The basis of the true doctrine of Gautama is everywhere too narrow to become a foundation of national religion. The genuine Buddhist ideas in their subtle philosophical character do not satisfy or grip the simple individual. They have to be coarsened and completed, therefore, in order to meet the common needs of humanity—as, for instance, by substituting Paradise for Nirvâṇa, and by a doctrine of God and the soul. But these changes are an absolute contradiction to the most important points in the Buddha's teaching.

2. Even these altered and limited Buddhist tenets

are only partially accepted by the people in general. The real task of education which ought to be undertaken by religion, to regulate the attitude and striving of the soul of the people, Buddhism has evidently been unable to accomplish. But few of its fundamental ideas—such as that of future recompense and retribution—have really won the general consent. Beyond that, in all Buddhist countries the life of the people is more or less dominated by pre-Buddhist underlying conceptions. These are mixed with the nominally dominant Buddhism, and where the latter dies out (as in Korea), these undercurrents reassert themselves with undiminished vitality.

3. Monasticism, in so far as it is made the centre of the religious life, is everywhere seen to be a bar to the progress of religion, of society, and of culture. Despite a certain educational work which it has accomplished in many ways, in the long-run it tyrannizes the laity, absorbs all moral energy; for the support of the monastic community becomes the highest duty, withdraws the most important factors from intellectual growth, and confines the latter to a narrow compass. The stagnation of so many Asiatic peoples, especially as it appears when coming in touch with the Western civilization, is mainly due to the monastic principle of Buddhism.

4. Taken as a whole, monasticism can nowhere show success in maintaining the character of a true discipleship of the Buddha Gautama. Although there is a great difference between the monks of Tibet and China on the one hand, and those of Ceylon and Burma on the other hand, even those of the last-

named countries in their overwhelming majority lag far behind what the Buddha Gautama would have required of his disciples. The monastic life, speaking generally, has not been the means of leading individuals to follow the master's way, but has become an institution governed by interested motives, teaching the use of the mendicant's garb and the mendicant's bowl in order to conceal idleness and dependence upon the charity of others.

If such results—stretching over a period of more than 2,000 years, amongst peoples of the most different kinds—are everywhere recurrent, it must be agreed that the main cause lies in the religion itself, in its fundamental character. There can be no doubt that this is the case. All those stereotyped defects manifesting themselves in the history of Buddhism spring from the nature of its original character. A religion which undertakes to solve the world's riddle by a specific Indian-hued, primitive philosophy, and which, in order to set man on his feet and to place him in the right environment, tears him from all the natural relationships of life, so that he may look upon the world from without and apart from its having any recognized positive value for him—such a religion bears within itself the germs of all those evils which we have met with. History has but more clearly demonstrated what was already latent in the founder's system. While not failing to recognize that Buddhism has been of some value for the civilization of the peoples under its influence, nor denying that great and true thoughts have been promulgated by it, above all without minimizing the ever-powerful and admirable personality of the Buddha himself, yet we must admit that as a religion Buddhism is entirely inadequate, and the defect is so closely allied to its deepest principle that it appears very questionable whether it could ever be remedied, except at the price of giving up its own fundamental ideas.

# LITERATURE

[This list, of course, does not aim at completeness, but is meant as a help for more detailed studies. A Buddhist bibliography is given by A. T. Edmunds in the Journal of the Pâli Text Society, 1903.]


### I. The Buddha and his Doctrine.

1. H. Oldenberg—Buddha: his Life, his Doctrine, his Order. Translated from the German by W. Hoey. London, 1888.
2. T. W. Rhys Davids—Buddhism; being a Sketch of the Life and Teachings of Gautama, the Buddha. S.P.C.K. Twenty-first thousand. 1907.
3. T. W. Rhys Davids—Buddhism: its History and Literature. (American Lectures on the History of Religions.) New York and London, 1904. Second edition.
4. T. W. Rhys Davids—Lectures on the Origin and Growth of Religion as illustrated by Some Points in the History of Indian Buddhism. London, 1881.
5. H. Kern—Manual of Indian Buddhism. Strasburg, 1896.
6. C. F. Koeppen—Die Religion des Buddha. 2 vols. Berlin, 1857-1859. Reprint, 1906. (The first volume deals with the Buddha and his doctrine.)
7. R. Pischel—Leben und Lehre des Buddha. Leipzig, 1906.
8. P. Dahlke—Buddhist Essays. Translated from the German by Bhikkhu Silacara. London, 1908.

### II. Translations from the Buddhist Canon.

9. T. W. Rhys Davids and H. Oldenberg—Vinaya Texts. 3 vols. (Sacred Books of the East, vols. xiii., xvii., xx.)
10. T. W. Rhys Davids—Buddhist Suttas. (Sacred Books of the East, vol. xi.)

11. T. W. Rhys Davids—Dialogues of the Buddha. London, 1899.
12. T. W. Rhys Davids—The Questions of King Milinda. (Sacred Books of the East, vols. xxxv., xxxvi.)
13. T. W. Rhys Davids—Buddhist Birth Stories; or, Jâtaka Tales. Vol. i. London, 1880.
14. F. Max Müller and V. Fausböll—The Dhammapada and the Sutta Nipâta. Translated. (Sacred Books of the East, vol. x.)
15. K. E. Neumann—Der Wahrheitspfad (Dhammapada).
16. C. Duroiselle—Dhammapada Atthakathâ: A Commentary to the Dhammapada. Translated in the periodical *Buddhism*, vol. ii., Rangoon, 1905-1908.
17. (Mrs.) C. A. F. Rhys Davids—Dhamma Sangaṇi: A Buddhist Manual of Psychological Ethics. (Oriental Translation Fund, New Series, vol. xii.) London, 1900.
18. H. C. Warren—Buddhism in Translations. (Harvard Oriental Series, vol. iii.) Cambridge, Mass., 1900. Second issue.
19. P. Carus—The Gospel of Buddha. Chicago, 1900. Seventh edition.
20. T. Dutoit—Das Leben des Buddha. (Translation of texts relating to the life of the Buddha.) Leipzig, 1906.

III. Early History of Buddhism in India.

21. V. A. Smith—The Early History of India. Oxford, 1908. Second edition.
22. V. A. Smith—Asoka. (Rulers of India Series.) Oxford, 1901.
23. T. W. Rhys Davids—Buddhist India. (Story of the Nations Series.) London, 1903.
24. A. F. R. Hoernle and H. A. Stark—A History of India. Cuttack, 1905.
25. A. Grünwedel and T. Burgess—Buddhist Art in India. London, 1901.
26. A. Foucher—L'Art Gréco-bouddhique du Ghandâra. Paris, 1905.

27. Megasthenis Indica, edited by E. A. Schwanbeck. Bonn, 1846.
28. L. de la Vallée Poussin—Les Conciles Bouddhiques: I. Les Deux Premiers Conciles. Louvain et Londres, 1905.
29. E. Hardy—König Asoka. Mainz, 1902.
30. A. Cunningham—The Stupa of Bharhut. London, 1879.

IV. LATER DOCTRINAL DEVELOPMENT (MAHÂYÂNA).

31. Târanâtha's Geschichte des Buddhismus in Indien. Uebers. v. A. Schiefner. Petersburg, 1869.
32. W. Wassiljew—Der Buddhismus: seine Dogmen, Geschichte, und Literatur. 1 Teil. Petersburg, 1860.
33. Açvaghosha's Discourse on the Awakening of Faith in the Mahâyâna. Translated by T. Suzuki. Chicago, 1900.
34. T. W. Rhys Davids—On the Eighteen Schools of Buddhism. *Journal of the Royal Asiatic Society*, 1891-92.
35. T. Minayeff—Recherches sur le Bouddhisme. Trad. par M. A. de Pompignan. Paris, 1894.
36. L. de la Vallée Poussin—Bouddhisme: Études et Matériaux. London, 1898.
37. T. Suzuki—Outlines of Mahâyâna Buddhism. London, 1907.
38. The Saddharma-Pundarîka; or, The Lotus of the True Law. Translated by H. Kern. (Sacred Books of the East, vol. xxi.)
39. Mahâyâna Texts. By E. B. Cowell, F. Max Müller, and S. Takakusa. (Sacred Books of the East, vol. xlix.)
40. The Fo-Sho-Hing-Tsan-King: a Life of Buddha. By Asvaghosha. Translated by S. Beal. (Sacred Books of the East, vol. xix.)
41. P. E. Foucaux—Le Lalita Vistara. Trad. du Sanscrit. (Annales du Musée Guimet, vol. vi.) Paris, 1884.

V. THE CHINESE PILGRIMS IN INDIA.

42. T. Legge—A Record of Buddhistic Kingdoms. By the Chinese monk Fâ-hien. Oxford, 1886.
43. H. A. Giles—Record of the Buddhistic Kingdoms. Translated from the Chinese. Shanghai, 1877.

44. St. Julien—Histoire de la Vie de Hiouen-Thsang et de ses Voyages dans l'Inde, depuis l'an 629 jusqu'en 645. Paris, 1853.

45. St. Julien—Mémoires sur les Contrées occidentales. Trad. du Sanscrit en Chinois en l'an 648, par Hiouen-Thsang, et du Chinois en Français. Paris, 1857.

46. S. Beal—Si-Yu-Ki: Buddhist Records of the Western World. Translated from the Chinese of Hiuen-Tsiang. 2 vols. London, 1906. (Reprint.)

47. S. Beal—The Life of Hiuen-Tsiang. London, 1888.

48. Th. Watters—On Yuan Chwang's Travels in India, 629-645 A.D. Edited by T. W. Rhys Davids and S. W. Bushell. 2 vols. London, 1904-05.

49. S. Beal—Travels of Fah-Hian and Sung-Yun, Buddhist Pilgrims from China to India. Translated from the Chinese. London, 1869.

50. J. Takakusu—A Record of the Buddhist Religion—by I-Tsing. Translated. Oxford, 1896.

51. S. Lévy et E. Chavannes—L'Itinéraire d'Ou Kong (751-790). Trad. et annoté. Paris, 1895.

### VI. Buddhism in Ceylon.

52. The Mahâvaṇsa. Translated by G. Turnour (first part) and L. C. Wijesiṇha (second part). Colombo, 1899.

53. The Dîpavamsa. Edited, with an English translation, by H. Oldenberg. London, 1879.

54. W. Geiger—Dîpavamsa und Mahâvamsa. Leipzig, 1905.

55. W. Geiger—The Dîpavamsa and the Mahâvamsa, and the Historical Tradition in Ceylon. (Indian Antiquary, vol. xxxv., part 443.)

56. R. Spence Hardy—Eastern Monachism. London, 1860.

57. R. Spence Hardy—A Manual of Buddhism in its Modern Development. Translated from Singhalese manuscripts. London, 1880.

58. R. S. Copleston—Buddhism, Primitive and Present, in Magadha and in Ceylon. London, 1908. Second edition.

59. Sir James E. Tennent—Ceylon. 2 vols. London, 1860. Fourth edition.
60. H. W. Cave—The Ruined Cities of Ceylon. London, 1900.
61. J. de Grey-Downing—Ceylon, Past and Present. *Buddhism*, vol. ii., p. 89 *et seq.*, p. 252 *et seq.*
62. The Dathâvansa; or, The History of the Tooth Relic of Gotama Buddha. Translated by M. C. Swamy.

### VII. Buddhism in Burma.

63. P. Bigandet—The Life or Legend of Gaudama, the Buddha of the Burmese. 2 vols. London, 1880. Third edition.
64. Shway Yoe—The Burman: his Life and Notions. London, 1896.
65. H. F. Hall—The Soul of a People. London, 1903.
66. Sangermano—The Burmese Empire a Hundred Years ago. With Introduction and Notes by J. Jardine. Westminster, 1893.
67. M. Symes—An Account of an Embassy to the Kingdom of Ava in the Year 1795. Edinburgh, 1827.
68. The Gazetteer of Upper Burma and the Shan States. Rangoon, 1900.
69. Taw Sein Ko: The Introduction of Buddhism into Burma. In the periodical *Buddhism*, vol. i., p. 585 *et seq.*
70. Reorganization of the Sangha in Upper Burma. *Buddhism*, vol. ii., p. 107 *et seq.*
71. Sir R. C. Temple—The Thirty-seven Nats: a Phase of Spirit Worship prevailing in Burma. London, 1906.
72. Sir R. C. Temple—A Native Account of the Thirty-seven Nats; being a Translation of a Rare Burmese Manuscript. *Indian Antiquary*, vol. xxxv., p. 217 *et seq.*

### VIII. Buddhism of the Shan States, Siam, Cambodja, Annam.

73. G. W. Bird—Wanderings in Burma. London, 1897. (On the Buddhism of the Shan tribes.)
74. H. Alabaster—The Wheel of the Law. London, 1871.

75. G. E. Gerini — A Retrospective View and Account of the Origin of the Thet Maha Ch'at Ceremony. Bangkok, 1892.

76. G. E. Gerini—Chulakanta Maṅgala; or, The Tonsure Ceremony as Performed in Siam. Bangkok, 1895.

77. G. E. Gerini — Siamese Archæology. In *Journal of the Royal Asiatic Society*, 1904, p. 233 *et seq.*

78. E. Lamairesse—La Vie de Bouddha, suivie du Bouddhisme dans l'Indo-Chine. Paris, 1892.

79. A. Leclère—Le Bouddhisme au Cambodge. Paris, 1899.

80. Dumoutier—Notes sur le Bouddhisme Tonkinois. *Revue d'Ethnographie*, 1888.

### IX. Buddhism in Tibet.

81. L. Feer—Analyse du Kandjour et du Tandjour. (Annales du Musée Guimet, vol. ii.) Paris, 1881.

82. L. Feer—Fragments Extraits du Kandjour. (Annales du Musée Guimet, vol. v.) Paris, 1883.

83. C. F. Koeppen. See No. 6 of this list.

84. E. Schlagintweit — Buddhism in Tibet. Leipzig and London, 1863.

85. L. A. Waddell — The Buddhism of Tibet, or Lamaism. London, 1895.

86. L. A. Waddell—Lhasa and its Mysteries. London, 1905.

87. L. A. Waddell—Translation of a Tibetan guide-book in *Journal of the Bengal Asiatic Society*, 1895, p. 259 *et seq.*

88. P. Landon—Lhasa. 2 vols. London, 1905.

89. E. Candler—The Unveiling of Lhasa. London, 1905.

90. Gr. Sandberg—Tibet and the Tibetans. London, 1906.

91. A. Grünwedel—Mythologie des Buddhismus in Tibet und der Mongolei. Leipzig, 1900.

92. G. Huth—Geschichte des Buddhismus in der Mongolei. Aus dem Tibetischen herausg. u. übers. 2 Bde. Strassburg, 1892, 1896.

93. W. Simpson—The Buddhist Praying-Wheel. London, 1896

94. J. de Grey-Downing — The Lama Praying-Wheel. *Buddhism*, vol. i., p. 613 *et seq.*

95. Chandra Das—Sam Ye. *Buddhism,* vol. ii., pp. 48-57.

96. Chandra Das—The Foundation of Lh'assa and its Two Great Shrines. *Buddhism*, vol. i., p. 575 *et seq.*

X. Buddhism in China.

97. Bunyiu Nanjio—A Catalogue of the Chinese Translation of the Buddhist Tripitaka. Oxford, 1883.

98. S. Beal—A Catena of Buddhist Scriptures from the Chinese. London, 1871.

99. S. Beal—Abstract of Four Lectures on Buddhist Literature in China. London, 1882.

100. S. Beal—Buddhism in China. S.P.C.K. London, 1884.

101. J. Edkins—Chinese Buddhism. London, 1893. Second edition.

102. J. Edkins—Religion in China. London, 1893. Second edition.

103. E. H. Parker—China and Religion. London, 1905.

104. I. I. M. de Groot—Le Code du Mahâyâna en Chine. Amsterdam, 1893.

105. I. I. M. de Groot—The Religious System of China. Vols. i. to v. Leyden, 1892-1907.

106. C. Puini—Enciclopedia Sinico-Giapponese. (A translation into Italian of parts of the Wa kan san sai tu ye.)

107. E. I. Eitel—Handbook of Chinese Buddhism; being a Sanskrit-Chinese Dictionary. Hongkong, 1888. Second edition.

108. C. de Harlez—Vocabulaire Bouddhique Sanscrit-Chinois. Leide, 1897.

109. A. Wylie—Notes on Chinese Literature. (Pages 204-215 on Buddhist books.) Shanghai, 1901. New edition.

110. C. de Harlez—Les Quarante-deux Leçons de Bouddha, ou le King des XLII Sections. Paris, 1899.

111. W. Schott—Über den Buddhaismus in Hochasien und in China. (Partly a translation of the book Ching t'u wen.) Berlin, 1846.

112. T. Richard—Guide to Buddahood; being a Standard Manual of Chinese Buddhism. Translated. Shanghai, 1907.

113. T. Watters—The Eighteen Lohan of Chinese Buddhist Temples. Shanghai, 1899.

114. D. T. Macgowan — Self-Immolation by Fire in China. *Chinese Recorder*, vol. xix., No. 11, p. 508 *et seq.*

115. G. Miles — Vegetarian Sects. *Chinese Recorder*, vol. xxxiii., No. 1, p. 1 *et seq.*

116. S. W. Bushell—Chinese Art. 2 vols. London, 1904, 1906.

(On the Chinese Pilgrims in India, see above, Nos. 42-51.)

### XI. Buddhism in Korea.

There exists no special work on Korean Buddhism. Some valuable material may be found in different articles of the following periodical—

117. *The Korea Review*, a monthly magazine. Seoul, 1901-1906.

### XII. Buddhism in Japan.

118. W. E. Griffis—The Religions of Japan. New York, 1896. Third edition.

119. Bunyiu Nanjio—A Short History of the Twelve Japanese Buddhist Sects. Tokyo, 1886.

120. Ryauon Fujishima—Le Bouddhisme Japonais. Paris, 1889.

121. G. W. Knox—The Development of Religion in Japan. New York, 1907.

122. E. M. Satow and A. G. S. Hawes—A Handbook for Travellers in Central and Northern Japan. London, 1884. (This *second* edition of Murray's Handbook contains more details on Buddhism than the other editions.)

123. G. Migeon—Au Japon: Promenades aux Sanctuaires de l'Art. Paris, 1908.

124. C. Netto and G. Wagener—Japanischer Humor. Leipzig, 1901.

125. W. Anderson—A History of Japanese Art. *Transactions of the Asiatic Society of Japan*, vol. vii., part iv. Tokyo, 1889.

126. L. Hearn — Gleanings in Buddha-Fields. Boston and New York, 1898.

127. L. Hearn—In Ghostly Japan. Boston, 1903.

128. L. Hearn—Kwaidan. Boston and New York, 1908.

129. Anesaki-Masahar—Religious History of Japan: An Outline. With two Appendices on the Textual History of the Buddhist Scriptures. Tokyo, 1907.

130. S. Kuroda—Outlines of the Mahâyâna. Tokyo, 1893.

131. A. Lloyd—Developments of Japanese Buddhism. *Transactions of the Asiatic Society of Japan*, vol. xxii., part iii., p. 337 *et seq.*

132. A. Lloyd — The Praises of Amida: Seven Buddhist Sermons, translated. Tokyo, 1907.

133. J. Troup—On the Tenets of the Shinshiu, or True Sect of Buddhists. *Transactions of the Asiatic Society of Japan*, vol. xiv., part i., p. 1 *et seq.* Yokohama, 1886.

134. J. Troup — The Gobunsho, or Ofumi, of Rennyo Shōnin. *Transactions of the Asiatic Society of Japan*, vol. xvii., part i., p. 101 *et seq.* Yokohama, 1899.

135. T. M. James—A Discourse on Infinite Vision. *Transactions of the Asiatic Society of Japan*, vol. vii., part iv., p. 267 *et seq.* Yokohama, 1889.

136. T. Suzuki—The Zen Sect of Buddhism. *Journal of the Pâli Text Society*, 1906-07.

137. H. Haas — Die Secten des Japanischen Buddhismus. Heidelberg, 1905.

138. H. Haas—Die Kontemplativen Schulen des Buddhismus. Tokyo, 1905.

139. Kobayashi—The Doctrines of Nichiren, with a Sketch of his Life. Shanghai, 1893.

# INDEX

[The numbers refer to the pages. Of names mentioned often in the book, only the most noticeable places are given.]

T.